What a blessing to be exposed to *Sacred Friendships*. It came at a great time, because I had just been wondering if we had any strongly historical books on women in ministry. This will be a great aid to those of us teaching in the area of women's ministry. I also see it guiding ministry approaches to both men and women in the area of spiritual formation. *Sacred Friendships* is a needed guide to understanding how the past can shape our theory and practice in the present-day conundrum of Christian counseling and ministry issues. Kellemen and Ellis have done a masterful job of interpreting the words and works of godly women from church history and have gleaned guiding principles for ministries concerned with spiritual formation in our day and age. *Sacred Friendships* is not just an anthology of these women's voices, but a thoughtful reflection on what they uniquely add to the stream of Christian counsel flowing through the waves of human history. The insights gathered by the authors and the penetrating discussion questions posed in each chapter provide helpful guidance for those who are interested in equipping others in soul care professions and ministries. This book would be useful for training soul care workers in academic and church-type settings because it enlists a broad spectrum of scholarship, but also connects that scholarship to practical issues. Bravo!

— **Christy Hill, Ph.D.,** Associate Professor of Spiritual Formation and Women's Ministry, Grace Theological Seminary

Sacred Friendships is a heartwarming historical anthology of women whose conviction and pluck shaped history. Rarely have I picked up a book to read that has so encouraged me to use my gendered gifting as a means to promote the growth of others. The stories contained in this book elevate the role of sister, friend, daughter, mother, wife, counselor, and spiritual director as the means God will use to shape lives. I learned there are no ordinary women: like the women in *Sacred Friendships* we leave a story behind to be told no matter when we live, or who we live among. What historical story will others tell about how you used your gift? The women in *Sacred Friendships* shaped ancient history, stepped up to be martyred for their faith, spoke words of comfort to soothe those they served, fought for justice when prejudice was unbridled, used wise words to encourage depressed church fathers, mentored theologians, and rebuked authorities. Each woman chose to follow in the footsteps of the Maker of gender by using her mind and words to reflect Him in unique ways.

> — **Penny Freeman, Ph.D.**, Associate Professor of Graduate Counseling, Philadelphia Biblical University

Dr. Robert W. Kellemen and Susan M. Ellis have sketched clearly and powerfully the portraits of the forgotten history and vision of women. Their echo of sacred friendship in the lives of women is irresistible. A 'must read' for every woman soul care-giver and spiritual director, and for all men who want to learn from these great women of the past.

> — **Jayanthi Benjamin,** Director of Field Education and Women Student Development, Moody Graduate School

Great read! These are important stories to tell and vital stories to read—great men of God were influenced and encouraged by great women of God. *Sacred Friendships* retraces the lives and perspectives of many women who walked their lives in faith. The authors sketch the spiritual words and deeds of women whose relationships with God caused them to minister grace and truth to those around them. This "cloud of witnesses" humbled and challenged me all at once, and inspired renewed commitment to live each day with an eternal perspective.

> — **Lynelle Buchanan, MA,** Chair, BA in Counseling, Baptist Bible College, Clarks Summit, Pennsylvania

Dr. Robert Kellemen and Susan Ellis have done a masterful job bringing together here a wonderful anthology of the stories and voices of Christian women throughout the history of the church. They steer a robust course between feminist misreadings on the one hand and irresponsible neglect on the other. A superb presentation!

— **Timothy George, Th.D.**, Founding Dean of Beeson Divinity School of Samford University; Senior Editor, *Christianity Today*

The stories of guides on the path to God are an important part of the resources that God has given to educate us in spiritual guidance. But most of the stories we have been told are stories of men, which means only half of the history of the Church is being recited, and this in an area where women have contributed so much. In such a context, *Sacred Friendships* must be counted a special treasure. Containing fifty-two stories of female travelers and guides to God, sampled from the breadth of the church's history and interpreted from a classical Christian perspective, this book does more than fill a void. It allows the lives of these women to educate us today and, by their example, to draw us into the holy love of God.

— **Eric Johnson, Ph.D.**, Professor of Christian Psychology, Southern Baptist Theological Seminary; Founder and Director, Society of Christian Psychologists

Sacred Friendships is a remarkable work! I invite you to come and be refreshed as you are enlightened by the many discoveries presented in this masterpiece. Every woman will see herself in this book and sometimes more than once. Every man will develop a deeper appreciation for the struggle, sacrifice and sensitivity for soul care of the women they have encountered. Bob and Susan take us on a journey of hope, help, and healing as they uncover the treasured stories of women who loved God and demonstrated their spirituality in numerous ways worth emulating. Through sustaining, healing, reconciling and guiding, the women of *Sacred Friendships* nurtured to maturity men and women of their day. And now we too can benefit from the graces they extended.

The "Learn Together Lessons" at the end of each chapter are also very helpful as we hear their hunger and thirst for righteousness. You can share in the dialogue of lessons they have learned while implementing practical application strategies from the context of the culture in which they gave their clarion call for Christlikeness. This text will help counselors, professors, pastors, ministry leaders, and care-givers move beyond ethics and skills to a place of compassion and mercy.

    — **Sabrina D. Black, Ph.D.,** Clinical Director, Abundant Life Counseling Center and A Healing Place Ministry

Though silent these many years, even centuries, the remarkable compilation in *Sacred Friendships* allows these world-influencing women to speak to us even today. We all will be wise to heed their many voices. These women's influence and spiritual vitality throughout history—captured and arranged so thoughtfully in *Sacred Friendships*—will both inspire your personal devotion and spark your imagination.

    — **Mindy Caligure,** Founder and President of Soul Care; Author of *Faith Books and Spiritual Journaling*

Sacred Friendships was exhilarating to read! I am recommending it to our students and professors ASAP. It unveils the rich heritage of diverse women in Christian ministry from a global perspective and presents a model of soul care that is powerful. It suggests an approach that provides all of the elements necessary for authentic spiritual transformation. This is a refreshing portrayal and celebration of the impact that women have made in the lives of others that has reflected the image of God in the healing process for those who are suffering. At last we see a book that promotes the fusion of biblical truth and loving grace as the foundation for the complexities of the sanctification process.

    — **Catherine Mueller-Bell, MA, LPC,** Assistant Professor of Counseling, Grand Rapids Theological Seminary

In a time when much is being said about advocating for the voiceless, little has been done to memorialize the specific contributions of godly women who teach, challenge, and encourage us to live lives worthy of the God who calls us His. *Sacred Friendships* fills a much-needed void by recording the imprint that known and unknown women have left throughout time on their families, their churches, their communities, and our history. I found myself hungry to read the stories of these women who made such a difference in their own unique and female way. Women whose strength and courage, wisdom and insight, leadership and followership challenged me as a woman to consider what my Father may be calling me to fulfill in the chapters of His story. Adding this important feminine element to our Christian heritage does not negate the powerful ways men have led, but rather gives a truer, more holistic, and richer perspective of the impact and modeling made by both genders. Women and men alike will be encouraged, inspired, surprised, transformed, and challenged by the stories and lessons found in the pages of *Sacred Friendships*.

— **Deb Musser, MA,** Assistant Professor, Department of Counseling and Interpersonal Relations, Grace College

Sacred
FRIENDSHIPS

CELEBRATING THE LEGACY OF WOMEN HEROES OF THE FAITH

ROBERT W. KELLEMEN, PH.D.
AND SUSAN M. ELLIS, M.A.

Sacred Friendships
Celebrating the Legacy of Women Heroes of the Faith
Copyright © 2009 by Robert W. Kellemen and Susan M. Ellis

Published by BMH Custom Books
PO Box 544, Winona Lake, Ind. 46590
www.bmhbooks.com

ISBN: 978-0-88469-264-5

RELIGION / Christian Life / Women

1. Pastoral counseling—Biblical teaching. 2. Spiritual life—Christianity. 3. Bible—Psychology. 4. History—Women's Ministry
253.5—dc 22

Contents

FOREWORD

Imagine 10,000 women lifting their hands to the God they love. Hundreds of them lining up at the altar. Some weeping. A few smiling. Many on their knees before the Lord. All of them hungry to know God more intimately. As president and host of *Extraordinary Women* conferences, I watch tens of thousands of women fill arenas and mega-churches across America to connect with other women, to be encouraged by God's Word, and to find hope and healing for the hurt in their lives. Who are these women? They are mothers. Grandmothers. Wives. Daughters. Women of influence—in their families and throughout their communities. Many are ministry leaders in their own churches. They are women who are making a difference in the lives of their children, marriages, churches, and communities. These amazing women of today long to be encouraged by equally remarkable women from the halls of church history.

Hebrews 12:1 speaks of a great cloud of spiritual witnesses. Ordinary people who lived extraordinary lives. For the past 2,000 years, that cloud has expanded exponentially. What we so often fail to hear is the incredible testimony of those extraordinary *women* in that great cloud, their godly lives, life lessons, and powerful ministries.

Dr. Bob Kellemen and Susan Ellis, in their compelling work, *Sacred Friendships*, provide a voice for the voiceless. Like never before, they tell "her story"—the story of our great female forbears in the faith. As they tell it, and as we listen, we do not simply learn historical facts; we are empowered and equipped to practice soul care and spiritual direction *today*.

By the way, please do not assume that *Sacred Friendships* is for women only! Nothing could be further from the truth. *Sacred Friendships* is a gift *from* women of the past to women *and* men of the present—a gift that teaches all of us how to use Christ's changeless truth to change lives in our ever-changing times.

That said, *Sacred Friendships* is also a gift *to* women. It validates the twin truths of the spiritual equality of women and of the spiritual giftedness of women. I promise you, you can't read this book without praising God for how He has and will continue to use women to advance His Kingdom purposes. As you read the previously untold stories of more than fifty extraordinary women, if you are a woman, you will never look at yourself the same way again. If you are a man, you will never look at your wife, daughter, mother, or sister the same way again.

Lay people—male and female, students, professional Christian counselors, pastors, and spiritual directors—will all glean a wealth of life-changing ministry principles from the unburied treasure of historic feminine soul care and spiritual direction. You will finish *Sacred Friendships* saying, "I never realized how fascinating church history is. I never fully appreciated the depth of the spiritual riches that arose through the previously unheard history of women's ministry. I never understood how relevant it is to my life and ministry today."

Sit back and enjoy this amazing gift.

Julie Clinton
President, *Extraordinary Women*

Acknowledgments

Sacred Friendships is not simply a book co-authored by Bob Kellemen and Susan Ellis. It is a book we have co-edited as we have uncovered the buried treasure of wisdom from that great cloud of female Christian witnesses who have gone before us. So we offer our first thanks to these amazing women believers whose stories we share and whose lives and ministries we desire to honor and hope to emulate.

I (Bob) would like to thank my co-author, Susan Ellis, whose partnership in this project has been a joy. Susan, your leadership in our Christian counseling department, your mentoring of women, and your launching of the Women's Concentration all flow from your heart of love for God and God's people. I'd also like to honor one who now stands in that great cloud of witnesses, the late Dr. Rembrandt Carter, past professor of church history at Baptist Bible College, Clarks Summit, Pa. Dr. Carter's passion for history stirred in me an already existing love for what we can learn from those who have walked the path before us.

I (Susan) especially thank Bob for inviting me to join him in such a worthwhile and grand adventure. As always, Bob has patiently mentored, nudged, challenged, and encouraged me as he has radiated the essence of spiritual friendship in my life.

Ceaseless gratitude goes to my family. My mom, Maxine, laid the foundation for me to be the woman I am with her unconditional love and guidance. My husband, Paul, makes me smile even in the hardest, darkest times. He lovingly reconciles me and has taught me much about myself and life. Our children, Paul and Samantha, have brought me boundless joy, brightening my days and refining my character. Paul reminds me to lighten up and to make room for grace. He makes me laugh. Our daughter, Samantha, resides in Paradise now, but while she was with us, she taught me a great deal about living life with gusto and passion. Our daughter-in-law, Kristen, warms my heart with her capacity to love with strength and tenderness. Our granddaughter, Jocelyn, lights up my world. Princess, may you find the King of kings within these pages and may you be comforted, encouraged, and challenged to be the woman the Lord created you to be.

Thank you, Father, Son, and Holy Spirit. Your mercies are new every morning.

WATER MY SOUL:
WOMEN AT THE WELL

> "It may surprise many to discover that tracing the history of women spiritual directors is a relatively easy task, because women have been exercising the ministry of spiritual direction quite extensively throughout the whole of Christianity's history." (Patricia Ranft)[1]
>
> "My suspicion is that there have been many more great women spiritual guides than the record shows, but who have remained in obscurity in the normative dominance of men in the positions of visible leadership. Hopefully, this 'negative learning' from Church history will be corrected in our time." (Tilden Edwards)[2]

As we've penned *Sacred Friendships*, one resounding passion has motivated our research and our writing: *to be a voice for the voiceless*. For far too long, people have silenced the voices of women believers throughout church history. We redress this imbalance by illuminating the forgotten history of more than half of the Christian community.[3]

G. K. Chesterton observes that history is democracy extended through time. History gives "votes to the most obscure of all classes, our ancestors. It is the *democracy of the dead*. Tradition refuses to submit to... those who merely happen to be walking around."[4]

Sacred Friendships gives vote and voice to our female forebears in the faith. It listens to their voices communicating the unique shapes and textures of their practice of soul care and spiritual direction.

A Sacred Legacy:
Uncovering Buried Treasure

Our purpose in writing *Sacred Friendships* is to uncover the buried treasure of wisdom about soul care and spiritual direction as practiced by women throughout the history of Christianity. Christian women from all races and nationalities have always helped hurting and hardened people through the personal ministries of *sustaining, healing, reconciling,* and *guiding.* (In chapter one, we explain these four terms and how they relate to our lives and ministries.) *Sacred Friendships* uncovers the great spiritual riches of this diverse feminine Christian tradition.

Sacred Friendships uses a Cross-based, four-dimensional model (sustaining, healing, reconciling, and guiding) of soul care and spiritual direction as a grid to map the marvels of historical women's ministry. This four-dimensional model is the traditional, time-tested, and widely-recognized pattern for understanding Christian spiritual care.

We purpose to inspire today's generation as they hear the voices of past female Christians speaking through the pages of *Sacred Friendships.* By listening to their historical narratives, we learn to speak to today's world with relevance—sharing Christ's changeless truth for our changing times. *Sacred Friendships* assists female *and* male lay spiritual friends, spiritual directors, pastoral care-givers, professional Christian counselors, and students of all races to become more spiritually aware and skillful by deriving modern implications from these recovered resources.

We aim to contribute to contemporary soul care and spiritual direction as seen through the eyes, experienced in the souls, and told from the lips of a multi-cultural rainbow of past female believers. As we drink at the well of these amazing women, they water our souls by helping us to develop contemporary models of lay spiritual friendship, spiritual direction, women's ministry, pastoral care-giving, and professional Christian counseling that are distinctively grounded *both* in the Word of God *and* in the sacred legacy of women's ministry.

A Spiritual Ministry: Telling the Untold Stories

To accomplish our goal, we tell the untold story of women's soul care and spiritual direction from the early Church to the modern era. *Sacred Friendships* listens to the voices of these previously voiceless women—hearing the feminine story told by women of all races and nationalities for the benefit of all women and men.

We begin our narrative where the amazing journey began—with the records of the lives and ministries of the Church Mothers and martyrs. Many of them were the physical mothers and biological sisters of the great Church Fathers. By listening to the voices of these courageous women of the faith, we detect new textures from the halls of church history.

The story continues with the sayings of the Desert Mothers who boldly provided feminine soul care and spiritual direction, not only for women, but for men. Their unsilenced voices provide readers with a new melody in the ancient ministry of spiritual friendship.

Moving to the Medieval times, we hear the feminine words of lay women, wives, single women, writers, and poets. Here, for the first time, whole books of spirituality furnish comprehensive manuals for soul care and spiritual direction from a feminine perspective.

The story also visits women of the Reformation and post-Reformation era. We hear the thought-provoking insights of wives of Reformers, pastors' wives, mothers of denominational leaders, and women who directed substantial ministries of their own.

We then trace the continued development and growth of women's soul care and spiritual direction in the modern era. Letters of spiritual counsel and books about women's ministry express the depth of individual and corporate mutual ministry.

Throughout each chapter, we weave together individual stories and highlight common themes. We invite you to enjoy the voices of diverse famous and not-so-famous women who tell their own stories. We pray that their stories will impact your life and ministry.

A Lifelong Calling: Introducing Your Story Tellers

If there is a story to tell, there must be storytellers. We (Bob and Susan) believe you deserve to know our perspective as we share the narratives of *Sacred Friendships*.

We like to think of ourselves less as co-authors and more as co-editors. Our job is not to write the stories; our job is to introduce each story, step back to allow these remarkable women to tell their own stories, and then ponder together possible themes and implications for our lives and ministries today.

As co-editors, we, of course, bring our own backgrounds to our task. We both minister in the context of Evangelical Protestant Christianity. That is our culture, context, and calling. However, *Sacred Friendships* is not only a book about Evangelical Protestant Christian women. As we've indicated, we move from the early Church to the modern era. Thus *Sacred Friendships* is a book about diverse Christian women soul care-givers and spiritual directors.

Frankly, we understand that some of our Evangelical Protestant Christian friends might wish we had studied only those women who might be identified as "within that camp." We make no apologies for the fact that we have not. We believe that every narrative presented within *Sacred Friendships* is representative of historic Christian orthodoxy, even if we might not personally agree with every aspect of every person's ministry represented in this book.

We also understand that some readers who would not self-identify as Evangelical Protestants might wonder about our ability to select and present our material in an unbiased way. Of course, recognizing one's biases is the first step toward eliminating them as much as is humanly possible. The second step we took was to research broadly and inclusively, looking for representative themes (theme saturation), and then incorporating the best, most stirring examples of those themes regardless of the "denomination" of the author. We have attempted to be good historians who accurately and fairly present the original sources so that you can discern the truth, and apply historical truth to post-modern life and ministry.

But why us? When I (Bob) present on the topic of women's ministry, I start every presentation with a PowerPoint slide showing the picture of an elephant in a living room. I ask the question, "Who or what is the elephant in our room today?" Inevitably some courageous audience member will point to me and shout, "You are! What's a male doing talking about the history of female soul care and spiritual direction?"

I take no offense. It is a legitimate question. For me, the journey began in 1981 when I was a seminary student witnessing rival factions debating which *current* model of biblical counseling could claim the mantle of accuracy and relevancy. During the ongoing and often heated discussions, I kept thinking, "Surely, the church has *always* been about the business of helping hurting and hardened people."

It seemed to me that few in the current debate were looking beyond the current options. I started looking *beyond*. I started looking *before*. I committed myself to a life-long search for the ancient paths and stumbled upon the buried treasure of historical soul care (sustaining and healing) and spiritual direction (reconciling and guiding).

Because I wrote my dissertation on how Martin Luther (a white male) exemplified soul care and spiritual direction, and since I co-authored *Beyond the Suffering: Embracing the Legacy of African American Soul Care and Spiritual Direction*[5] (African American males and females), the time was right to join with Susan to pen *Sacred Friendships*. This "voice-for-the-voiceless" view is for me not academic, but personal. God has built into my DNA and my history a passion for empowering those who have been robbed of their voice. It's not just what I do; it's who I am.

The elephant in the room? It is me—a male who cares deeply about those who have been stifled and who has learned profoundly from female Christians.

When I (Susan) began my seminary education I was excited about all my counseling courses, except one, *History of Soul Care and Spiritual Direction*. Up to that point, my experience with history was boring lectures full of useless dates and dry facts. But my dislike of history quickly melted during that class. I was surprised by the inspiring stories of my brothers and sisters in Christ. I was amazed by the relevance of all they had to teach us. I wanted to know more.

At the same time, my formal and informal ministry to women continued to increase. I found myself assisting women from different races, cultures, life stages, and ages. As my involvement with women grew, so did my passion for them. I look forward to helping them overcome pain from a traumatic experience or throw off the shackles of sin that disrupt their relationship with God, family, and friends. I treasure all they teach me along the way and delight in watching the Lord's daughters blossom into the women He intended them to be.

When Bob asked me to be a part of this project, I couldn't say no. It was the marriage of two of my passions. The more I researched, the more energized I became. I was fascinated with the treasures we were unearthing and thrilled to meet my sisters from yesteryear. I have been inspired, encouraged, motivated, comforted, and convicted by the women we've studied and I can't wait to introduce them to others. My hope is that *Sacred Friendships* will be only the beginning for many; that readers will get a taste of life and wisdom from the women presented within these pages, and will dig deeper to learn more about the women who lovingly provided soul care and spiritual direction through the centuries.

Listening to the Silenced Voices

Throughout *Sacred Friendships* we will listen to the previously silenced voices of more than fifty godly Christian women spanning nearly 2,000 years, five continents, and a great diversity of nationalities and races. Centuries later, surrounded by so great a cloud of witnesses, we build upon the foundation they laid.

Our prayer as you read *Sacred Friendships* is that you will marvel at the depth of the spiritual riches that arose through the previously unheralded history of women's soul care and spiritual direction. More than that, whether you are female or male, it is our desire that when you finish *Sacred Friendships* you will be empowered to sustain, heal, reconcile, and guide the people you love based upon the wisdom and practice of these female predecessors in the faith.

CHAPTER ONE

SO GREAT A CLOUD OF WITNESSES:
IN HER OWN WORDS

"Women's history has certainly come a long way in a very short time. Perhaps the reason for this phenomenal progress is the fact that so much of it was there, just waiting to be rescued from obscurity by interested historians." (Patricia Ranft)[1]

"'Where were the women?' 'What did they have to say?' 'How did they shape the life and thought of the church?' For many of us, the courses we took in church history or the history of Christian theology left these questions unanswered." (Amy Oden)[2]

The early Christians addressed in Hebrews desperately needed godly counsel. They lived in a cosmopolitan world with a myriad of questions and competing answers, and they faced persecution from every direction that forced them to ponder the goodness of God during the badness of life. The author of Hebrews, in addition to providing them with words of inspired counsel, offers them inspiring examples of living counsel. "Therefore, since we are surrounded by such a great cloud of witnesses, let us throw off everything that hinders and the sin that so easily entangles, and let us run with perseverance the race marked out for us" (Hebrews 12:1).

Far too many of us forget the "therefore" of the verse, and we imagine the scene as if the Roman Coliseum is filled with fifty-thousand out-of-shape, couch-potato fans cheering on Olympic athletes. When we remember the "therefore," then our minds return to Hebrews 11 and the great spiritual "Hall of Faith" with spiritual athletes like Abel, Enoch, Noah, Abraham, Joseph, Moses, and Rahab. Then we grasp the truth—it is these spiritual Olympic champions who fill the stands. Their robes of white look like a cloud—a great cloud of amazing witnesses whose lives testify to the validity and veracity of faith.

Standing in unison, they cheer on the struggling, exhausted, battered Christians of Hebrews. They cry out, "Don't quit!" "You can do it!" "Throw off that extra weight!" "Abandon that besetting sin!" "Run your marathon... for Jesus... in His strength... like we did!" "Fix your eyes on Jesus. Consider how He endured such persecution from sinners, so that you will not grow weary or lose heart!"

A Forgotten Art: Reclaiming Our Historical Mantle of Mutual Ministry

Is our situation so different from the early Christians? Do we not need inspiring spiritual athletes who have already run the race to encourage and empower us? Yet, in our swiftly changing times, as we desperately search every which way for spiritual solutions, we tend to turn a deaf ear to the experienced voices of the past.

However, we could drink deeply from the rivers of historic Christianity. Specifically, we could quench our thirst for spiritual wisdom in the waters of the great cloud of Christian *women* witnesses. Given the persecution they endured, given the mistreatment they overcame, history has equipped them to be our soul care-givers and spiritual directors as we run the race of faith.

The history of women's soul care and spiritual direction provides a deep spiritual root system able to withstand high winds and parching drought so that our souls can be nourished and our spiritual lives can flourish. By following in their footsteps, we can reclaim the ancient gifts of soul care and spiritual direction, restore the forgotten arts of sustaining, healing, reconciling, and guiding, and experience a reformation in how we minister to one another.

Sacred Friendships joins a rising chorus beckoning Christians back to their roots. The voices in this chorus advise that we explore historic models of spiritual care for their relevance for ministry today. They recommend that we examine how Christians faced spiritual and emotional issues *before* the advent of modern secular psychology.

Too often we build personal ministry models without the wisdom of the historic voices of the church. Thomas Oden explains that some Christians are willing to listen only to their own voice or the voices of contemporaries in the dialogue. "Christians have usually been losers when they have neglected the consensual writers of their own history and tradition."[3]

According to Wayne Oates, Christians "tend to start over from scratch every three or four generations." Therefore, we do not consolidate the communal wisdom of the centuries because of our "antipathy for tradition." As a result, we "have accrued less capital" in the form of proverbs, manuals of mutual ministry, and a theology of body life.[4]

William Clebsch and Charles Jaekle present a convincing explanation for our lack of connection with the history of Christian mutual care. "Faced with an urgency for some system by which to conceptualize the human condition and to deal with the modern grandeurs and terrors of the human spirit, theoreticians of the cure of souls have too readily adopted the leading academic psychologies. Having no pastoral theology to inform our psychology or even to identify the cure of souls as a mode of human helping, we have allowed psychoanalytic thought, for example, to dominate the vocabulary of the spirit."[5]

Today's crying needs drown out yesterday's relevant answers. Why? We lack a sufficient awareness of the victorious ways in which people have faced life issues in centuries past.

The Sound of Silence: Listening to Inspiring Feminine Voices from the Past

In particular, we lack awareness of how Christian women assumed the ancient roles of soul physicians and spiritual friends and how they modeled the ancient arts of soul care and spiritual direction. Even well-researched books on the history of spiritual care often primarily view women as the objects of care and rarely as caregivers themselves, and not as the source of new ideas.[6] The soul care and spiritual direction roles of women have been overlooked and flagrantly neglected to such an extent that women have virtually disappeared. It is time to give them back their voices and their visibility.

Having said that, it is important to realize that *Sacred Friendships* is not a feminist history of soul care and spiritual direction. Rather, it is a history of feminine soul care and spiritual direction. The difference is huge. We have doggedly endeavored to offer an objective account—one not filtered through a personal philosophy.

One need not be a feminist (and neither of us is) to understand that God is the God of the widow, of the powerless, of the hurting (Psalm 68:5). Voiceless, invisible women like Hagar perceive by faith that God is the God who hears and sees the oppressed (Genesis 16:13). The historical silencing of women has significance to God— the God who sees, hears, cares, and empowers.

Because of their Hagar-like faith in God, rather than succumbing to their mistreatment, women of faith have risen above the trials of life lived east of Eden. Lettie Burd Cowman (1870-1960), missionary to Japan and famous for her *Streams in the Desert* daily devotional, emphasized that part of the depth of women's spirituality arises from their wilderness experiences. She took her theme from Isaiah 35:6, "Water will gush forth in the wilderness and streams in the desert."

Her core spirituality taught that *life is hard in order to make us hardier.*[7] Her notion of powerlessness as the route to power rang true for her feminine readers and rings true for us in light of the history of feminine spirituality. "It is the difficulty encountered on the hills that drives us to the throne of grace and brings the showers of blessing. Yes, it is the hills, the cold and seemingly barren hills of life, that we question and complain about, that bring down the showers.... And how many would have been killed by the cold, destroyed or swept desolate of their fruitfulness by the wind, if not for the hills—stern, hard, rugged, and so steep to climb."[8]

Despite the hills of silence and the valleys of invisibility, women have ministered significantly throughout church history. As *Sacred Friendships* repeatedly demonstrates, the role of women has been an honored one; we simply have to uncover the evidence. For instance, early in church history this prayer recited at the ordination of a deaconess speaks volumes to women's high honor.

> O eternal God, the Father of our Lord Jesus Christ, the Creator of man and of woman, who did fill with the Spirit Miriam, Deborah, Anna, and Huldah, who did not deem unworthy that your only-begotten Son should be born of a woman, who also in the tent of witness in the Temple ordained women as keepers of your holy gates: now look upon this your servant who is being ordained as a deaconess, and give her the Holy Spirit, and purify her from any defilement of flesh and spirit (2 Cor. 7:1), so that she may worthily accomplish the work entrusted to her and to your glory and the praise of your Christ, with whom to you and to the Holy Spirit be glory and adoration forever. Amen![9]

For those with eyes to see and ears to hear it is not hard to uncover the buried historical treasure of women's spiritual care. Once it is unburied, our calling is to derive a universally applicable contemporary model of soul care and spiritual direction grounded in the historical experience of Christian women— as they have lived it and told it.

Reading God's Treasure Map[10]

Imagine that we stumble upon a treasure map directing us to the riches of biblical insights for living found in messages from our feminine Christian forebears. Using our map and arriving at our destination, we find an immeasurable treasure. In fact, we find so much truth for life that we're overwhelmed. How do we sort it all out, decode it, translate it? How do we integrate the changing with the changeless and balance today's demands with yesterday's treasures?

Somehow we must enter into enduring companionship with those who have gone before us. From our personal connection with them, we need to formulate an approach to spiritual care that is vital for our time *and* firmly grounded in the best traditions of the past.[11] We require a model, a map, or a grid that can alert us to currently forgotten but time-tested modes for meeting people's spiritual needs.

We have various means available for unearthing the riches of historical Christian women's spiritual care resources. As we noted in the Introduction, we've chosen to use the traditional model of soul care (sustaining and healing) and spiritual direction (reconciling and guiding) as a probe into the past beliefs and practices of our female ancestors in the faith.

Our use of this model is not an attempt to conceal the complexity of mutual ministry. Nor is it an effort to force feminine spiritual care into our own image. We recognize that spiritual care is an extremely complex activity that has taken place in countless ways over 2,000 years of church history. Therefore, we need to define carefully our terms in order to use sustaining, healing, reconciling, and guiding to explore what female believers have done to provide soul care and spiritual direction.

Once we understand these specific definitions, we can use them to ask concrete questions when reading letters of spiritual counsel, letters of consolation, personal narratives, manuals of spirituality, and other primary historical documents. This aids us in uncovering the richness and diversity of feminine Christian care as it has been exercised in the past. It also helps us to distill relevant applications for our current practice of Christian care-giving.

Plotting the Map of Soul Care and Spiritual Direction: The Twin Themes

Experts who examine the history of spiritual care have consistently identified the twin historical themes of soul care and spiritual direction. John McNeil's *A History of the Cure of Souls* traces the art of soul care throughout history and various cultures. "Lying deep in the experience and culture of the early Christian communities are the closely related practices of mutual edification and fraternal correction," he writes. Speaking of the Apostle Paul, McNeil notes, "In such passages we cannot fail to see the Apostle's design to create an atmosphere in which the intimate exchange of spiritual help, the mutual guidance of souls, would be a normal feature of Christian behavior."[12]

Throughout his historical survey, McNeil explains that mutual edification involves *soul care* through the provision of sustaining (consolation, support, and comfort) and healing (encouragement and enlightenment). Fraternal correction includes *spiritual direction* through the provision of reconciling (discipline, confession, and forgiveness) and guiding (direction and counsel).

In *Clinical Theology*, Frank Lake clarifies that historically soul care deals with *suffering* while spiritual direction deals with *sin*. He summarizes his classification by explaining that "pastoral care is defective unless it can deal *thoroughly* with these evils we have suffered as well as with the sins we have committed."[13] Throughout church history, biblical care-givers have dealt with both suffering *and* sin, deprivation *and* depravity, hurting hearts *and* hard hearts, comforting *and* confronting, soul care *and* spiritual direction.[14]

Plotting the Map of Sustaining, Healing, Reconciling, and Guiding: The Four Tasks

Clebsch and Jaekle offer the classic description of traditional spiritual care. The care of souls has historically involved "helping acts, done by *representative Christian persons*, directed toward the *healing, sustaining, guiding, and reconciling* of *troubled persons* whose troubles arise *in the context of ultimate meanings and concerns.*"[15]

Kenneth Leech observes that Clebsch and Jaekle's definition has become the standard definition for pastoral care and spiritual counseling, noting that the Association for Pastoral Care and Counseling adopted the definition into its constitution.[16] Thomas Oden suggests that the four tasks of sustaining, healing, reconciling, and guiding "try to absorb and work seriously with a wide variety of confessional and denominational viewpoints on ministry." They try to "reasonably bring all these voices into a centric, historically sensitive integration, with special attention to historical consensus."[17]

The framework of the two themes and four tasks provides a perspective—a historical way of viewing and thinking about spiritual friendship, pastoral care, and professional Christian counseling. It is the map we will use to organize systematically what Christian women have done as they provide Christian care-giving.

Combining the two themes and the four tasks creates the following profile of historic spiritual care.

- ◆ Soul Care: Comfort for Suffering
  - ◆ Sustaining
  - ◆ Healing
- ◆ Spiritual Direction: Confrontation for Sinning
  - ◆ Reconciling
  - ◆ Guiding

The following chart expands this outline. The rest of this chapter provides illustrative examples of these terms as practiced by past Christian women and explains how we use the terms throughout *Sacred Friendships* to distill personal applications and ministry implications.

Soul Care and Spiritual Direction
Sustaining, Healing, Reconciling, and Guiding

Soul Care: The Evils We Have Suffered

"God Is Good Even When Life Is Bad"

Soul care givers compassionately identify with people in pain and redirect them to Christ and the Body of Christ to sustain and heal their faith so they experience communion with Christ and conformity to Christ as they love God (exalt God by enjoying and trusting Him) and love others.

Sustaining: *"It's Normal to Hurt"*

Sense Your Spiritual Friend's Earthly Story of Despair

Empathize with and Embrace Your Spiritual Friend

Healing: *"It's Possible to Hope"*

Stretch Your Spiritual Friend to God's Eternal Story of Hope

Encourage Your Spiritual Friend to Embrace God

Spiritual Direction: The Sins We Have Committed

"God Is Gracious Even When I Am Sinful"

*Spiritual directors understand spiritual dynamics
and discern root causes of spiritual conflicts,
providing loving wisdom that reconciles and guides people so they
experience
communion with Christ and conformity to Christ
as they love God (exalt God by enjoying and trusting him) and love
others.*

Reconciling: *"It's Horrible to Sin, but Wonderful to Be Forgiven"*

Strip Your Spiritual Friend's Enslaving Story of Death

Expose Your Spiritual Friend's Sin and Reveal God's Grace

Guiding: *"It's Supernatural to Mature"*

Strengthen Your Spiritual Friend with Christ's Empowering
Story of Life

Equip and Empower Your Spiritual Friend to Love[18]

Roadmap Marker Number One: Soul Care through Sustaining— "It's Normal to Hurt"

Susannah Spurgeon's (1832-1903) biographer highlighted Susannah's soul care ability. Speaking of the year she was engaged to her future husband, Pastor Charles H. Spurgeon, he notes of her, "Even in these early days, C. H. Spurgeon was abused in the press, and he found some consolation in writing to his fiancée, who did much to comfort and sustain him."[19] In a letter Charles wrote to Susannah in May 1855, he shared how "down in the valley" he was.

And he affirms his need for her sustaining ministry. "My love, were you here, how you would comfort me..."[20]

We know from records of their relationship exactly the type of sustaining comfort Susannah provided for Charles. Pastor Spurgeon would expend such energy preaching that Susannah worried about his health. Of her concern she would write, "Oh how my heart ached for him! What self-control I had to exercise to appear calm and collected and keep quietly in my seat up in that little side gallery! How I longed to have the *right* to go and comfort and cheer him when the service was over! But I had to walk away, as other people did—I who belonged to him and was closer to his heart than anyone there!"[21]

Her empathy for him continued all through their married life. When Pastor Spurgeon felt that he had not been earnest enough in preaching, they would "sob and weep together," he "from the smiting of a very tender conscience towards God" and she because she "loved him and *wanted to share his grief.*"[22]

Susannah embodies historic sustaining. For more than 2,000 years, Christian sustaining has emphasized consolation and *compassionate commiseration* believing that *shared sorrow is endurable sorrow.* Its practitioners have offered *empathy* in the original sense of the word—feeling deeply the feelings of another. Historic sustainers have joined others in their pain by communicating that *"It's normal to hurt."* When the fallen world fell on their spiritual friends, they connected with them by acknowledging that *"Life is bad."* When their friends, like the Apostle Paul in 2 Corinthians 1:8-9, felt the sentence of death and despaired even of life, they *climbed in the casket* with them, identifying with their feelings of despair.

They have also provided *comfort* in the original sense of the word—offering "co-fortitude"—by coming alongside to lend support and to instill courage in a hurting heart. They have purposed to help hurting people endure and transcend irretrievable loss. Finding people facing such loss, practitioners of sustaining offered wise pilotage for souls in danger of floundering in external distress (level one suffering) and inner doubt (level two suffering). Their ministry drew a line in the sand of the soul finding a stopping place against full retreat by rejecting denial and surrender, replacing them with candor and the will to survive.

With this understanding of historic sustaining, as we engage first-hand accounts of feminine soul care by sustaining, we have specific questions that we can ask. We have specific compass points on our map of sustaining soul care that we can use to plot the nature of care-giving. When ministering to hurting people, how did Christian women:

* Communicate compassionate commiseration?
* Employ the principle that shared sorrow is endurable sorrow?
* Practice empathy by feeling deeply the feelings of others?
* Join others in pain by communicating that *"It's normal to hurt"*?
* Connect with others by acknowledging that *"Life is bad"*?
* Climb in the casket to identify with feelings of despair?
* Provide comfort by coming alongside to lend support and to instill courage?
* Help others to endure and transcend irretrievable loss?
* Offer wise pilotage for souls in danger of floundering?
* Draw a line in the sand of the soul, finding a stopping place against full retreat?
* Enhearten others to find strength to face and survive life's difficulties?

In all of these probes, our task is to uncover the unique ways in which female believers practiced the historic soul care art of sustaining. Then we can prayerfully apply their ancient practices to our current situations.

Roadmap Marker Number Two: Soul Care through Healing—"It's Possible to Hope"

John Wesley had been dead only sixteen years when Phoebe Worrall (1807-1874) was born. Her father, Henry Worrall, had been powerfully moved by Wesley's preaching at Bradford, England. At age nineteen, Phoebe married Walter C. Palmer, a Rutgers-educated New York physician, on September 28, 1827. Their first two children (of six) died in infancy.[23]

Phoebe reflected on the trials and victory of her faith during her time of grieving and healing from the death of her first two children. "These trials, through they sometimes arose from outward causes, were generally inward and the struggle they caused is indescribable; in the midst of which she was often called to lean so entirely, 'with *naked* faith, upon a *naked* promise,' that nature was sometimes tempted in its shrinkings to say, 'My God, why hast thou forsaken me?', but still holding with unyielding grasp upon that promise, 'I will never leave nor forsake thee...'"[24]

Her cup of parental grieving, sadly, was yet unfulfilled. On July 29, 1836, Phoebe's eleven-month-old daughter, Eliza, died in a tragic crib fire. During her dark night of the soul, Phoebe agonized over this third death. "Never have I passed through a trial so severe, as since the last date. If it were not that the Heavenly Physician had applied the healing balm, I should shrink utterly from a review of the scene."[25]

She then spoke of an inexpressible bewilderment of grief accompanied by an unshakable faith in a loving God and a purposeful existence. "While pacing the room, crying to God, amid the tumult of grief, my mind was arrested by a gentle whisper, saying, 'Your Heavenly Father loves you. He would not permit such a great trial, without intending that some great good proportionate in magnitude and weight should result.'"[26]

Palmer personifies historic healing. For more than 2,000 years, Christian healing has underscored the encouragement that comes through enlightened eyes that see God at work behind life's miseries and mysteries. Its practitioners have understood that *when life stinks, our perspective shrinks.* Therefore, they have diligently listened for God's eternal story of deliverance. They have asked, in the midst of messes, "What is God up to in this?" They have worked with suffering people to co-create faith stories and Exodus narratives so that people can rejoice in the truth that *"It's possible to hope."*

When all seemed dark and hopeless, they communicated that *"God is good. He's good all the time!"* Healing soul physicians enabled their spiritual friends to say with the Apostle Paul, "But this happened that we might not rely on ourselves but on God, who raises the dead"

(2 Corinthians 1:9b). They *celebrated the resurrection* and rejoiced because of the empty tomb.

They have also emphasized faith eyes or spiritual eyes by using scriptural truths to enlighten people entering new dimensions of spiritual insight and empowering them to cross the threshold toward new levels of spiritual maturity. If sustaining brought *surviving*, then healing produced *thriving*. Even when situations could not change, attitudes and character could. Historic healers followed a biblical sufferology (theology of suffering) that taught that crisis provides a door of opportunity which can produce forward movement from victim to victor. Through creative suffering, they placed themselves and their spiritual friends on God's anvil to be master-crafted according to His perfect will.

With this understanding of historic healing, we can ask precise questions as we sift through first-hand accounts of women's soul care. When ministering to hurting people, how did female Christians:

- Encourage and enlighten people to see God at work behind the scenes?
- Co-create new faith stories and Exodus narratives?
- Help people to experience the truth that *"It's possible to hope"*?
- Communicate that *"God is good"*?
- Celebrate the resurrection and the empty tomb?
- Enable people to enter deeper dimensions of spiritual insight?
- Empower people to cross the threshold toward new levels of spiritual maturity?
- Help people to thrive in parched conditions?
- Develop and share a biblical sufferology?
- Equip people to move from being victims to victors?
- Practice the art of creative suffering?

Through such probing questions, we'll learn together the essence of historic healing as practiced by female believers. As we learn, we'll grow in our abilities as physicians of the soul who bring Christ's healing touch to hurting human hearts.

Roadmap Marker Number Three: Spiritual Direction through Reconciling—"It's Horrible to Sin, but Wonderful to Be Forgiven"

We know little about Elizabeth White's (1630-1669) short life. Her spiritual memoir provides the only detailed account we have of a seventeenth-century Puritan woman.

She was raised in a Christian home and brought up in the nurture and admonition of the Lord, but pride gripped her sinner's heart. "I was ready to think myself somebody, and with the proud Pharisee, to thank God that I was not as others, not considering that I was but like a Wolf chained up, which keeps its Nature still, as I by the Goodness of God have seen, since the Lord was pleased to lay his Eye Salve upon me."[27]

Elizabeth was one month from marriage and her father wanted her to receive her first communion, but she felt herself unworthy and perhaps unconverted. Three weeks later her minister visited her. "O how loath was I to acquaint him with my sad State! I was ashamed to tell him that I was yet a Stranger to God and all Goodness, till it was forced from me.... then there came many Sins to my Remembrance, which I had taken no notice of before, counting them small Sins... I remembered with bitter Grief, and I thought that there was no Mercy for me, but he persuaded me there was hope of Mercy for such as I, and that the Lord waited to be gracious to poor Sinners..."[28]

Elizabeth exemplifies historic reconciling. For more than 2,000 years, Christian reconciling has focused upon guilt *and* grace, sin *and* forgiveness, repentance *and* mercy, shame *and* shalom. Its practitioners have understood that reconciliation with God requires a personal awareness of the truth that *"It's horrible to sin, but wonderful to be forgiven."* Therefore, they practiced the arts of loading the conscience with guilt and lightening the conscience with grace. They helped people to see that *"God is gracious even when they were sinful."* Historic reconcilers were *dispensers of grace.*

In their understanding of human nature, they emphasized God's original *Creation* of humanity in His image, humanity's *Fall* into sin, and believers' *Redemption* through Christ's grace. They also underlined a three-fold need for reconciliation—with God (due to alienation), with others (due to separation), and with self (due to dis-integration). Thus they focused upon restoring people to a right relationship with

God, others, and self through confrontation, repentance, confession, and forgiveness.

Using this model of historic reconciling, we can map what Christian women did when providing reconciling spiritual direction. We can ask, when ministering to hardened people, how did female believers:

- Maintain an integrated focus on guilt *and* grace, sin *and* forgiveness?
- Help people to personalize the complementary truths that *"It's horrible to sin, but wonderful to be forgiven"*?
- Enlighten people to the truth that *"God is gracious even when we are evil"*?
- Load the conscience with guilt?
- Lighten the conscience with grace?
- Dispense grace to each other?
- Teach about Creation, Fall, and Redemption?
- Restore people through reconciliation and restoration with God, others, and self?
- Confront sin?
- Grant forgiveness?

Probing questions like these cause us to examine our own hearts. Are we in right relationship with God, others, and ourselves? Are we practicing the soul physician art of reconciliation from a biblical perspective in a biblical way?

Roadmap Marker Number Four: Spiritual Direction through Guiding—"It's Supernatural to Mature"

Sojourner Truth (1797-1883) was born a slave named Isabella Baumfree around 1797 in Hurley, Ulster County, New York, on the estate of a Dutch family, the Hardenberghs. She and twelve siblings lived with her parents in deplorable conditions in the Hardenberghs' cellar.[29]

Sojourner's mother inspired her devotion to Christ. In the evening her mother would teach her 13 children of "the only Being that could effectually aid or protect them." She would say, "'My children, there is a God, who hears and sees you.' 'A *God*, mau-mau! Where does he live?' asked the children. 'He lives in the sky,' she replied; 'and when you are beaten, or cruelly treated, or fall into any trouble, you must ask help of him, and he will always hear and help you.'"[30]

Sojourner treasured and held sacred these instructions from her mother. "Thus, in her humble way, did she endeavor to show them their Heavenly Father, as the only being who could protect them in their perilous condition; at the same time, she would strengthen and brighten the chain of family affection, which she trusted extended itself sufficiently to connect the widely scattered members of her precious flock."[31]

Speaking of her own experience of being sold at the slave auction, and of her memory of her mother's spiritual direction, Sojourner records, "In these hours of her extremity, she did not forget the instructions of her mother, to go to God in all her trials, and every affliction; and she not only remembered, but obeyed: going to Him, 'and telling Him all—and asking Him if He thought it was right,' and begging Him to protect and shield her from her persecutors."[32]

Sojourner Truth and her mother typify historic guiding. For more than 2,000 years, Christian guiding has concentrated on the wisdom necessary to apply God's Word in trying situations in order to promote spiritually mature lifestyles. Its practitioners have understood the prerequisite for wise specific choices—a redeemed, maturing, God-dependent heart and mind. Rather than presenting self-sufficient sources for wisdom for living, they taught that *"It's supernatural to mature."* They did so by *stirring up the gift of God* that already resided within the new creation God redeemed. They taught about the new nature (sainthood) and the new nurture (sonship).

Building upon these foundations, practitioners of guiding performed *devil craft*—shared discovery of biblical principles for spiritual victory over Satan during times of spiritual warfare. They also engaged in the mutual exploration of scriptural principles to help perplexed people make confident choices in matters of the soul. Together, guide and disciple discovered practical, proverbial wisdom that equipped the disciple to love God and others in increasingly mature ways.

Following this paradigm of guiding, we can detect characteristic methods used by female mentors as they guided others. We can ask, when ministering to perplexed people, how did Christian women:

- Convey the God-dependent attitude that *"It's supernatural to mature"*?
- *Stir up the gift of God* within redeemed people?
- Teach biblical principles of the new nature and new nurture?
- Jointly discern the biblical wisdom principles necessary to help perplexed people find scriptural guidance?
- Practice *devil craft*—discover biblical principles for spiritual victory over Satan?
- Help others to find practical, proverbial wisdom?
- Equip disciples to love God and others more maturely?

Our purpose is to use these probes to identify the noteworthy methods that female predecessors in the faith used to guide people. Through better understanding their special style of historic guiding, we can appreciate their creativity and emulate their ingenuity.

Listening to the Silenced Voices

Throughout *Sacred Friendships* our passion is to listen carefully to the previously silenced voices of women soul care-givers and spiritual directors. Our ears will repeatedly hear the profound messages of sustaining, healing, reconciling, and guiding. No, they did not have these terms readily available to outline what they said. Rather, they lived, breathed, and embodied the essence of these four soul care and spiritual direction tasks.

Susannah Wesley (1669-1742), mother of Wesleyan pioneers John and Charles, exemplifies in one breath these four interrelated callings. "We are to be instructed, because we are ignorant [guiding]; and healed, because we are sick [healing]; and disciplined, because we are so apt to wander and go astray [reconciling]; and succored and supported, because we are so often tempted [sustaining]."[33]

Susannah Wesley and uncountable Christian women like her followed a spiritual compass. Instead of N-S-E-W, their soul care and spiritual direction compass points read S-H-R-G: Sustaining, Healing, Reconciling, and Guiding. Throughout *Sacred Friendships*, they will gift us with their wisdom—wisdom for ministry today to God's glory forever.

Learning Together from Our Great Cloud of Witnesses

1. Who are your heroines and heroes in the faith like the women and men of Hebrews 11-12? What lessons have you applied to your life from the great cloud of witnesses who cheer you on?

2. Why do you think that our society prefers the latest trends and newest fads over the time-tested wisdom of our Christian predecessors?

3. What negative results occur when we ignore the wisdom of those who have gone before us?

4. Are you at all surprised by our assertion that past female Christians have a tremendous contribution to make to current Christian ministry?
   a. If so, why?
   b. If not, what wonderful contributions can you identify that past female believers have made toward the way you live your Christian life and practice ministry?

5. Concerning soul care and spiritual direction, along with sustaining, healing, reconciling, and guiding:
   a. Have you ever heard of these terms before? If so, where? Have you implemented them in your ministry? If so, how?
   b. Do you have a "model" that you follow as you seek to help suffering people and as you minister to people overcome by besetting sins? Where did you learn it? How effective do you find it?
   c. To what extent are you open to learning a new model of mutual ministry?

6. Of sustaining, healing, reconciling, and guiding:
   a. Which one do you think you most naturally tend toward?
   b. Which one do you most desire to further learn about and develop?

7. On a scale of one to ten, with one being "like unwrapping my third wedding toaster" and ten being "like a kid unwrapping his/her longed-for gift on Christmas morning," how excited are you about receiving ministry gifts from these past female believers?

CHAPTER TWO

HANDMAIDS OF THE LORD: THE FORGOTTEN CHURCH MOTHERS

"From ancient times, examples of the faith have been committed to writing in order to verify God's grace and provide guidance for human-kind. The aim of recalling the past through the written word has also been to honor God and reassure humanity" (Introductory exhortation to *The Martyrdom of Perpetua*, Marcelle Thiebauz).[1]
"Early in the third century, when persecutions against Christians were raging like a virus in the North African city of Carthage, a young woman named Vibia Perpetua was arrested with four friends. At twenty-one she was their leader and guiding spirit, rallying them in their last crisis and urging them to 'stand fast in the faith'" (Marcelle Thiebauz).[2]

*W*hen we ponder early church history, our minds naturally focus on the Church *Fathers*. Sadly, we normally fail even to consider the Church *Mothers*. Yet, these godly women heroically waged spiritual warfare against the world, the flesh, and the devil. Their losses and their victories, their pain and their joy, their walk with Christ and their journey with one another are all an inheritance from which each of us is eligible to draw. There is a mighty company of gallant women believers from whom we can learn.

From Victim to Victor

Vibia Perpetua (181-203) heads that company. The early church preserved her manuscript (*The Martyrdom of Perpetua*) as a martyr's relic because it is one of the oldest and most descriptive accounts of death for Christ. It is also the earliest known document written by a Christian woman.

Anyone who has ever suffered for the faith or has been oppressed by the powerful can carry on a conversation and feel a bond with Perpetua. In fact, in the introduction to her story, we read that it was "written expressly for God's honor and humans' encouragement" to testify to the grace of God and to edify God's grace-bought people.[3]

Of course, even reading the word "martyr" likely causes us to imagine that Perpetua was a spiritual "super woman" whose life and ministry we could not possibly emulate. The story of her life, however, demonstrates just the opposite.

Perpetua lived in Carthage in North Africa during the persecution of Christians under Septimius Severus. At the time of her arrest in 202 AD, she was a twenty-one-year-old mother of an infant son. Born into a wealthy, prominent, but unbelieving family, she was a recent convert with a father who continually attempted to weaken her faith and a husband who was, for reasons unknown to us, out of the picture. Nothing in Perpetua's situation or background prepared her for the titanic spiritual struggle God called her to face.

Perpetua, her brother, her servant (Felicitas), and two other new converts were discipled by Saturus. We learn from Perpetua of the arrest of all these faithful followers of Christ. "At this time we were baptized and the Spirit instructed me not to request anything from the baptismal waters except endurance of physical suffering. A few days later we were imprisoned."[4]

A Light in the Darkness: Experiencing the Pain of Others

Perpetua candidly faced her fears and expressed her internal and external suffering. "I was terrified because never before had I experienced such darkness. What a terrible day! Because of crowded conditions and rough treatment by the soldiers the heat was unbearable. My condition was aggravated by my anxiety for my baby."[5]

This very human woman exudes superhuman strength. In the midst of her agony, she empathizes with and consoles *others*. Her father, completely exhausted from his anxiety, came from the city to beg Perpetua to recant and offer sacrifice to the emperor. "I was very upset because of my father's condition. He was the only member of my family who would find no reason for joy in my suffering. I tried to comfort him saying, 'Whatever God wants at this tribunal will happen, for remember that our power comes not from ourselves but from God.' But utterly dejected, my father left me."[6]

On the day of her final hearing, the guards rushed Perpetua to the prisoners' platform. Her father appeared with her infant son, guilting her and imploring her to "have pity on your son!" He caused such an uproar, that Governor Hilarion "ordered him thrown out, and he was beaten with a rod. My father's injury hurt me as much *as if* I myself had been beaten. And I grieved because of his pathetic old age."[7]

Perpetua provides a classic portrait of biblical empathy. Her *as if* experience of her father's pain is the essence of sustaining soul care.

She not only finds in Christ the strength to empathize with her father, she also summons Christ's power to console and encourage her family and her fellow martyrs. "In my anxiety for the infant I spoke to my mother about him, tried to console my brother and asked that they care for my son. I suffered intensely because I sensed their agony on my account. These were the trials I had to endure for many days."[8] Incredibly, Perpetua's greatest pain was her ache for others who hurt for her!

A few days passed after the hearing and before the battle in the arena commenced. During this interval, Perpetua witnessed to her persecutors and ministered to other detainees. "Pudens, the official in charge of the prison (the official who had gradually come to admire us for our persistence), admitted many prisoners to our cell so that we might mutually encourage each other."[9]

The Road to Hope: Maintaining Perpetual Persistence

Felicitas was in her eighth month of pregnancy. As the day of the contest approached, she became very distressed that her martyrdom might be delayed, since the law forbade the execution of a pregnant woman. An eyewitness to their eventual death shares his account of their journey together. "Her friends in martyrdom were equally sad at the thought of abandoning such a good friend to *travel alone on the same road to hope.* And so, two days before the contest, united in grief they prayed to the Lord."[10] Immediately after their prayers, her labor pains began and Felicitas gave birth to a girl whom one of her sisters reared as her own.

This eyewitness records their witness for Christ to the very end. "On the day before the public games, as they were eating the last meal commonly called the free meal, they tried as much as possible to make it instead an *agape*. In the same spirit they were exhorting the people, warning them to remember the judgment of God, asking them to be witnesses of the prisoners' joy in suffering, and ridiculing the curiosity of the crowd.... Then they all left the prison amazed, and many of them began to believe."[11]

To the very end, Perpetua maintained her perpetual persistence. "The day of their victory dawned, and with joyful countenances they marched from the prison to the arena as though on their way to heaven. If there was any trembling, it was from joy, not fear. Perpetua followed with a quick step as a true spouse of Christ, the darling of God, her brightly flashing eyes quelling the gaze of the crowd."[12]

As they were led through the gates, they were ordered to put on different clothes; the men, those of the priests of Saturn, the women, those of the priestesses of Ceres. "But that noble woman *stubbornly resisted* even to the end. She said, 'We've come this far voluntarily in order to protect our rights, and we've pledged our lives not to recapitulate on any such matter as this. We made this agreement with you.' Injustice bowed to justice and the guard conceded that they could enter the arena in their ordinary dress. Perpetua was singing victory psalms as if already crushing the head of the Egyptian."[13]

Here we witness not only Perpetua's courageous example of persistence, but also her model of biblical confrontation. She provides riveting testimony to Christ's power at work in the inner life of a Christian woman whose spirit could never be overpowered.

The Lasting Legacy of Macrina the Elder

Like Perpetua before her, Macrina the Elder (270-340) learned the Christian life in the school of suffering. She was born sometime near A. D. 270 in Neocaesarea in Pontus (Asia Minor). During the persecution of Diocletian, Macrina fled the city with her husband

and they lived in hiding in a forest near Pontus for seven years, nearly starving several times.

Macrina's family is a fitting place to continue our exploration of women soul care-givers and spiritual directors. They are unique in the history of Christianity. Her grandsons, Basil the Great and Gregory of Nyssa, both church fathers, are the most famous of her lineage. However, they are not the only reason why generations have long revered the family. She nurtured three generations of Christian leaders, passing the torch of faith from herself to her daughter Emmelia, and then to Emmelia's children Macrina the Younger, Peter, Basil, and Gregory, all of whom history has honored as saints. Most importantly, "what is pertinent here is the fact that the family recognized the women to be the guides directing them all to their spiritual ends."[14]

Truth and Life: Passing on the Faith

Macrina's grandson, Basil, wrote admiringly of his grandmother's mentoring. "What clearer proof of our faith could there be than that we were brought up by our grandmother, a blessed woman. I am speaking of the illustrious Macrina, by whom we were taught the words of the most blessed Gregory (Thaumaturgus), which, having preserved until her time by uninterrupted tradition, she also guarded, and she formed and molded me, still a child, to the doctrines of piety."[15]

What a fascinating concluding phrase, "formed and molded me... to the *doctrines* of *piety*." Macrina's discipleship model focused not just on doctrine, not just on piety, but on *both*—truth *and* life. In this, she followed in the heritage of the Apostle Paul who passed on the faith to Timothy with these words: "Watch your life *and* doctrine closely. Persevere in *them*..." (1 Timothy 4:16a, emphasis added).

Like Macrina the Elder, her daughter Emmelia played a dynamic part in the spiritual development of her children, especially her firstborn, Macrina the Younger. Gregory of Nyssa tells us in his story of his sister: "The education of the child was her mother's task; she did not, however, employ the usual worldly method of education, but such parts of inspired Scripture as you would think were incomprehensible to young children were the subject of the girl's studies; in particular the Wisdom of Solomon, and those parts of it especially which have an ethical bearing. Nor was she ignorant of any part of the Psalter, but at stated times she recited every part of it."[16] Indeed, "When she rose from bed, or engaged in household duties, or rested, or partook of food, or retired from table, when she went to bed or rose in the night for prayer, the Psalter was her constant companion, like a good fellow-traveler that never deserted her."[17]

Like mother, like daughter. Emmelia's guiding emphasized truth *and* life by inculcating the "ethical bearing" of Proverbs. She also followed the pedagogical insight and teaching methodology of Deuteronomy 6:7, "Impress them on your children. Talk about them when you sit at home and when you walk along the road, when you lie down and when you get up."

From Generation to Generation: Mentoring Other Mentors

Emmelia's life lessons stuck. Macrina the Younger discipled her younger brother, Peter. She "took him soon after birth from the nurse's breast and reared him herself and educated him on a lofty system of training, practicing him from infancy in his holy studies" and eventually became "all things to the lad—father, teacher, tutor, mother, giver of all good advice."[18]

In turn, Peter applied well his sister's life lessons. "Scorning to occupy his time with worldly studies, and having in nature a sufficient instructor in all good knowledge, and always looking to his sister as the model of all good, he advanced to such a height of virtue that in his subsequent life he seemed in no whit inferior to the great Basil. But at this time he was all in all to his sister and mother, co-operating with them in the pursuit of the angelic life."[19] In later years, Peter and Macrina the Younger administered the double monastery at Annesi, discipling yet another generation of young believers.

Thus in yet another way, Macrina's family followed the discipleship model of the Apostle Paul who exhorted Timothy, "And the things you have heard me say in the presence of many witnesses entrust to reliable men who will also be qualified to teach others" (2 Timothy 2:2). Macrina the Elder's family mentored four generations and beyond. Macrina the Elder provided guidance to Emmelia; Emmelia provided spiritual direction to Macrina the Younger; Macrina the Younger discipled Peter; Peter mentored those at the double monastery; and those at the monasteries passed the torch of truth to still others.

Mothers of the Church Fathers

When discussing the great church fathers, names like the three Cappadocian Fathers (Basil the Great, Gregory of Nyssa, and Gregory of Nazianzus) come to mind, as do John Chrysostom and Augustine. However, in most cases, we have forgotten their mothers: Emmelia, whom we just considered; Nonna, the mother of Gregory of Nazianzus; Anthusa, the mother of John Chrysostom; and Monica, the mother of Augustine. It is to this lost tradition that we now turn our attention.

Nonna: Stirring Up the Gift of God

The two brothers, Basil the Great and Gregory of Nyssa, along with their close friend and fellow theologian, Gregory of Nazianzus, were the principal formulators of the classic doctrine of the Trinity. Gregory of Nazianzus was the son of Gregory the Elder and Nonna. He became the Bishop of Constantinople and a preacher of orthodoxy who wrote extensively on both theological and devotional topics. After the victory of Nicene Orthodoxy at the Council of Constantinople I in 381, Gregory of Nazianzus retired as a bishop and led a monastic life.

Long before he became famous, his lesser-known mother guided his spiritual life and that of his father. Nonna was born around A. D. 300 and passed away on August 5, 374. Gregory described in glowing terms her holiness of life and the beautiful conformity of her actions to the highest standards of Christian excellence. "She is a woman who while others have been honoured and extolled for natural and artificial beauty, has acknowledged but one kind of beauty, that of the soul, and the preservation, or the restoration as far as possible, of the Divine image."[20]

To her example, aided by her prayers, he ascribed the conversion of his father from a strange medley of paganism and a heretical

Christian sect. Unwilling to accept his status as an unbeliever, Nonna "fell before God night and day, entreating for the salvation of her head with many fastings and tears, and assiduously devoting herself to her husband, and influencing him in many ways, by means of reproaches, admonitions, attentions, estrangements, and *above all* by her own character with its fervour for piety, by which the soul is specially prevailed upon and softened, and willingly submits to virtuous pressure."[21]

Nonna's example provides hope and direction for any Christian wife who struggles with how to relate to a beloved unbelieving husband. She certainly was no "wallflower." Her method of reconciling combined the strong medicine of reproaches and admonitions with continual doses of character and piety. We see in her example the power of persistent prayer and the plan of God to combine prayer and action in all our reconciling relationships.

Her ministry to her newly-saved husband did not end at reconciling. Gregory goes so far as to attribute his father's spirituality and ministry success to Nonna. "But she who was given by God to my father became not only, as is less wonderful, his assistant, but even his *leader*, drawing him on by her influence in deed and word to the highest excellence; judging it best in all other respects to be overruled by her husband according to the law of marriage, but not being ashamed, in regard to piety, even to offer herself as his *teacher*."[22]

Her spiritual guidance was so extensive and intensive that when Gregory the Elder became a bishop, he learned how to shepherd from her example. At his sister's funeral, Gregory of Nazianzus said of his father and mother, "This good shepherd was the result of his wife's prayers and guidance, and it was from her that he learned his ideal of a good shepherd's life."[23]

Here we have a Christian wife guiding her husband. More than that, we find a wife teaching her husband how to shepherd. In church history, women have not taken a back seat to anyone in providing reconciling and guiding spiritual direction.

Nonna's ministry did not stop with her husband, but continued with her son. Like Hannah with Samuel (1 Samuel 1:1-28), Nonna committed her son to the Lord and His service even before Gregory's birth. Reflecting on it years later, Gregory noted about his mother, "That which concerns myself is perhaps undeserving of mention, since I have proved unworthy of the hope cherished in regard to me: yet it was on her part a great undertaking to promise me to God before my birth, with no fear of the future, and to dedicate me immediately after I was born. Through God's goodness has it been that she has not utterly failed in her prayer, and that the auspicious sacrifice was not rejected."[24]

What enabled Nonna to maintain such a relentless prayer life? "These were the objects of her prayers and hopes, in the fervour of faith rather than of youth. Indeed, none was as confident of things present as she of things hoped for, from her experience of the generosity of God."[25] Nonna believed in a good God with a good heart. She knew that her God was a generous rewarder of those who diligently seek Him (Hebrews 11:6). In the ebb and flow of soul care and spiritual direction, Nonna embodied the truth that it is our certainty about God's generosity that leads to our capacity to minister steadfastly.

Anthusa: Lamenting Loss, Gripping Grace

Endeared as one of the four great doctors of the church, John Chrysostom was born in A.D. 347 in Antioch, Syria, and was prepared for a career in law under the renowned Libanius, who marveled at his pupil's eloquence and foresaw a brilliant vocation for him as statesman and lawgiver. But John decided, after he had been baptized at the age of twenty-three, to abandon law in favor of service to Christ. In his renowned pulpit ministry, he emerged as "Golden Mouth," a preacher whose oratorical excellence gained him a reputation throughout the Christian world.

Unfortunately, we know little about John's upbringing and even less about his mother, Anthusa. What we do know should resonate with every woman who has ever been left bereft of a husband.

Anthusa repeats her story of widowhood to her son on the occasion of his plan to leave home at age twenty to share a residence with his best friend, Basil. John recounted the scene. "But the continual lamentations of my mother hindered me from granting him the favor, or rather from receiving this boon at his hands. For when she perceived that I was meditating this step, she took me into her own private chamber, and, sitting near me on the bed where she had given birth to me, she shed torrents of tears, to which she added words yet more pitiable than her weeping, in the following lamentable strain."[26]

Anthusa then shares and bares her soul. "My child, it was not the will of Heaven that I should long enjoy the benefit of thy father's virtue. For his death soon followed the pangs which I endured at thy birth, leaving thee an orphan and me a widow before my time to face all the horrors of widowhood, which only those who have experienced them can fairly understand. For no words are adequate to describe the tempest-tossed condition of a young woman who, having but lately left her paternal home... is suddenly racked by an overwhelming sorrow, and compelled to support a load of care too great for her age..."[27]

Though distressing, Anthusa's candor is refreshing. Sometimes we have the false impression that the "saints of old" sailed through life's sorrows without a single word of complaint or even a blip on their emotional EKG. Anthusa reminds us that this is fictitious. She also models for us the great Old Testament tradition of lamentation, which is so vital in the sustaining process.

Anthusa offered insight into the healing process as she shared with her son how she survived and eventually thrived. "None of these things, however, induced me to enter into a second marriage, or introduce a second husband into thy father's house: but I held on as I was, *in the midst of the storm and uproar*, and did not shun the iron furnace of widowhood. My foremost help indeed was *the grace from above*.[28] In the midst of our storms, our foremost healing help is always grace from above.

Monica: Mingling Spiritual Friendship and Spiritual Direction

The name of Monica (331-387), mother of Augustine, is perhaps the best known of the church mothers. What we know about Monica we learn almost entirely from her son's autobiography *Confessions*. Ranft cogently notes, "Because we are fortunate enough to have *Confessions*, we can easily identify the most influential person in his spiritual life. Monica, his mother, stands out above all others as the spiritual guide and anchor, indeed, as the determinative relationship in his life."[29]

Monica was born in North Africa near Carthage in what is now Tunisia, perhaps around A.D. 331, of Christian parents, and was a committed believer throughout her life. She married an unbelieving husband, Patricius, a man of hot temper who was often unfaithful to her. It was her greatest joy to see both him and his mother ultimately receive the Gospel. Monica also spent years suffering over her son's pagan lifestyle until his conversion and commitment to Christian ministry.

In the *Confessions*, which Augustine addressed to God, we hear of her reconciling witness to her wayward son. "In fact, as a boy I had heard about the eternal life that had been promised to us through the humility of the Lord our God's lowering himself to our pride, and already I was stamped with the sign of his cross, already seasoned with his salt from the womb of my mother, who put great hope in You.... My fleshly mother was disturbed, because she more lovingly brooded over my eternal salvation, with a pure heart in Your faith."[30]

Coming to faith, Augustine describes a scenario to which every believing woman with an unbelieving husband can relate. "Thus already I believed, as did my mother and all the household, my father alone excepted, who nonetheless did not drive out the authority of my mother's piety so that I did not believe in Christ, inasmuch as he did not yet believe. For my mother busied herself in order that You might be my Father, my God, rather than he, and in this matter You helped her so that she might overcome her husband, to whom she was subject...."[31]

Christian mothers need to hear Monica's voice. She confidently spoke and personified the reality that a mother's piety can drown out a father's irreverence. She also reminds mothers that they do *not* have to be both mother and father. In the absence of a believing father, Monica pointed her son to his ultimate Father, rather than trying to be a surrogate father.

Of course, none of this implies that Monica was indifferent to her husband's spiritual plight. "She concerned herself to win him for You, speaking of You through her behavior, by which You made her beautiful, respectfully lovable, and admirable to her husband. Moreover, she thus endured the wrongs to her bed, so that she never had any feuding with her husband on account of this matter. She waited for Your compassion to come upon him, so that believing in You, he might become chaste."[32]

Monica lived to see the fruit of the seeds of life that she planted. "At last she won for You even her own husband, now at the end of his earthly life. In him as a believer she did not now bewail that which she endured when he was not yet one of the faithful."[33]

Monica's ministry extended beyond her home. As she journeyed to join Augustine in Milan, the faith that she exercised with her family strengthened her to comfort, console, and bring courage even to sailors in a storm. "Already my mother had come to me, strong in her piety, following me over land and sea, secure in You against all dangers. For during the hazards at sea she comforted the sailors themselves (to whom inexperienced travelers at sea customarily go for consolation when they become anxious), promising them a safe arrival, because You had promised her this in a vision."[34]

Augustine reserved his final testimonial to his mother's spiritual direction for her spiritual conversations with him in her dying days and hours.

> Thus we were talking alone together very sweetly, forgetting past events and stretching out to those ahead of us. We were seeking between us in the presence of truth, which You are, to think how the future eternal life of the saints would be, the life "which eye has not seen nor ear heard, nor had it entered the heart of man" (Is. 64:4; 1 Cor. 2:9). We opened wide the mouth of our heart to the supernatural streams of Your fountain, the fountain of life, which is with You, so that being sprinkled from it according to our power of comprehension, we might in some way reflect on so great a thing.[35]

Picture it. Mother and son. Leaning on a window, viewing the garden of their house, talking of eternal hope, knowing that she would soon be leaving this world behind. Imagine the encouragement in the midst of sadness that Monica brought her son.

> And when our discussion arrived at the conclusion that the pleasure of the carnal senses, however great it may be, in however great corporeal light, seemed not comparable to the pleasantness of that life, indeed, not even worth speaking about, we raised ourselves by our more ardent passion toward Him, and we gradually traveled through all corporeal things and Heaven itself, whence sun and moon and stars shine above the earth. We were still ascending by our inner reflection and speech. We admired Your words. We came to our minds and transcended them, that we might reach the region of unfailing fruitfulness, where You feed Israel forever with the food of truth…[36]

Nine days later, in the fifty-sixth year of her life, and in the thirty-third year of Augustine's life, Monica passed from life to death to eternal life.

Augustine expressed his grief mingled with hope.

> Then gradually did I call back my earlier feeling for Your handmaid, her devout conversation with You, her gentleness to and compliancy with us in holiness, of which suddenly I was destitute. It was pleasing to weep in Your sight for her and over her, for myself and over myself. And I released the tears which I had restrained, that they might flow as much as they wished, spreading them under my heart, which rested in them, since Your ears were there, not those of a man, who would interpret my weeping in a haughty spirit. And now, Lord, I will confess to You in writing.

Let him read it who will, and let him interpret it as he will, and if he finds a sin in my weeping for my mother for a small part of an hour—a mother who was meanwhile dead to my eyes, who had wept over me for many years that I might live in Your eyes—let him not laugh, but rather, if he is a person of lofty charity, let him weep for my sins against You, the Father of all the brothers of Your Christ.[37]

Augustine wept. He lost his best spiritual friend. He lost the most important person in his life. He lost the earthly mother who led him to know his heavenly Father. Augustine grieved. But he grieved with hope because Monica had encouraged him with words of life.

Listening to the Silenced Voices

When we listen to the silenced voices of the forgotten church mothers we lean back hearing a loudspeaker blaring, *"Women are worthy!"* Remember, this was nearly 2,000 years ago—not exactly an era perceived to be the height of the women's movement. Yet repeatedly, the great church fathers testify of their spiritual debt to the great church mothers.

When we listen to the silenced voices of the forgotten church mothers we also lean over to hear a calm, quiet voice whispering, *"Women are God-empowered."* We do not detect even a trace of arrogance or anger in these powerful women. In fact, it seems they would blush at the word "powerful." Rather, they would choose the word "empowered." These church mothers saw themselves as God-called and God-empowered lights in the darkness. They reflected the light of hope coming from the Son of God as they journeyed gently, yet confidently, with other women and men.

Learning Together from Our Great Cloud of Witnesses

1. Think about a situation where you are suffering for your faith or are being mistreated by an overpowering person.
   a. Like Perpetua, how can you candidly face your fears and express your internal and external suffering?
   b. What would it take for you, *in the midst of* your personal suffering, to empathize with and console *others*?

2. Perpetua modeled the essence of biblical empathy: experiencing another person's pain *as if* it is your own.
   a. Who lives this kind of *as if* life for you?
   b. In what relationship can you apply *as if* empathy? How will you do it?

3. Perpetua and her spiritual friends modeled traveling together on the road to hope.
   a. Think about a dark path that you are facing in your life. How can you invite others to help you to find the road to hope? Who will you invite to journey with you?
   b. Who do you know that needs you to travel with them down their road toward hope? How will you journey with them?

4. Rate your own level of "perpetual persistence" with 10 being "trusting God to the very end regardless of the obstacles," and with 1 being "giving up at the least sign of resistance." What can you do to increase your persistence barometer?

5. Macrina the Elder "balanced" truth *and* life (doctrine *and* application) in her guiding spiritual direction. Do you tend more toward the doctrine side or more toward application? Why? How can you better integrate the two, as Paul did with Timothy in 1 Timothy 4:16?

6. Reflecting on Nonna's witness to her unsaved husband, ponder what applications you can make in your reconciling witness to unsaved family members and friends.

7. In church history, women have not taken a back seat to anyone in providing reconciling and guiding. Whether you are a man or a woman, what do you *do* with this reality?

8. Anthusa both lamented loss (sustaining) and gripped grace (healing). Which do you need in your life? In your ministry to others?

9. What would it be like to have a mother like Monica who uses spiritual conversations to provide authentic spiritual friendship and spiritual direction? What can the church today do to equip more Monicas?

CHAPTER THREE

SPIRITUAL FRIENDS TO SPIRITUAL
GIANTS: DAUGHTERS OF THE CHURCH

"Books surveying the history of Christianity have been traditionally 'his stories'—describing the flaws and celebrating the achievements of great theologians, eloquent preachers, and powerful administrators" (Barbara MacHaffie).[1]

"But what is most excellent and honorable, she also won over her husband to her side, and made of him a good fellow-servant, instead of an unreasonable master" (Gregory Nazianzus, speaking of his sister, Gorgonia).[2]

*T*he ancient Roman world in which early Christian women lived was ruled by notions about women such as these from Aristotle who saw "the female sex as defective and the male as normative."[3] Going back to the earliest days of the Republic, throughout their lives women were under the complete domination of a male figure. Women passed from the control of their fathers to that of their husbands *in manu*—under the total jurisdiction of males. Though women's experiences were varied, "the only general comment to make is that no woman was perceived as equal to a man in terms of her worth."[4]

Into this inequitable situation burst the Christian faith. While respecting the distinctives roles discussed in Scripture, early Christian leaders honored women as their spiritual equals. In fact, in the early church many of the great male leaders of the faith such as Gregory of Nazianzus, Peter, Basil, Gregory of Nyssa, and John Chrysostom were nurtured by their physical and spiritual sisters. Women like Gorgonia, Macrina the Younger, and Olympias demonstrated how the seeds of feminine spiritual friendship blossomed into the giants of the faith.

In Praise of My Sister

We first met Gorgonia's family in chapter two where we learned how to stir up the gift of God from Nonna. Nonna and her husband, Gregory the Elder, were the parents of Gregory of Nazianzus and Gorgonia (A.D. 325-375). Gorgonia and her husband Alypius lived in Iconium where they raised three godly daughters and two sons who became bishops.

All that we know of Gorgonia we derive from her brother Gregory of Nazianzus' funeral oration on her life. Gregory went to great extremes to convey the historical accuracy of his eulogy of Gorgonia. "In praising my sister, I shall pay honour to one of my own family; yet my praise will not be false, because it is given to a relation, but, because it is true, will be worthy of commendation, and its truth is based not only upon its justice, but upon well-known facts. For, even if I wished, I should not be permitted to be partial; since everyone who hears me stands, like a skilful critic, between my oration and the truth, to discountenance exaggeration...."[5]

An Empowering Heroic Narrative: Applying Life Lessons

Gregory modeled the soul physician art of producing a heroic narrative for the purpose of empowering others. "Come, let me proceed with my eulogy... performing, as a most indispensable debt, all those funeral rites which are her due, and further instructing everyone in a zealous imitation of the same virtue, since it is my object in every word and action to promote the perfection of those committed to my charge."[6] Like the author of Hebrews in chapters 11 and 12, Gregory shepherds his living flock by reminding them of the faithfulness of the great cloud of witnesses who have gone before them. Though dead, their lives still speak.

Gorgonia's life spoke from heaven because while on earth she was so heavenly minded that she was of great earthly good.

> Gorgonia's native land was Jerusalem above, the object, not of sight but of contemplation, wherein

is our commonwealth, and whereto we are pressing on: whose citizen Christ is, and whose fellow-citizens are the assembly and church of the first born who are written in heaven, and feast around its great Founder in contemplation of His glory, and take part in the endless festival... which is produced by reason and virtue and pure desire, ever more and more conforming, in things pertaining to God, to those truly initiated into the heavenly mysteries; and in knowing whence, and of what character, and for what end we came into being.[7]

Gorgonia lived with spiritual eyes focused on her native land—heaven. Her life teaches us how to discover our where, who, and why. By focusing on eternity, we learn our origin (where), our identity (who), and our purpose (why). Gorgonia modeled the lesson that we do not find the answers to the great philosophical, existential questions of life by focusing exclusively on this life, but rather by focusing intensely on the next life.

Godly Character Leading to Godly Counsel: Walking the Talk

Her godly character provided the firm foundation necessary for her godly counsel. In fact, Gregory directly linked her "prudence and piety" when speaking of Gorgonia's fame as a wise counselor. "What could be keener than the intellect of her who was recognized as a common adviser not only by those of her family, those of the same people and of the one fold, but even by all men round about, who treated her counsels and advice as a law not to be broken? What more sagacious than her words? What more prudent than her silence?... Who had a fuller knowledge of the things of God, both from the Divine oracles, and from her own understanding?... Who so presented herself to God as a living temple?"[8]

Gorgonia, like all biblical counselors, based her counsel upon the Word of God filtered through the discernment that develops from a lifelong commitment to God. She practiced the competency of using her human reason redeemed by grace to prudently listen to the specific situations of each unique individual in order to provide a timely, insightful word fit seamlessly for the exact occasion.

Gorgonia's soul care was not of the "professional/office variety," but earthly, real, and practical.

> Who opened her house to those who live according to
> God with a more graceful and bountiful welcome?…
> Whose soul was more sympathetic to those in trouble?
> Whose hand more liberal to those in want? I should
> not hesitate to honour her with the words of Job: Her
> door was opened to all comers; the stranger did not
> lodge in the street. She was eyes to the blind, feet to
> the lame, a mother to the orphan. Why should I say
> more of her compassion to widows, than that its fruit
> which she obtained was, never to be called a widow
> herself? Her house was a common abode to all the
> needy of her family; and her goods no less common
> to all in need than their own belonged to each.[9]

In the spirit of 1 Thessalonians 5:14, Gorgonia practiced holistic ministry. "And we urge you, brothers, warn those who are idle, encourage the timid, help the weak, be patient with everyone." In the spirit of James 1:27, she practiced true spirituality. "Religion that God our Father accepts as pure and faultless is this: to look after orphans and widows in their distress and to keep oneself from being polluted by the world." In the spirit of Acts 2:44-45, she practiced sacrificial giving. "All the believers were together and had everything in common. Selling their possessions and goods, they gave to anyone as he had need."

Her counsel and care rang true and pure because she walked the talk. We see this when her maddened mules ran away with her carriage, overturning it, and dragging her along, causing serious injuries to her bones and limbs. Gregory recorded her response to her suffering, a response that teaches us much about biblical sufferology. "…the suffering being human, the recovery superhuman, and giving a lesson to those who come after, exhibiting in a high degree faith in the midst of suffering, and patience under calamity, but in a still higher degree the kindness of God to them that are such as she. For to the beautiful promise to the righteous 'though he fall, he shall not be utterly broken,' has been added one more recent, 'though he be utterly broken, he shall speedily be raised up and glorified.'"[10] Reflecting back upon her silence during the recovery period, Gregory concluded, "...that was the time to be silent, this is the time to manifest it, not only for the glory of God, but also for the consolation of those in affliction."[11]

Gorgonia's sufferology provides a lasting lesson for all to learn: we must mingle enduring patience with deep faith in the goodness of God during the badness of life. Such faith not only brings God glory, it also offers comfort to those currently facing hardships.

As she lived; she died. On her deathbed, Gorgonia offered words of healing hope and guiding direction as she spoke God's truth in love. "After many injunctions to her husband, her children, and her friends, as was to be expected from one who was full of conjugal, maternal, and brotherly love, and after making her last day a day of solemn festival with brilliant discourse upon the things above, she fell asleep, full not of the days of man, for which she had no desire, knowing them to be evil for her, and mainly occupied with our dust and wanderings, but more exceedingly full of the days of God."[12] In serene calmness she whispered her final benediction, "I will lay me down in peace, and take my rest."[13] Even in death, Gorgonia focused on offering life-giving comfort to those she loved.

An Amazing Sister in an Amazing Family

In the previous chapter, we learned that Macrina the Younger (327-379) came from one of the most amazing families in all of church history. Her paternal grandmother was Macrina the Elder, her mother was Emmelia, and her brothers were Peter, Basil, and Gregory of Nyssa. It is from Gregory's work *The Life of St. Macrina* that we learn of her skill as a soul physician.

Spiritual Friend to Her Physical Family: Drawing Her Family to Christ

Although Macrina had no desire for marriage, she acceded to her father's wishes, who arranged for her to marry a noted lawyer. But before the wedding ceremony, her fiancé died unexpectedly. Soon thereafter, her father also died, leaving her mother Emmelia with ten children. Macrina, as the eldest, took over the care of the youngest, the infant Peter. Even more, she became her mother's soul care-giver and spiritual director. "In all these matters she shared her mother's toil, dividing the cares with her, and lightening her heavy load of sorrow.... By her own life she instructed her mother greatly, leading her to the same mark, that of philosophy [Christian theology] I mean, and gradually drawing her on to the immaterial and more perfect life."[14]

Macrina's brother, Basil, returned to the family home after a long period of education, already a practiced rhetorician. "He was puffed up beyond measure with the pride of oratory and looked down on the local dignitaries, excelling in his own estimation all the men of leading and position."[15] Macrina would have none of that. "Nevertheless Macrina took him in hand, and with such speed did she draw him also toward the mark of philosophy [Christian theology] that he forsook the glories of this world and despised fame gained by speaking."[16] With deft guiding, Macrina changed the course of Basil's entire life, swaying him from the torrents of self to the current of Christ.

Sustaining and healing care were also a major focus of Macrina's ministry to her family. The second of her four brothers, Naucratius, died unexpectedly in an accident. She grieved because her "natural affection was making her suffer as well. For it was a brother, and a favorite brother, who had been snatched away." Yet now Macrina displayed her selflessness. Facing the disaster, "she both preserved herself from collapse and becoming the prop of her mother's weakness, raised her up from the abyss of grief, and by her own steadfastness... taught her mother's soul to be brave.... She so sustained her mother by her arguments that she, too, rose superior to her sorrow."[17]

Here we view Macrina practicing classic historical Christian sustaining. She allowed grief, and even embraced it. However, her sustaining drew a line in the sand of retreat. Through it, she forestalls despair by the infusion of hope and by the sharing of sorrow.

An Invincible Athlete: Coaching Others in the Spiritual Olympics

Approximately a decade later, Macrina's brother Basil also "departed from men to live with God." When Macrina heard the news of the calamity in her distant retreat, "she was distressed indeed in soul at so great a loss—for how could she not be distressed at a calamity, which was felt even by the enemies of the truth?" Though grieving greatly, she never surrendered hope. "So she remained, like an invincible athlete in no wise broken by the assaults of troubles."[18]

Her brother Gregory, pained by his own sorrows, traveled to Annesi where Macrina led a spiritual community of women. Upon his arrival, he discovered that Macrina herself was on her deathbed. Yet once again, her focus was on the pain of others. "I journeyed to her, yearning for an interchange of sympathy over the loss of her brother. My soul was right sorrow-stricken by this grievous blow, and I sought for one who could feel it equally, to mingle my tears with.... Well, she gave in to me for a little while, like a skillful driver, in the ungovernable violence of my grief."[19]

After engaging in sustaining through this skillful interchange of sympathy, Macrina slowly shifted the focus to healing hope.

> And in every way she tried to be cheerful, both taking the lead herself in friendly talk, and giving us an opportunity by asking questions. When in the course of conversation mention was made of the great Basil, my soul was saddened and my face fell dejectedly. But so far was she from sharing in my affliction that, treating the mention of the saint as an occasion for yet loftier philosophy, she discussed various subjects, inquiring into human affairs and revealing in her conversation the divine purpose concealed in disasters. Besides this, she discussed the future life, as if inspired by the Holy Spirit, so that it almost seemed as if my soul were lifted by the help of her words away from mortal nature and placed within the heavenly sanctuary.[20]

Macrina was dying, yet she consoled her brother. How? She seamlessly moved from sustaining empathy to healing encouragement. She drew him out by giving him a chance to talk, and then used his human emotions as a starting point for erecting a biblical way of thinking about loss. In classic healing fashion, she unfolded God's eternal plan in the midst of sad human events, focusing on heavenly hope. The result? Gregory's spirit soared because he now could view this life through the lens of the life to come.

Returning the next day, Gregory opened up about his troubles. "First there was my exile at the hands of the Emperor Valens on account of the faith, and then the confusion in the Church that summoned me to conflicts and trials." Perhaps expecting sympathy, he instead received reconciling confrontation. "Will you not cease to be insensible to the divine blessings? Will you not remedy the ingratitude of your soul?… Churches summon you as an ally and director, and do you not see the grace of God in it all? Do you fail to recognize the cause of such great blessings, that it is your parents' prayers that are lifting you up on high, you that have little or no equipment within yourself for such success?" Rather than being floored by her chastisement, he "longed for the length of the day to be further extended, that she might never cease delighting our ears with sweetness."[21] Her capacity to exude love while speaking truth enabled Gregory to hear her words as the faithful wounds of a friend.

The next day would be her last… on earth. She had her couch turned toward the east, facing the *sun* and symbolically facing the *Son*. She then prayed her own benediction. "Thou, O Lord, hast freed us from the fear of death. Thou hast made the end of this life the beginning to us of true life.… Thou hast shown us the way of resurrection, having broken the gates of hell, and brought to naught him who had the power of death—the devil.… But when she had finished the thanksgiving, and her hand brought to her face to make the sign that signified the end of the prayer, she drew a great deep breath and closed her life and her prayer together."[22] As with Gorgonia, even in death, Macrina spoke words of life to those yet living.

A Spiritual Sister to a Church Father

Much of our knowledge of Olympias comes from an anonymous fifth-century document (*The Life of Olympias*) composed by someone who knew her well and from the church father John Chrysostom, who poured out his heart to her in seventeen letters he wrote from his exile. Olympias' grandfather, Ablabius, was a Christian and a senator in Constantine's Roman government. He had a daughter who married Secundus, one of the emperor's "companions," a noble order created by Constantine. Olympias was born to this pair between A.D. 360 and 370. She was orphaned early in life, after which Procopius, the prefect of Constantinople, served as her guardian.[23]

She married Nebridius in 384, but was widowed just days later around age twenty. Pressured to remarry, she instead chose a single life, explaining her position to the emperor Theodosius. "If my King, the Lord Jesus Christ, wanted me to be joined with a man, he would not have taken away my first husband immediately."[24]

The Loving Deaconess: Providing Spiritual Direction through Spiritual Example

By now a rich, pious widow, Olympias gave of her immense wealth to those in need and to many religious leaders. By age thirty she was named a deaconess, which usually did not occur until age sixty. The *Didascalia of the Apostles* mentions deaconesses assisting at baptisms, discipling new believers in the faith, teaching women, visiting unbelievers and believers in their homes, and serving the sick.[25]

During this time she took on the task of spiritual leadership for fifty young single women in Constantinople. Of them, Olympias' biographer notes, "One was struck with amazement at seeing certain things in the holy chorus and angelic institution of these holy women: their incessant continence and sleeplessness, the constancy of their praise and thanksgiving to God, their 'charity which is the bond of perfection,' their stillness."[26] As spiritual directors of these female spiritual friends, Olympias led them in the consistent practice of life-changing spiritual disciplines.

Summarizing her life and ministry among them, Olympias' biographer poetically recalled her Christlike character. "She had a life without vanity, an appearance without pretence, character without affection… a mind without vainglory, intelligence without conceit, an untroubled heart, an artless spirit, charity without limits, unbounded generosity… immeasurable self-control, rectitude of thought, undying hope in God, ineffable almsgiving; she was the ornament of all the humble…"[27]

She was so humble that she readily invited Chrysostom to take over the spiritual leadership of her small community when he arrived in Constantinople in 398 after having been appointed bishop. He and Olympias became close spiritual friends and he became spiritual director for these women. He "visited them continuously and sustained them with his most wise teachings. Thus fortified each day by his divinely-inspired instruction, they kindled in themselves the divine love so that their great and holy love steamed forth to him."[28]

The Spiritual Warrior with Spiritual Courage: Standing Strong against Wrong

One could assume, falsely, that such a humble, servant-hearted woman might lack commensurate courage and conviction. History tells a markedly different story. Olympias' loyalty to her spiritual leaders caused her great persecution and immense suffering. "And due to her sympathy for them, she endured many trials by the actions of a willfully evil and vulgar person; contending eagerly not in a few contests on behalf of the truth of God, she lived faultlessly in unmeasured tears night and day…"[29] In fact, her biographer, in one breath, spoke both of what he called "her manly courage," and of how "she cultivated in herself a gentleness so that she surpassed even the simplicity of children themselves."[30]

Throughout *Sacred Friendships* you will find this theme saturated everywhere. Godly women of old integrated into their Christlike character both *humble care* and *bold courage*. They saw no dichotomy between the two; they experienced no contradiction between tender soul care and tenacious spiritual direction.

Olympias faced the greatest test of her courage when Chrysostom's enemies slandered him in respect to his relationship to her. With Chrysostom sent into exile, one might expect an accused woman in this time period to meekly retreat. Not Olympias. Forced to appear before the city prefect for interrogation, she refused to recant her innocence and her defense of Chrysostom. Sent into exile herself, "she, strengthened by the divine grace, nobly and courageously, for the sake of the love of God, bore the storms of trials and diverse tribulations which came upon her."[31]

Chrysostom, using the language of spiritual warfare, extolled the virtues of her steadfastness. "You are like a tower, a haven, and a wall of defense, speaking in the eloquent voice of example, and through your sufferings instructing either sex to strip readily for these contests, and descend into the lists with all courage, and cheerfully bear the toils which such contests involve."[32]

He then contrasts Olympias' resilience with the weakness of others. He notes that she deserves "superlative admiration" because "so many men" when facing trials "have been turned to flight" but "you on the contrary after so many battles and such a large muster of the enemy are so far from being unstrung, or dismayed by the number of your adversities, that you are all the more vigorous, and the increase of the contest gives you an increase of strength."[33]

In exile, she maintained both her care for those under her direction and the courage of her convictions. "Victorious in the good fight, she crowned herself with the crown of patience, having turned over the flock to Marina, who was her relative and spiritual daughter.... Having done this, she escaped from the storm of human woes and crossed over to the calm haven of our souls, Christ the God."[34]

The Soul Physician's Soul Physician: Vulnerably Receiving Spiritual Care

One might also falsely think that a woman of this era such as Olympias was so pious, or perhaps even so pretentious, that she never felt deeply the pangs of despair. Again, history paints a truer, more humane portrait. We learn of this human, vulnerable, real, and raw side of Olympias from the letters of spiritual consolation Chrysostom penned to her. While we only have his side of the correspondence, his words give us a glimpse into her soul. In his first letter to her, he responded to her previous correspondence with him by saying, "Come now let me relieve the wound of thy despondency, and disperse the thoughts which gather this cloud of care around thee."[35]

Chrysostom proceeded to sketch a lengthy litany of "fierce black storm" clouds engulfing Olympias. Yet he realized that words do not suffice. "But how much further shall I pursue the unattainable? For whatever image of our present evils I may seek, speech shrinks baffled from the attempt."[36] He shifted instead to worthier imagery—the imagery of Christ—to offer his hurting spiritual friend hope. "Nevertheless even when I look at these calamities I do not abandon the hope of better things, considering as I do who the pilot is in all this—not one who gets the better of the storm by his art, but calms the raging waters by his rod."[37]

In Chrysostom's second letter, we learn again of her humanness. He referred to Olympias having received his letter of consolation and yet having "sunk so deeply under the tyranny of despondency as even to desire to depart out of this world."[38] He responded with a prolonged second attempt to comfort her. Finally, in his third letter, he rejoiced that her spirits are lifted. "And now I am exceedingly glad and delighted to hear, not only that you have been released from your infirmity, but above all that you bear the things which befell you so bravely...."[39]

Though in Chrysostom's words we do not hear the soul physician ministry of Olympias, we do learn about Olympias the soul physician. Her lesson is a lesson that every soul physician must heed. While some quote the proverb "Physician, heal thyself!", Olympias applied the proverbial wisdom that in much counsel there is great wisdom. She understood what all soul care-givers and spiritual directors must understand: *soul physicians need soul physicians!* Though a skilled, mature spiritual director herself, she humbled herself to receive soul care and spiritual direction from Chrysostom. She did not feel the modern/post-modern need to be a "super woman," independent, self-sufficient. She understood that she could be strong and simultaneously admit her need. Women, and men, in leadership today would be wise to follow her example.

Listening to the Silenced Voices

When we listen to the silenced voices of Gorgonia, Macrina, and Olympias we hear three spiritual sisters whose lives speak to us still today. When we listen to the voices of Gregory of Nazianzus, Gregory of Nyssa, and John Chrysostom we hear three spiritual brothers whose respect for these three women speaks volumes, especially given the day in which they lived. Swimming against the Aristotelian tide of the Greco-Roman world, these men in no way saw these females as defective. Rather, they treated them as spiritual equals. More than that, *they received spiritual care from their spiritual sisters.*

In fact, it is not going too far to say that these church fathers stood in awe of these church sisters. Gregory Nazianzus listened to the life of his biological sister, Gorgonia, and heard the voice of an empowering heroine. Gregory of Nyssa listened to the life of his biological sister, Macrina, and heard the voice of an invincible athlete. John Chrysostom listened to the life of his spiritual sister, Olympias, and heard the voice of a spiritual warrior.

These daughters of the church truly were spiritual friends to spiritual giants. Without Gorgonia, Macrina, and Olympias it is doubtful that we would have ever heard of Gregory Nazianzus, Gregory of Nyssa, or John Chrysostom. And thankfully, because of these men and their love and respect for these women, we have heard of and learned life lessons from Gorgonia, Macrina, and Olympias—a great cloud of feminine witnesses.

Learning Together from Our Great Cloud of Witnesses

1. What unbiblical views of women are prevalent today that women must fight against? What encouragement can women today find from Gorgonia, Macrina, and Olympias in this fight?

2. Gorgonia's focus on heaven teaches us how to find our origin, identity, and purpose. How could focusing on eternity help you to understand better where you came from, who you are, and where you are headed?

3. Gorgonia, like so many of the women in *Sacred Friendships*, practiced holistic spiritual care—caring for the body and the soul, meeting physical and spiritual needs. Why do you think the feminine soul tends toward this holistic balance? What application can you make in your ministry from this tendency?

4. Macrina saw her brother Basil's arrogant worldly focus and deftly guided him toward a humble Christ-focus.
   a. How hard is it for you to courageously and lovingly expose error in others?
   b. Who might God be calling you to minister to so that they move from self to Christ, from arrogance to humility?

5. Like Macrina, how is God calling you to exude love while speaking truth so that people hear your words as the faithful wounds of a friend?

6. Olympias, like so many godly women of old, integrated into her Christlike character both *humble care* and *bold courage*.
   a. Which comes *more* naturally for you: humble care or bold courage? Why do you suppose that is?
   b. Which comes *less* naturally for you: humble care or bold courage? How might you go about developing a more biblical balance?

7. Olympias vulnerably received spiritual care. She teaches all of us that soul physicians need soul physicians.
   a. How well are you able to admit your needs to others?
   b. Who is a soul physician for you? If you do not have one, what could you do to find one?

8. Gregory of Nazianzus, Gregory of Nyssa, and John Chrysostom also teach us. They teach us that we must not be conformed to this world's views of women, but we must be transformed by the renewing of our minds to follow Christ's view of women. What transforming does your mind need?

CHAPTER FOUR

PILGRIMAGE OF THE HEART:
THE DESERT MOTHERS

"We carry ourselves wherever we go and we cannot escape temptation by mere flight" (Amma Matrona).[1]
"If I prayed God that all people should approve of my conduct, I should find myself a penitent at the door of each one, but I shall rather pray that my heart may be pure toward all" (Amma Sarah).[2]

*D*uring the first five centuries of the early church, two diverse Christian lifestyles developed. Thus far in *Sacred Friendships* we have explored the lifestyle of women who were spiritual friends and spiritual mentors to the church fathers. These women and men typically lived in thriving cities, debated current theological issues, and, in the case of the men, served as clerics, bishops, and church council leaders. Theirs was the life of the sociable scholar.

History tell us of another group of men and women. These desert fathers and mothers typically rebuffed the hustle and bustle of the cities, concerned themselves more with experiencing the life of Christ than with debating the doctrines of the church, and were, for the most part, lay people. They lived the life of the contemplative spiritual warrior. This chapter reveals the untold stories of these desert mothers—women such as Theodora, Syncletica, Marcella, and Paula. These "Ammas" provided soul care and spiritual direction to women and men alike.

Ammas: Spiritual Mothers

Admittedly, the word "Amma" can be puzzling. We're more familiar with the word "Abba" from Romans 8:15 where we learn that through the Spirit of sonship we cry, "Abba, Father." "Amma" comes from the same cultural context. Both Abba and Amma were terms of family endearment conveying honor and closeness. Calling a woman "Amma" communicated that she was a spiritual mother, loved and respected by all her spiritual children.

Desert Spirituality: Experiencing the Geography of the Heart

Hearing the phrase "Desert Mother" or "desert spirituality" can also sound odd, ancient, foreign, and irrelevant to anything we experience today. And for some, these terms can even seem "unbiblical." Yet, we will find that the desert spirituality of these desert mothers was scriptural and is relevant.

"Desert" did not necessarily mean a barren wasteland. Some of the desert mothers that we learn from simply moved away from the city to rural, less-inhabited areas. Others did not move at all, instead selling most of their possessions in order to acquire enough land and lodgings to house a spiritual community of women and to accommodate the frequent spiritual pilgrims who sought them.

Regardless of location, the motivation remained the same. The desert mothers believed that the greatest enemies of the inner journey were hurry, crowds, and noise. They sought to create an environment that quieted the inner noise which kept them from hearing God's Spirit speaking to their spirit through God's inspired Word.[3] Desert mothers like Amma Syncletica focused on the geography of the heart. "There are many who live in the mountains and behave as if they were in the town, and they are wasting their time. It is possible to be a solitary in one's mind while living in a crowd, and it is possible for one who is a solitary to live in the crowd of his own thoughts."[4]

To understand further and relate to their movement of desert spirituality, we have to understand two characteristics of the early church—it was a *city-centered faith* and a *home-centered faith*. The book of Acts tells us that the apostles shared the message of Jesus in the urban centers of the day. The apostles targeted the mass of hungry, hurting people in thriving cities like Jerusalem, Antioch, Philippi, Thessalonica, Athens, and Rome.

The destruction of the temple in A.D. 70 and the persecution of the church in ensuing years resulted in domestic dwellings becoming the place for community meetings. Local believers gathered in homes for the Lord's Supper, baptism, worship, and teaching. Lay men and women were involved in personal evangelism and works of mercy to the poor, the orphaned, and to prisoners.[5]

Desert spirituality sprang from this city-centered and home-centered culture. The movement away from urban centers was motivated by the belief that the church in the city was compromising with the culture of the secular world. The desert mothers and fathers believed that the church was losing its prophetic voice as it yielded to cultural and political pressures and became organized more like the government than like a living organism.[6] Sound familiar? Sound relevant?

As patriarchs and matriarchs of extended families became more and more disenchanted with the political correctness of the church and the spiritual expediency of its leaders, they left the cities (or at least the secular attitude of the city), but rarely did they leave alone. The first "desert communities" usually included relatives, dependents, and household slaves (then considered family members). This inclusiveness had a deep impact upon desert spirituality. Life was centered around times of communal prayer, the group study and application of Scripture, joint ministry to the poor, and the collaborative application of the writings of the leaders of the movement.[7]

The desert mothers based their decision to leave the worldliness of the secular city upon Christ's model. They read and desired to apply passages like Luke 4:1, "Jesus, full of the Holy Spirit, returned from the Jordan and was led by the Spirit in the desert" (see also Matthew 4:1). "At daybreak Jesus went out to a solitary place." (Luke 4:42a). "Very early in the morning, while it was still dark, Jesus got up, left the house and went off to a solitary place, where he prayed" (Mark 1:35). "Then, because so many people were coming and going that they did not even have a chance to eat, he said to them, 'Come with me by yourselves to a quiet place and get some rest.' So they went away by themselves in a boat to a solitary place" (Mark 6:31-32). "After he had dismissed them, he went up on a mountainside by himself to pray. When evening came, he was there alone" (Matthew 14:23).

The desert mothers noticed and applied at least two major lessons from passages such as these. They saw the need for God's people to find a respite *from* the worldliness of the world. Reading the verses that followed the ones quoted above, they also recognized the call for God's people to return from their rest refreshed and renewed to be Christ's servants *in* the world. The desert mothers we study in this chapter were not secluded hermits. They were remembered as much for their public ministry to the poor and hurting as they were for their private spirituality. Their communal retreat away from secular urban centers was for the purpose of growing closer to Christ so they could be empowered to share Christ's truth in love to a lost and lonely world. While we might respond differently to our increasingly secular culture, and while we might apply these passages differently, at least we can relate to their social motivation and biblical conviction.

Spiritual Direction: Entering the Heart of Spiritual Matters

Escaping the sinfulness of daily city life might make us think the Ammas focused on external manifestations of evil. Actually, the opposite was true. They were concerned with the source of sin in the human heart. Moreover, they were careful to note that external spiritual disciplines (such as fasting, silence, solitude, prayer without ceasing, meditation, giving to the poor, etc.) might lead to the worst sin of all—pride.[8] The desert mothers sought the Spirit's discernment to perceive and repent of secret idols of the heart, and to live constantly aware of the presence of Christ's grace and in anxious anticipation of Christ's soon return. In the desert waiting, they were loyal sons and loving daughters watching for their father's return.[9]

While trying to live humbly in extended family communities, their relentless pursuit of spirituality produced stories that spread their fame. Spiritually committed believers came to these Ammas seeking a spiritual elder. Christians saw an Amma as someone seasoned in the spiritual life "who was known to have reached a level of maturity and wisdom and had experience in teaching by example, exhortation, story, and instruction."[10] Often the disciple, if not already a member of the family, moved into the elder's home. "A deep spiritual bond formed as the Amma taught—more often by example than by words."[11]

The Amma normally took less the role of a spiritual friend—which would be mutual in nature—and more of the role of a spiritual director with a one-sided, sacrificial, unselfish focus on the spiritual growth of the disciple. Ammas were "practiced in peeling back the layers of silence, pierced to the core the hearts of fellow seekers and laid bare for them the voice of the living God."[12] People viewed these ancient soul physicians as the true psychologists of the day.

The Amma "journeyed and struggled alongside her disciple but maintained the detachment necessary for discernment." Their communication was candid. "The disciple shared her heart's struggles, and the Amma did not hide her own humanity."[13] The Ammas gained the insight and discernment to deal with unruly or false passions by long, hard living. They were aware of the necessity of self-understanding and they emphasized the importance of taking personal responsibility for one's actions.[14]

The Ammas' pilgrimage into the desert was a pilgrimage of the heart. They cultivated solitude in order to intensify their inner journey toward their goal of intimacy with Christ so they would be empowered to disciple others toward that same intimacy.[15] Their practice should speak volumes to soul care-givers and spiritual directors today who are often too busy, too exhausted, and too much like Martha to be of any spiritual good.

Martha "had a sister called Mary, who sat at the Lord's feet listening to what he said. But Martha was distracted by all the preparations that had to be made. She came to him and asked, 'Lord, don't you care that my sister has left me to do the work by myself? Tell her to help me!' 'Martha, Martha,' the Lord answered, 'you are worried and upset about many things, but only one thing is needed. Mary has chosen what is better, and it will not be taken away from her'" (Luke 10:39-42). While few of us can take a literal pilgrimage to the desert, none of us can afford to live a Martha lifestyle. The desert Ammas modeled how to live like Mary in a Martha world.

Daughters of Eve: Nourished by Wise Women Counselors

Because of their humility and solitude, we know little about most of the Ammas. What we do know, we derive from collections of their sayings shared with their followers. Their ancient words of wisdom instruct and nourish us today.

Amma Theodora: Ministering with Humility, Praying with Vitality

Amma Theodora (350-395) lived in the fourth century in Egypt. She displays tremendous insight into the character and competence of the spiritual director. "A teacher ought to be a stranger to the desire for domination, vain-glory, and pride; one should not be able to fool him by flattery, nor blind him by gifts, nor conquer him by the stomach, nor dominate him by anger; but he should be patient, gentle and humble as far as possible; he must be tested and without partisanship, full of concern, and a lover of souls."[16] Many today chafe at the idea of a spiritual *director* because they sense that it grants far too much control to the director. Theodora disabuses us of this notion. The only "thing" Theodora wanted to dominate was her own soul, never the soul of her directee. True spiritual directors love Christ, love their counselees, and point them to the ultimate Lover of their soul.

Theodora also offered relevant counsel for anyone struggling with darkness, despair, hopelessness, and lack of motivation. The ancients labeled this "accidie." Some list it as one of the seven deadly sins and describe it as sloth. But sloth hardly portrays the depth of meaning behind this term. Spiritual giants of old experienced it as spiritual weariness, distress of heart, and apathy. They saw it as spiritual warfare in which the Evil One sought to deceive spiritual warriors into thinking they were weak, worthless, and lacking any giftedness to help others or to advance God's kingdom.

Theodora's first prescription included acknowledging how universal spiritual depression is and exposing the customary source. "You should realize that as soon as you intend to live in peace, at once evil comes and weighs down your soul through accidie, faintheartedness, and evil thoughts."[17] Here she *normalizes* and *spiritualizes* (in the best sense of that word) an experience that makes most sufferers feel abnormal and unspiritual.

Theodora next prescribed the cure as the spiritual discipline of perpetual prayer. "But if we are vigilant, all these temptations fall away. There was, in fact a monk who was seized by cold and fever every time he began to pray, and he suffered from headaches, too. In this condition, he said to himself, 'I am ill, and near to death; so now I will get up before I die and pray....' So, by reasoning in this way, the brother resisted, and prayed and was able to conquer his thoughts."[18] Using the heroic narrative of an unnamed believer, Theodora outlined the battle strategy. When we are tempted by Satan to believe that all our spiritual resources are impotent, that is the exact time when we must place our faith in God's power to demolish strongholds and take captive every thought to make it obedient to Christ (2 Corinthians 10:4-5).

Amma Syncletica: Putting Up the Cross for Our Sail

We know of Amma Syncletica (380-460) from *The Life and Regimen of the Blessed and Holy Teacher Syncletica*, a fifth-century work that survives to this day. She was born in Alexandria into a well-respected Christian family that saw to it that she was well-educated. Her two brothers died at a relatively young age and her sister was blind. At the death of her parents, she sold her possessions, giving them to the poor, and moved with her sister outside Alexandria.[19]

Feminine imagery is one of the beauties we discover when we unearth the riches of women's spirituality. Amma Syncletica, speaking of healing hope, encourages us to focus on the life to come, using the language of the womb. "Whatever we do or gain in this world, let us consider it insignificant in comparison to the eternal wealth that is to come. We are on this earth as if in a second maternal womb.... We have sampled the nourishment here; let us reach for the Divine! We have enjoyed the light in this world; let us long for the sun of righteousness! Let us regard the heavenly Jerusalem as our homeland."[20]

Lest we think that only a female can speak with such imagery, we should recall that the Apostle Paul used similar language in a similar healing context when he described the attitude we should have toward suffering in this life and our hope for the life to come. "We know that the whole creation has been groaning as in the pains of childbirth right up to the present time. Not only so, but we ourselves, who have the firstfruits of the Spirit, groan inwardly as we wait eagerly for our adoption as sons, the redemption of our bodies" (Romans 8:22-23).

We would also be wrong to assume that a woman like Syncletica could use only stereotypical feminine imagery. When offering guiding counsel, she powerfully applied a sailing metaphor.

> If you have begun some good work, you should not be turned from it by the enemy's attempts to hinder you, indeed your endurance will overthrow the enemy. Sailors beginning a voyage set the sails and look for a favorable wind, and later they meet a contrary wind. Just because the wind has turned, they do not throw the cargo overboard or abandon ship; they wait a while and struggle against the storm until they can set a direct course again. When we run into headwinds, *let us put up the cross for our sail*, and we shall voyage through the world in safety.[21]

Syncletica smashes the notion that the feminine soul is weak or that feminine counsel only empathizes. Her sailing metaphor empowers, and it derives from a potent soul and a resilient will.

This is unsurprising given Syncletica's insistence that the spiritual director must be mature, or her direction would be damaging. "It is dangerous for a man to try teaching before he is trained in the good life. A man whose house is about to fall down may invite travelers inside to refresh them, but instead they will be hurt in the collapse of the house. It is the same with teachers who have not carefully trained themselves in the good life; they destroy their hearers as well as themselves. Their mouth invites salvation, their way of life leads to ruin."[22]

Her warning is just as accurate and required today as it was then. Training in soul care and spiritual direction must focus first on the soul and the spiritual maturation of the trainee, not simply on developing helping competencies. Otherwise we send into a hurting world unhealed wounders instead of wounded healers.

Marcella: The Aquila of Her Day

Marcella (325-410) endured life's deprivations early and often. Her father's death left her an orphan, and she had been married just half-a-year when her husband died. By birth she was the scion of the highest Roman nobility, but she adopted the life of desert spirituality late in her teens after her husband's passing. She gathered around herself a circle of high ranking women who turned their homes into spiritual retreats. Under her leadership and example they became eager students of Scripture under tutors such as Jerome.[23]

Spiritual Training: Living Like You Are Dying

It is from Jerome's correspondence with Marcella and his memoir of her life that we glimpse snapshots of her character and ministry. Jerome addressed Marcella's memoir to her closest spiritual friend, Principia, but he had to wait two years to pen it owing "to an incredible sorrow which so overcame my mind" when she died. Finally bringing himself to write, he spoke first of her love for and application of God's Word.

> Her delight in the divine scriptures was incredible. She was for ever singing, "Your words have I hid in mine heart that I might not sin against thee," as well as the words which describe the perfect man, "his delight is in the law of the Lord; and in his law does he meditate day and night." This meditation in the law she understood not of a review of the written words as among the Jews the Pharisees think, but of action according to that saying of the apostle, "whether, therefore, you eat or drink or whatsoever ye do, do all to the glory of God."[24]

Marcella modeled the spiritual training needed by every spiritual director. She believed that biblical information, plus personal meditation, combined with the right motivation (daily action for Christ's glorification) were God's design for spiritual preparation.

Such spiritual exercise empowered and equipped her for spiritual friendships. Jerome said of Marcella, "My revered friend Paula blessed with Marcella's friendship, and it was in Marcella's cell that Eustochium, that paragon of virgins, was gradually trained. Thus it is easy to see of what type the mistress was who found such pupils."[25]

Jerome also informed us of the philosophy of life that enabled Marcella to be such an accomplished spiritual mentor. "She often quoted with approval Plato's saying that philosophy consists in meditating on death. A truth which our own apostle endorses when he says: 'for your salvation I die daily.' Indeed according to the old copies our Lord himself says: 'whosoever does not bear his cross daily and come after me cannot be my disciple....' She *passed her days and lived always in the thought that she must die.* Her very clothing was such as to remind her of the tomb, and she presented herself as a living sacrifice, reasonable and acceptable, unto God."[26]

In sustaining, we talk about "climbing in the casket." For Marcella, guiding meant "living in light of the casket." It meant living as one who has already died with Christ to the things of this world and who has already been raised with Christ to the things of the next world.

Versed in God's Word: Blending Grace and Truth

As with other godly women we have studied, one might expect that such a sacrificial attitude could lead to an overly meek approach to others, perhaps especially to male spiritual leadership. Such was not the case in Marcella's relationship with the distinguished Jerome. "And, as in those days my name was held in some renown as that of a student of the scriptures, she never came to see me that she did not ask me some question concerning them, *nor would she at once acquiesce in my explanations but on the contrary would dispute them; not, however, for argument's sake but to learn the answers to those objections* which might, as she saw, be made to my statements.[27] Marcella displayed a "Berean" attitude (Acts 17:11)—examining the Scriptures to see if what Jerome said was indeed true.

So thoroughly versed was she in God's Word that Jerome could say:

> Whatever in me was the fruit of long study and as such made by constant meditation a part of my nature, this she tasted, this she learned and made her own. Consequently after my departure from Rome, in case of a dispute arising as to the testimony of scripture on any subject, recourse was had to her to settle it. And so wise was she… that when she answered questions she gave her own opinion not as her own but as from me or some one else, thus admitting that what she taught she had herself learned from others… and she would not seem to inflict a wrong upon the male sex many of whom (including sometimes priests) questioned her concerning obscure and doubtful points.[28]

Consider her blending of insight, shrewdness, and humility—especially given the day in which she lived. Even priests would seek her interpretation of difficult biblical passages and theological concepts. So well had she learned under Jerome, that she was deemed most fit to explain God's Word. But rather than acting in a condescending manner toward those seeking her insight, she discreetly gave praise to another (Jerome). Marcella was a woman full of grace and truth.

She embodied grace and truth not only in her relationship with leading men like Jerome and various priests, but also with numerous women in Rome, including her spiritual friend Principia. Jerome reflected on the nature of Marcella and Principia's mentoring relationship. "I am told that my place with her was immediately taken by you, that you attached yourself to her, and that, as the saying goes, you never let even a hair's-breadth come between her and you. You both lived in the same house and occupied the same room so that every one in the city knew for certain that *you had found a mother in her and she a daughter in you*."[29] There certainly was no "arms-length" spiritual direction relationship between these two women.

What they shared, they modeled for others. "For a long time you lived together, and as many ladies *shaped their conduct by your examples, I had the joy of seeing Rome transformed into another Jerusalem.*[30] Their discipleship emphasized the living lesson plan.

Marcella could be a student (to Jerome), a teacher (to Principia), and she could equally "adjust" and enjoy the role of mutual spiritual friend, even with her teacher, Jerome. When she and he were parted, they *"consoled each other for our separation by words of mutual encouragement*, and discharged in the spirit the debt which in the flesh we could not pay. We always went to meet each other's letters, tried to outdo each other in attentions, and anticipated each other in courteous inquiries. Not much was lost by a separation thus effectually bridged by a constant correspondence."[31]

Though a woman of grace, Marcella would never wink at error. While she was living in what Jerome called "holy tranquility," a "tornado of heresy" arose that "introduced a ship freighted with blasphemies into the port of Rome itself." It was then that "the holy Marcella, who had long held back lest she should be thought to act from party motives, threw herself into the breach." Confronting the heresy and the heretics, she then *"publicly withstood its teachers choosing to please God rather than men."*[32]

This was no easy battle, but Marcella engaged it fully and faithfully. "She it was lastly who called on the heretics in letter after letter to appear in their own defense. They did not indeed venture to come, for they were so conscience-stricken that they let the case go against them by default rather than face their accusers and be convicted by them. This glorious victory originated with Marcella, she was the source and cause of this great blessing."[33] Here we witness Marcella offering public reconciling—exposing the horrors of doctrinal sin through open confrontation.

Marcella's last days mirrored how she lived all her days. In 410 the Goths, while looting Rome, entered Marcella's home and tortured her to reveal the whereabouts of her wealth. They simply could not believe her when she told them she had given it all to the poor.

Even during this time, Marcella's focus remained on others and on God. She "burst into great joy" and "thanked God" for having kept her spiritual friend, Principia, unharmed. She also expressed thanks that "Christ satisfied her needs so that she no longer felt hunger, that she was able to say in word and in deed: 'naked came I out of my mother's womb, and naked shall I return thither: the Lord gave and the Lord has taken away; blessed be the name of the Lord.'"[34]

After a few days "she fell asleep in the Lord; but to the last her powers remained unimpaired." When "she closed her eyes, it was in your arms; when she breathed her last breath, your lips received it; you shed tears but she smiled conscious of having led a good life and hoping for her reward hereafter."[35] She ever remained a loving spiritual friend and a trusting daughter of God.

Paula: The Lydia of Her Day

Of Paula's birth and life (347-404), Jerome writes, "Noble in family, she was nobler still in holiness; rich formerly in this world's goods, she is now more distinguished by the poverty she embraced for Christ."[36] Marrying Toxotius, she joined an equally aristocratic Roman family. Together they bore five children. "When he died, her grief was so great that she nearly died herself," Jerome informs us. Able to follow the dictum that "it's normal to hurt," Paula also pursued the truth that "it's possible to hope." "Yet so completely did she then give herself to the service of the Lord, that it might seem that she had desired his death."[37]

Holistic Care and Confrontation: Modeling by Example

As with so many of the feminine soul care-givers in church history, Paula practiced care for the body as well as for the soul. Like the Good Samaritan, Jerome was able to record of her, "What poor man, as he lay dying, was not wrapped in blankets given by her? What bedridden person was not supported with money from her purse? She would seek out such with the greatest diligence throughout the city."[38]

Years after her husband passed, and when her children were older, Paula sensed God leading her to go on a pilgrimage to the

Holy Lands with one of her daughters, Eustochium. After the end of her lengthy journey, she and Eustochium established a spiritual community for women in Bethlehem. Here, too, Paula displayed her Good Samaritan spirit. Jerome asked rhetorically, "How shall I describe her kindness and attention towards the sick or the wonderful care and devotion with which she nursed them?"[39]

Her life is reminiscent of the words of the Apostle John. "If anyone has material possessions and sees his brother in need but has no pity on him, how can the love of God be in him? Dear children, let us not love with words or tongue but with actions and in truth" (1 John 3:17-18). Her life is a chastisement to those today who claim to be spiritual counselors but refuse to trouble themselves with others' physical needs. James warns against such one-dimensional care: "Suppose a brother or sister is without clothes and daily food. If one of you says to him, 'Go, I wish you well; keep warm and well fed,' but does nothing about his physical needs, what good is it?" (James 2:15-16).

On the other hand, to help people with material and physical needs and to omit concern for their souls would be eternally disastrous. Paula demonstrated no such secular-sacred dichotomy. The young women under her care came from quite distinct social classes, "some of whom are of noble birth while others belonged to the middle or lower classes." Wanting them to be one in Christ, "these three companies met together for psalm-singing and prayer." No one was permitted to remain behind or to exclude himself. Paula always arrived first, "urging them to diligence rather by her own modest example than by motives of fear."[40]

Her guiding consisted not only of modeling, but also of biblical training via meditation and memorization. "No sister was allowed to be ignorant of the psalms, and all had every day to learn a certain portion of the holy scriptures."[41]

Paula practiced idiosyncratic reconciling. That is, she understood that different methods of spiritual confrontation worked better with different personality types. "When a sister was backward in coming to the recitation of the psalms or shewed herself remiss in her work, Paula used to approach her in different ways. Was she quick-tempered? Paula coaxed her. Was she phlegmatic? Paula chided her, copying the example of the apostle who said: 'What will ye? Shall I come to you with a rod or in love and in the spirit of meekness?'"[42]

Paula also recognized that different spiritual approaches were necessary when reconciling and confronting different patterns of sins. "When the sisters quarreled one with another she reconciled them with soothing words. If the younger ones were troubled with fleshly desires, she broke their force by imposing redoubled fasts... If she chanced to notice any sister too attentive to her dress, she reproved her for her error with knitted brows and severe looks...."[43]

Personal Care and Confrontation: Speaking to Herself about God's Word

Of course, it would have been hypocritical of Paula to confront others while ignoring the mote in her own eye. In fact, she was so hyper-conscientious that Jerome had to balance her focus on "it's horrible to sin" with his and God's focus on "it's wonderful to be forgiven." "Her tears welled forth as it were from fountains, and she lamented her slightest faults as if they were sins of the deepest dye. Constantly did I warn her to spare her eyes and to keep them for the reading of the gospel."[44] Jerome's shrewd counsel is a reminder to all spiritual directors that where sin abounds, the gospel of Christ's grace superabounds.

Paula not only practiced the art of self-confrontation, she also applied the skill of self-consolation. Jerome noted that "envy always follows in the track of virtue"[45] and that Hadad the Edomite became Paula's thorn in the flesh, buffeting her day after day with false accusations. Her response involved self-trialoguing—she defeated the voice of the devil's condemnation by speaking to herself about God's Word.

> Why may I not by my patience conquer this ill will? Why may I not by my humility break down this pride, and when I am smitten on the one cheek offer to the smiter the other? Surely the Apostle Paul says "Overcome evil with good." Did not the apostles glory when they suffered reproach for the Lord's sake?

Did not even the Saviour humble Himself, taking
the form of a servant and being made obedient to
the Father unto death, even the death of the cross,
that He might save us by His passion? If Job had
not fought the battle and won the victory, he would
never have received the crown of righteousness, or
have heard the Lord say: "Thinkest thou that I have
spoken unto thee for aught else than this, that thou
mightest appear righteous." In the gospel those only
are said to be blessed who suffer persecution for
righteousness' sake.[46]

Paula's self-consolation through self-trialogue won the victory.
"My conscience is at rest, and I know that it is not from any fault
of mine that I am suffering; moreover affliction in this world is a
ground for expecting a reward hereafter." Jerome further explained
that, "When the enemy was more than usually forward and ventured
to reproach her to her face, she used to chant the words of the psalter:
'While the wicked was before me, I was dumb with silence; I held my
peace even from good' and again, 'I as a deaf man heard not; and I
was as a dumb man that openeth not his mouth' and 'I was as a man
that heareth not, and in whose mouth are no reproofs.'"[47]

When she felt herself tempted again, Jerome noted that she
meditated "upon the words in Deuteronomy: 'The Lord your God
proveth you, to know whether ye love the Lord your God with all your
heart and with all your soul.' In tribulations and afflictions she turned
to the splendid language of Isaiah: 'Ye that are weaned from the milk
and drawn from the breasts, look for tribulation upon tribulation, for
hope also upon hope: yet a little while must these things be by reason
of the malice of the lips and by reason of a spiteful tongue.'"[48]

Jerome astutely summarized Paula's personal application of
Scripture.

This passage of scripture she explained *for her own
consolation* as meaning that the weaned, that is, those
who have come to full age, must endure tribulation

upon tribulation that they may be accounted worthy to receive hope upon hope. She recalled to mind also the words of the apostle, "we glory in tribulations also: knowing that tribulation worketh patience, and patience experience, and experience hope: and hope maketh not ashamed" and "though our outward man perish, yet the inward man is renewed day by day" and "our light affliction which is but for a moment worketh in us an eternal weight of glory; while we look not at the things which are seen but at the things which are not seen: for the things which are seen are temporal but the things which are not seen are eternal."[49]

What an amazingly practical example of the personal application of Scripture. No wonder her peers knew Paula as a skillful soul physicians of others—she first practiced her art on her own soul.

Listening to the Silenced Voices

When we listen to the silenced voices of the desert mothers we hear their focus on *soul* geography not *soil* geography. Godly women like Theodora, Syncletica, Marcella, and Paula took spiritual samples of the *inner* person, not geological samples of the *external* world.

Their voices speak volumes to us about the soul physician's need to escape from the worldly attitude that church programs and counseling techniques are the route to Christian discipleship. They reveal wisdom that has taken the church nearly 2,000 years to grasp. "It's the heart, Christian!" We don't need to pay consultants millions of dollars and spend years surveying church members and seminary students to discover that biblical discipleship prioritizes changing lives with Christ's changeless truth. All we have to do is listen to the humble yet powerful voices of ancient Christian women whose words are as relevant as anything emerging from church life today. God's truth spoken in Christ's love first to our own souls and then to the souls of our spiritual friends is God's time-tested vocational calling.

Learning Together from Our Great Cloud of Witnesses

1. After reading this chapter, how have your views of terms like "Desert spirituality" and "Desert Mothers and Fathers" changed?

2. What factors in society today keep us from hearing God's Spirit speaking to our spirit through God's inspired Word? What lifestyle changes could we make that might help us to find a respite from the worldliness of the world?

3. In today's world, how could we cultivate solitude in order to intensify our journey toward the goal of intimacy with Christ? How could we become more like Mary and less like Martha (Luke 10:39-42)?

4. When you are discipling another person, how can you, like Amma Theodora, avoid dominating that person and instead focus on gently leading that person to Christ as the ultimate Spiritual Director?

5. Like Amma Syncletica, when you run into headwinds (suffering, obstacles, persecution, problems, etc.) what would it look like for you to *put up the cross for your sail*?

6. Amma Syncletica and all four of the women we learned from in this chapter emphasized the need for soul care-givers/spiritual directors to focus first on their own heart.
   a. Why is this so seldom the focus of much current-day training in discipleship, soul care, spiritual direction, pastoral ministry, seminary education, and biblical counseling?
   b. To what neglected area of your own heart geography do you need to attend?

7. Marcella believed that biblical information plus personal meditation, combined with the right motivation (daily action for Christ's glorification) were God's design for spiritual preparation.

Which areas of that design might God be calling you to highlight in your life and ministry?

8. Paula counseled herself through self-confrontation and self-consolation. How effectively do you counsel your own soul? What could you apply from her model?

9. What revolution might occur if today's church listened to this message from yesterday's feminine spiritual sisters: "God's truth spoken in Christ's love first to our own souls and then to the souls of our spiritual friends is God's time-tested vocational calling"?

CHAPTER FIVE

COACHING OTHERS IN THE SPIRITUAL OLYMPICS: WOMEN SPIRITUAL ATHLETES

"But I… cannot weep enough, even though in all my wretchedness I were to swim in a lake of tears. Each person had an individual lament. I alone pour forth laments for all, since the public grief is a private grief for me" (Radegund of Poitiers, 520-587, recounting her lament over the loss of her loved ones in battle).[1]

"I am forced to weep not only for the dear ones slain; I weep as well for those whom kindly, life has preserved. Often I press my eyes shut, my face wet with tears. My sighs lie quelled, but my cares are not silent!" (Radegund of Poitiers expressing, "it's normal to hurt").[2]

Often today when we think of the process of spiritual direction and especially the practice of guiding, our minds focus primarily on *words* of guidance. However, in this chapter we repeatedly find the common theme of guiding by *personal example*. The women of this chapter teach us how to coach others spiritually by first being "player-coaches"—spiritual champions others can emulate.

Guidance-By-Modeling: Studying the Lives of Invincible Spiritual Athletes

Palladius (363-431), Bishop of Helenopolis and church historian, powerfully explained the importance of guidance-by-modeling. His work *The Lausiac History* is a biography of early church leaders written at the encouragement of Lausus in A.D. 420. Palladius recorded the virtuous and "marvelous manner of life" of holy men and women "with a view of stirring to rivalry and imitation" those who wish to progress along the path of spiritual maturity. It contained the "memoirs of aged women and illustrious God-inspired matrons" who serve as a "model and object of desire for those women" who long to hear their heavenly Father's "Well done!"[3]

Lausus arouses Palladius "to the contemplation of better things, to imitate and attempt to rival" the virtues of holy spiritual fathers and mothers. "Having studied the lives of these invincible athletes," Palladius collated their life stories because he was aware of "the benefit accruing to the readers" by a summary of "the main contests and achievements of the noble athletes... not only illustrious men who have realized the best manner of life, but also blessed and highborn women who have practiced the highest life."[4]

In a letter to Lausus, Palladius congratulated Lausus for wanting "to be taught the words of true edification" learned through the examples of mature believers. Speaking of those who refuse to learn from the example of the great cloud of witnesses, Palladius noted, "now those who think they need no teacher... are afflicted with the disease of ignorance, which is the mother of overweening pride." He further observed that "words and syllables do not constitute teaching," for some teachers possess great words but live "disreputable in the extreme." Historically, teaching and guiding consist of "virtuous acts of conduct, of freedom from injuriousness, of dauntlessness, and of an even temper. To all these add an intrepidity which produces words like flames of fire."[5]

Palladius supported his conviction with the words of Christ. "For if this were not so, the great Teacher would not have told His disciples: 'Learn of me, because I am meek and humble of heart.' He did not use fine language when teaching them, but He required rather the formation of their character..."[6]

Palladius continued his prologue by explaining that his purpose in penning his history of godly women and men is "for the edification and safety of those who follow the teachings of the Saviour with trusting intention" and "to your spiritual progress." He wrote about these male and female spiritual athletes as "a sacred reminder for the good of your soul and a constant medicine against forgetfulness. May it dispel the drowsiness which arises from senseless desire, indecision, and pettiness in necessary affairs. May it free your character of hesitation and meanness of spirit. May it rid you of excitability, disorders, worldly conceit, and irrational fear. May it improve your never failing desire and your pious intention, and may it be a guide both to you and to those who are with you, not only your subordinates but your rulers as well."[7]

How different from our perspective. We assume that the only "solutions" to lust, character defects, relational bitterness, and emotional struggles are medication and "talk therapy." Palladius believed that the study of church history equips us to put off these sins, put on piety, and find healing from our suffering. In fact, guidance-by-modeling, according to Palladius, empowers us to empowers others—guided by the lives of great women spiritual athletes, we can guide our spiritual friends, our disciples, and even spiritual leaders.

Deaconess Melania the Elder: Spiritual Guiding by Spiritual Modeling

Of all the godly men and women Palladius highlighted, Deaconess Melania the Elder (342-411) stands out due to her exemplary guiding-by-modeling. Palladius began his narrative of her life by noting that she was "a Spaniard by origin," and the daughter of the axcounsul and the wife of a high ranking official. Widowed at twenty-two, Melania "sold her goods and turned them into money" and traveled to the Mount of Olives accompanied by numerous women whom she discipled.[8]

Modeling Boldness and Gentleness: The Backbone of a Warrior, the Soul of a Servant

When a number of church leaders were banished to Palestine, Melania ministered to them from her own funds. Because Melania was wearing the attire of a young slave, the consul of Palestine, not knowing her background or her backbone, "thought he would terrify her." Thrown into prison, she told him, "For my part, I am So and So's daughter and So and So's wife, but I am Christ's slave. And do not despise the cheapness of my clothing. For I am able to exalt myself if I like, and you cannot terrify me in this way or take any of my goods." The consul, now himself terrified that he had mistreated a woman of high birth, "made an apology and honored her, and gave orders that she should succor the saints without hindrance."[9]

Like so many other women studied in *Sacred Friendships*, Melania clung tenaciously to her identity in Christ: "I am Christ's slave." And, like others, her understanding of who she was in Christ led to a fearlessness and boldness for Christ and a gentleness and tenderness toward those in need.

After her short imprisonment, Melania spent the next thirty-seven years ministering in Jerusalem. Along with Rufinus, a priest, they "edified all who visited them, and they reconciled the schism of Paulinus... and winning over every heretic that denied the Holy Spirit... and they honored the clergy... with gifts and goods, and so continued to the end, without offending anyone."[10]

Melania not only reconciled and guided believers, she also sustained and healed them through acts of mercy. "For no one escaped her benevolence, neither East nor West nor North nor South. For thirty-seven years she had been giving hospitality, and at her own costs had succored both churches and monasteries and strangers and prisoners."[11] Melania practiced holistic care—she ministered to body and soul, physically and spiritually.

Sharing Scripture and Soul: Hard Words of Confrontation from a Tender Heart of Love

Melania's passion for discipleship extended to her granddaughter, Melania the Younger. Afraid that her granddaughter would "be injured by bad teaching or heresy or evil living, though an old woman of sixty years, she flung herself into a ship and sailing from Caesarea reached Rome in twenty days."[12] What an intrepid woman.

Arriving in Rome she evangelized Apronianus—"she instructed him and made him a Christian." All in a day's work, she "also strengthened the will of her own granddaughter Melania, with her husband Pinianus, and instructed her daughter-in-law Albina, wife of her son."[13]

When many of the elite of Rome—senators and their wives—tried to prevent her from taking her disciples back with her to Jerusalem, she engaged in spiritual conversations and scriptural exploration with them. "Little children, it was written 400 years ago, It is the last hour. Why do you love to linger in life's vanities? Perchance the days of antichrist will surprise you, and you will cease to enjoy your wealth and your ancestral property."[14]

Never one to mince words, yet always one to speak the truth in love, Melania did just that with Jovinus the priest. Coming into an intense heat, Jovinus "took a basin and gave his hands and feet a thorough wash in ice cold water, and after washing flung a rug on the ground and lay down to rest." Seeing this, Melania "came to him like a wise mother of a true son and began to scoff at his softness." She challenged him, saying: "How dare you at your age, when your blood is still vigorous, thus coddle your flesh, not perceiving the mischief that is engendered by it? Be sure of this... that I am in the sixtieth year of my life and except for the tips of my fingers neither my feet nor my face nor any one of my limbs have touched water, although I am a victim to various ailments and the doctors try to force me. I have not consented to make the customary concessions to the flesh, never in my travels have I rested on a bed.'"[15] Hard words of confrontation about a soft life of pampering.

This was not a one-time confrontation event, but a life pattern. In a letter to Sulpicius Severus, Paulinus of Nola wrote, "A woman of more elevated rank, she loftily cast herself down to a humble way of life, so that as a strong member of the weak sex she might censure indolent men, so that as a rich person appropriating poverty, and as a noble person adopting humility, she might confound people of both sexes."[16]

One might expect that such an active life would leave little or no time for the life of the mind. Such certainly was not the case with Melania. "Being very learned and loving literature she turned night into day by perusing every writing of the ancient commentators, including 3,000,000 (lines) of Origen and 2,500,000 (lines) of Gregory, Stephen, Pierius, Basil, and other standard writers. Nor did she read them once only and casually, but she laboriously went through each book seven or eight times. Wherefore also she was enabled to be freed from knowledge falsely so called (1 Tim. 6:20) and to fly on wings, thanks to the grace of these books; elevated by kindly hopes she made herself a spiritual bird and journeyed to Christ."[17] Clearly one of the "secrets" to Melania's spiritual maturity was her spiritual discipline of study.

Olympias, from whom we learned in chapter three, in turn learned from Melania. "That most venerable and devoted lady Olympias followed the counsel of Melania, attending to her precepts and walking in her footsteps."[18] And now we know the rest of the story—the story behind Olympias' story. Notice how Melania's "counsel" consisted both of content ("precept") and character ("footsteps"). Like the Apostle Paul, she loved her disciples so much that she was delighted to share with them not only the Scriptures but her soul as well (1 Thessalonians 2:8).

Tetta and Leoba: Christ's Disciples Discipling Others

In Winbourne, England, two spiritual directors are forever linked in history and ministry: Tetta (650-720) and Leoba (700-779). Their biographer, Rudolf of Fulda, wrote their story in A. D. 836, having interviewed four of their disciples.[19]

Though most of Rudolf's narrative focused on Leoba, he declared that, "Before I begin the narration of her [Leoba] remarkable life and virtues, it may not be out of place if I mention a few of the many things I have heard about her spiritual mistress and mother, who first introduced her to the spiritual life and fostered in her a desire for heaven." He further explained that Leoba "learned the elements of the spiritual life from so noble a mistress."[20]

Integrating Content and Character: Instruction by Deeds Rather Than Words

As with Melania, Tetta discipled more through actions than words. Speaking of Tetta's character, Rudolf observed that though "a woman of noble family (for she was a sister of the king)," she was "more noble in her conduct and good qualities." She guided "with consummate prudence and discretion. She gave instruction by deed rather than by words, and whenever she said that a certain course of action was harmful to… souls she showed by her own conduct that it was to be shunned."[21] When we ponder Melania, Tetta, Leoba, and Dhuoda (see below), we are forced to ask ourselves why so much discipleship today is via talk and not walk. How might the power of soul care and spiritual direction be elevated if we more successfully integrated content and character, talk and walk, words and deeds into modern-day mentoring?

None of this means that Tetta, these other women, or anyone today should refrain from words of counsel. Tetta certainly did not. There was a certain abbess who was "too incautious and indiscreet in enforcing discipline over those under her care, she aroused their resentment, particularly among the younger members of the community." Rudolf remarked that "though she could easily have mollified them and met their criticisms, she hardened her heart against taking such a course of action and went so far in her inflexibility that even at the end of her life she would not trouble to soften their hearts by asking their pardon. So in this stubborn frame of mind she died and was buried."[22] When she died, her spiritual daughters "climbed onto her tomb, as if to stamp upon her corpse, uttering bitter curses over her dead body to assuage their outraged feelings."[23]

When Tetta heard of this, "she reprehended" these young women "for their presumption and vigorously corrected them." She called them together and "began to reproach them for their cruelty and hardness of heart. She upbraided them for failing to forgive the wrongs they had suffered and for harboring ill feelings on account of the momentary bitterness caused by harsh discipline."[24]

To reconciling, Tetta added guiding. "She told them that one of the fundamental principles of Christian perfection is to be peaceable with those who dislike peace, whereas, they, far from loving their enemies as God had commanded, not only hated their sister whilst she was alive but even pursued her with their curses now that she was dead." Tetta also "counseled them to lay aside their resentment, to accept the ill-treatment they had received and to show without delay their forgiveness."[25] As usual, she then led the way in prayer and confession—walking her talk.

Connecting Soul-to-Soul: Ministry by Example and Word

Leoba was born in Wessex, England, to aged parents, Dynno and Aebba, who named her Leoba meaning "beloved." They sent her to Winbourne as a youth to study Scripture under Abbess Tetta. More than a teacher-student relationship developed for Rudolf described Leoba as Tetta's "spiritual daughter."[26]

Like mother, like daughter, Leoba not only heard the Word, she lived the Word. "Fired by the love of Christ, she fixed her mind always on reading or hearing the Word of God. Whatever she heard or read she committed to memory, and put all that she learned into practice.... In this way she so arranged her conduct that she was loved by all the sisters."[27]

Her depth of community connection did not occur by accident. Leoba humbly sought to model their best virtues. "She learned from all and obeyed them all, and by imitating the good qualities of each one she modeled herself on the continence of one, the cheerfulness of another, copying here a sister's mildness, there a sister's patience. One she tried to equal in attention to prayer, another in devotion to reading. Above all, she was intent on practicing charity, without which, as she knew, all other virtues are void."[28] In selecting spiritual disciplines and virtues, Leoba models for us the important practice of imitating the finer traits of others.

When "Leoba's reputation for learning and wisdom had spread far and wide," her cousin, Boniface, requested that she join him in his mission to preach the Word of God to the German people. He received her "with deepest reverence" not so much "because she was related to him" but because "he knew that by her holiness and wisdom she would confer many benefits by her *word and example.*"[29]

Leoba eventually settled in Bischofsheim where she trained a large community of women who "made such progress in her teaching that many of them afterwards became superiors of others" so that there was hardly a community "which had not one of her disciples as abbess."[30] Leoba was an "equipper of the equippers."

She followed timeless, biblical equipping principles. "She was ever on her guard not to teach others what she did not carry out herself." It might appear to some that such a woman would come across "too spiritual" to be widely loved and accepted. Yet her four followers from whom Rudolf learned of Leoba all concurred that "in her conduct there was not arrogance or pride; she was no distinguisher of persons, but showed herself affable and kindly to all." She was "universal in her charity." When disagreements arose, as they inevitably will, "the sun never went down upon her anger."[31]

As Leoba's reputation spread, even kings were impressed with her holiness and wisdom. "Pippin, King of the Franks, and his sons Charles and Carolman, treated her with profound respect.... Queen Hiltigard also revered her with a chaste affection and loved her as her own soul. She would have liked her to remain continually at her side so that she might progress in the spiritual life and profit by her words and example."[32] Word and example, content and character—repeatedly Leoba mentors us in the art of spiritual mentoring by modeling that who we are and how we relate are just as important as what we share in our "counseling interactions."

It's fascinating that "Leoba detested the life at court like poison." Though it wasn't her calling or her passion, she served there faithfully. "The princes loved her, the nobles received her, the bishops welcomed her with joy. And because of her wide knowledge of the Scriptures and her prudence in counsel they often discussed spiritual matters and ecclesiastical discipline with her."[33] This is an important reminder and caution. All this talk about the importance of our "walk," should never minimize the importance of prudent counsel derived from an in-depth knowledge of God's Word and how to relate His truth to human relationships. For Leoba, it was never either/or; it was both/and—the content of the Word of God *and* the character of the servant of God.

As her life moved toward its last days, Leoba sculpted one final soul care and spiritual direction lesson—this one about community and connecting. Hearing of her illness and impending death, Queen Hiltigard begged Leoba to visit her because "she longed to see her before she passed from this life." Leoba "agreed for the sake of her longstanding friendship." Staying for several days, Leoba left her spiritual friend with these words of remembrance. "Farewell for evermore, my dearly beloved lady and sister; farewell, most precious half of my soul. May Christ our Creator and Redeemer grant that we shall meet again without shame on the day of judgment. Never more on this earth shall we enjoy each other's presence."[34] What tender intimacy—"most precious half of my soul." Leoba did not practice aloof, arm's-length ministry. She engaged in soul-to-soul attachment.

Dhuoda: A Soul Burning for Her Son

All that we know of Dhuoda (803-843), we know from her *Manual* written to her son, William, in A.D. 843 in proverbial fashion, much like Solomon penned Proverbs. As she put quill to scroll, Dhuoda was facing another Christmas without the three men in her life: her husband Bernhard, her young son William, and her infant son Bernhard.

Married on June 29, 824, she gave birth to William on November 29, 826. On March 22, 841, Bernhard entered the world. Sadly, due to political intrigue and a less-than-loving husband, Dhuoda spent most of her life in semi-abandonment in her husband's castle in southern France. In the summer of A. D. 841, Bernhard sent William as a semi-hostage to Charles the Bald. Her husband took her second son from her in the first days of the boy's life, so that two years later Dhuoda still did not know his name.[35]

Mirroring God's Word: Life Words from a Living Example

Being brutally honest about her level one external suffering, Dhuoda described the cause of her desolation. "As the misery and calamities of this world grew and continued to grow, amid many vicissitudes and discords of the reign, the aforementioned emperor [Louis who was favorable to Dhuoda and her family] went the way of all flesh."[36] He was replaced by Charles the Bald, who was to Dhuoda like "the Pharaoh who knew not Joseph," and her life came crashing down as the children of her womb were ripped from her.

Dhuoda was equally candid about her resulting level two internal suffering. "Having noticed that most women in this world are able to live with and enjoy their children, but seeing myself, Dhuoda, living far away from you, my dear son, William, I am filled with anxiety because of this..."[37]

Resiliently refusing to give in or give up, Dhuoda determined to mother her son from a distance. "With the desire to be of aid to you, I am sending you this little manual, written by me, for your scrutiny and education, rejoicing in the fact that, though I am absent in body, this little book will recall to your mind, as you read it, the things you are required to do for my sake."[38] One wonders how many of us, under similar or even less dire circumstances, would display such heroic endurance and such other-centered focus.

Because of Dhuoda's enforced absence, we might assume that her letter of guidance fits exclusively in the category of guidance by words rather than guidance by personal example. Yet in her prologue, Dhuoda clearly states that William should see her words as guidance by modeling. Urging her son to "read frequently this my little work," she explained that "you will find in it all you desire to know, set down briefly; you will also find a mirror..."[39]

Later, even more pointedly, she exhorted him, "Your admonisher, Dhuoda, is always with you, son, and if I be absent because of death... you will have this little book of moral teaching as a memorial; and in it you will be able to *see me as a reflection in a mirror...* Son, you will have teachers who will teach you other documents of greater utility, but not under the same conditions, *not with a soul burning in their breasts as I, your mother, have,* O firstborn son."[40]

Her metaphor of a mirror (*speculum*) for a spiritual handbook was widespread during the Middle Ages. Because of the intimacy of their mother-son relationship, Dhuoda is able to communicate something uniquely appropriate to William. She conveys not simply words, but life lessons which she has learned and now applies to his life. Her life story becomes the spectacles through which her son can read his life story.

Where else to begin the narrative of one's life story than with her son's image of God and personal relationship to God? Though presenting herself as unlearned, Dhuoda insightfully explained that her son's relationship *to* God will always be based upon his image *of* God. "He is to be feared, loved, and certainly to be believed to be immortal Who without diminution is Ever-Powerful King, commanding and performing whatever He wishes.... He Himself is the God of the universes; He is the power, the kingdom, and the empire."[41]

Dhuoda poetically and powerfully described God's nature and William's necessary response to this loving and holy God. "He is good, for His mercy endureth forever! And believe Him to be above, below, inside, and outside, for He is superior, inferior, interior, and exterior... *Since He is thus* and so great that no one can comprehend His essence, I beg you to fear Him and to love Him with all your heart, all your mind, all your understanding, to bless Him in all your ways and deeds..."[42] Dhuoda concluded her opening salvo by further connecting William's walk *with* God to his view *of* God. "Beseech Him, cherish Him, love Him; if you do so, He will be a Keeper, a Leader, a Companion, and a Fatherland to you, the Way, the Truth, and the Life."[43]

Mentoring from God's Word: Words of Life from the Word of God

While starting with a focus on William's spiritual relationship to God, Dhuoda next moved to his social relationship to others. She counseled him to have in his life a "Paul" (a spiritual director), a Jonathan (a spiritual friend), and a Timothy (a spiritual disciple).

William was to accept spiritual counsel from his elders. "Act according to the counsel of those who prepare you for faithful action as to the body and the soul. It is written, 'Do all things with counsel, and thou shalt not repent when thou hast done.'"[44] Dhuoda also advised him to connect with godly peers, giving and receiving mutual spiritual friendship. "I also urge you not to neglect getting together with the young who love God and seek wisdom."[45] She further implored William to minister to the least of these, even as Christ did. "And if He, great as He is, comports Himself thus toward the lesser ones, what should we, small as we are, do toward those who are worse off? Those who are able ought to help them, and, according to the urgings of the words of the Apostle Paul, bear one another's burdens."[46]

Dhuoda's spiritual guidance not only taught William about spiritual relationships, but also about spiritual formation and spiritual warfare. She instructed him to lead a spiritually disciplined life. "To attain model behavior for a human being requires a great effort and studious labor. Contrary remedies are to be opposed to contrary illnesses, and not only against the men of this world, burning with envy, must one fight, but also, as Saint Paul says, against spirits of wickedness in high places."[47] Dhuoda likewise encouraged William to practice the spiritual disciplines of reading and meditation. "You have and will have books in which you may read, page through, ruminate on, scrutinize, and understand, or even teachers to instruct you, and these will furnish you with models to follow in the performance of both your duties."[48]

Practicing the ancient art of "devil craft," Dhuoda counseled William with principles of spiritual warfare. "If, because of the persuasion of Satan, author of death, fornication or any other thorn in the flesh should touch your heart, oppose charity to it and remember the continency of the blessed patriarch Joseph, or of Daniel, or of others..."[49] As she so often did, here Dhuoda saturated her words of counsel with scriptural exploration and examples.

Dhuoda's "balanced" approach to spiritual direction carries over in the area of reconciling sin. She encouraged William to remember that it's horrible to sin, but that's it's wonderful to be forgiven. "If it should happen, my son, that you do something bad, or even if you perceive that your soul is afflicted, hasten as soon as you can to make amends in all things. Turn to Him Who sees everything; always bear witness, externally as well as internally, of your guilt and worthlessness until you have given complete satisfaction, saying 'The sins of my youth and my ignorances, do not remember.'"[50]

Having exhorted him to load his conscience with guilt, she then tenderly reminded William to lighten his conscience with grace by praying to God: "In accord with Thy ancient clemency, and Thy great goodness, come to my aid, for Thou art merciful."[51]

Dhuoda concluded her *Manual* with guiding words of empowerment. "Have frequent recourse to this little book. Always be, noble child, strong and brave in Christ!" William, heeding his mother's advice, stood firm in his convictions to the end, when, seven years later, he was beheaded by Charles the Bald in 850. But not before he was able to reflect upon and apply to his life the mirror of his mother's guidance-by-modeling.

Listening to the Silenced Voices

When we listen to the silenced voices of women spiritual athletes for Christ we hear not only their voices, but moreso we hear the messages of their lives. They understood that if they were to coach others spiritually, they first had to be world-class champions for Christ.

In an earlier chapter we learned that *women are God-empowered.* In this chapter we discover that *women are God-empowerers.* God empowers women to empower others. They do so not like a screaming, out-of-shape, overweight coach on the sidelines, but like a participating, fine-tuned, well-disciplined player-coach on the field. Their personal training regimens produce a model spiritual specimen who trains others by example.

Much so-called "training" today in discipling, Christian counseling, spiritual friendship, soul care, and spiritual direction misses the mark by training only the head and not the heart. While these women knew and counseled from God's Word, they did not stop there. To biblical content they added biblical application that led to Christ-like character and Christians connecting in community.

Additionally, much modern-day equipping emphasizes "talk therapy" while deemphasizing "be-with-me-in-order-to-be-like-me-therapy." While these women talked, they didn't stop there. "Office only" therapy would have been completely foreign to them. Their therapy of choice was living Christianity in community. We have much to learn from them.

Learning Together from Our Great Cloud of Witnesses

1. Think about a recent situation where you needed guidance and direction.

   a. Did you primarily think about asking someone for advice and words of counsel? What might have happened if your mind focused on a question like, "Whose life example could I ponder in order to discern godly ways to handle this situation?"

   b. When someone guided you concerning this situation, did they do so primarily through their words or through their example? If it was only via words, how might things have been different if they had coached you also by modeling?

2. When people seek guidance and spiritual direction from you, do you tend to guide them by "talk" (words of advice) or by "walk" (actions, deeds, example, being with them, etc.)?

   a. Why do you think you are prone to one or the other "methods"?

   b. How could you better integrate talk and walk, content and character/community into your spiritual direction?

3. Melania the Elder was able to model boldness *and* gentleness. How difficult do you find it to do both: bold confrontation and gentle comforting? Which do you tend toward the most? How could you "balance" these two "sides" better in your life and ministry?

4. Melania the Elder also emphasized her identity in Christ, because of which she could not be terrified by those who tried to degrade her.

   a. If you were to capture your identity in Christ in one phrase or image, what would it be?

   b. How can your identity in Christ impact how you respond to others who attempt to identify you in worldly ways?

5. Rudolf praised Tetta for her nobility of conduct and good qualities. By God's grace and empowering, what noble conduct and good qualities could others legitimately praise you for?

6. Leoba modeled soul-to-soul intimate connecting. How would your spiritual friendships grow if you related more and more with others as "soul mates"?

7. Dhuoda encouraged her son to participate in relationships where he receives spiritual direction, where he gives and receives spiritual friendship, and where he gives spiritual direction. Do you have at least one relationship in each of these areas? If so, how could you strengthen them? If not, how could you pursue them?

8. What would it be like to have a spiritual coach like Melania the Elder, Tetta, Leoba, or Dhuoda? What can the church today do to equip more spiritual coaches like these godly women?

CHAPTER SIX

THE LIFE OF THE SOUL, THE LIFE OF THE MIND: THE MEDIEVAL SOUL PHYSICIANS

> "The devil sinned in three ways: by pride, because I [God] had created him good; by desire, to be not only similar to me, but superior to me; and by lust to enjoy so much my divinity that he willingly would have killed me, had he been able to, so that he might reign in my place. Because of this he fell from heaven, filled the earth with these three sins and so violated all mankind" (Birgitta of Sweden).[1]
>
> "There is no doubt that the kind and merciful God himself would immediately be as ready to receive that person [who had committed every sin against God] back into his grace with great joy and happiness as would be a loving father who saw returning to him his only, dearly beloved son, now freed from a great scandal and a most shameful death" (Birgitta of Sweden).[2]

During the Middle Ages (800-1400) the two groups of Medieval men who wrote about women were those who knew the least about women: the clergy and the aristocracy. "The ideas about women were formed on the one hand by the clerkly order, usually celibate, and on the other hand by a narrow caste, who could afford to regard its women as an ornamental asset, while strictly subordinating them to the interests of its primary asset, the land."[3]

Nevertheless, women did write in the Middle Ages sharing their spiritual practices and perceptions.[4] In fact, male writers praised their superior counsel. "And so, in our days... has the art arisen amongst women. Lord God, what art is this that an old woman better understands than a man of wit?"[5] "Art" is the word *kunst* meaning understanding and expressing spiritual realities. The writer, von Regensburg, marvels that mature women were more skillful in the soul physician art than men of wisdom. He reasons that perhaps this is due to the fact "that in her desire she understands better the wisdom flowing from Heaven than does a hard man who is clumsy in these things."[6]

Note that the author links *desire* and *understanding*. This is a common thread sewn through much of women's ministry in the Medieval period. Brunn argues that Medieval women's originality and power reside in "the perfect amalgamation of their doctrine with their spiritual experience."[7] They were masters of living rather than only masters of reading Scripture. They were not tied to doctrine that remained fettered to the intellect, but to doctrine applied to life relationships. In their counsel, they used not only the rational capacity, but also the relational capacity.[8]

From their feminine model we learn how to speak *and* live the truth in love (Ephesians 4:15), how to offer others the Scriptures *and* our souls (1 Thessalonians 2:8), and how our love can abound more and more in knowledge and depth of insight (Philippians 1:9). All of these encompass the classic soul physicians' art.

Hildegard of Bingen: Integrating Head and Heart

Some might assume that Medieval women's emphasis on love led to de-emphasizing the life of the mind. Though no one perfectly integrates head and heart, the women of this chapter exemplify a balance.

Hildegard of Bingen (1098-1179) has been called "one of the greatest intellectuals of the West."[9] She clearly linked love and logic. "This is what your Creator does. He loves you exceedingly, for you are His creature; and He gives you the best treasures, a vivid intelligence." And for what reason? "That He, the Good Giver, may thereby be clearly known."[10] Out of love, the God of love gives us reason so that we can come to understand how good, gracious, and beautiful He is.

Hildegard practiced what she preached. Hazzecha, an abbess in Strasbourg, showed a craving for dependence upon Hildegard and her advice. While responding with relational words of connection,

Hildegard insisted that Hazzecha pursue the way of wisdom. "Daughter of God, you that in God's love call me—poor little creature—mother, learn to have discretion, which, in heavenly things and earthly, is the mother of us all, since by this the soul is directed, and the body nurtured in appropriate restraint."[11] Hildegard gently urged her disciple to wean herself off of her spiritual mother, and to depend upon her heavenly Father. This mindset is one we all could heed. It says to our spiritual friends, "Take direction, but take it responsibly as an adult under God's ultimate spiritual direction."

Unmistakably, Hildegard's manner of speaking the truth in love was effective. Of the three hundred letters preserved from Hildegard's correspondence, the vast majority request or contain her spiritual direction.[12] For example, Hermann, Bishop of Constance, introduced himself by telling her "the fame of your wisdom has spread far and wide and has been reported to me by a number of truthful people, reports that have made me desire to seek out your solace and support even from these far distant regions."[13]

Hildegard not only combined truth and love, she mingled confrontation and comfort. Elisabeth of Schonau (1128-1164) struggled with acute depression and anxiety, even wishing for death on more than one occasion. She wrote to Hildegard admitting that her mind was clouded with shadows, sadness, and despair.[14] Instead of chastening her, Hildegard sustained her, as Elisabeth reported. "For you have been kind and compassionate to me in my distress, as I have understood from the words of my Comforter—whom you have earnestly reminded to console me."[15]

Not only did Hildegard comfort the afflicted, she also afflicted the comfortable. She wrote a letter of confrontation to Emperor Frederick, holding up to him the mirror of princely conduct. In a second letter, she included a ferocious warning because he was behaving "childishly, like one whose mode of life is insane."[16]

None of this was easy for her. Even in her 70s, when famous as a reformer and spiritual director, Hildegard confided to a friend that, "For my part I am always in fear and trembling." She could only speak the truth in love because God sustained her "as on wings whose flight is beyond comprehension and which soar in the heavens in spite of contrary winds."[17] What a needful reminder that courageous counseling does not mean the absence of fear, but the sustaining presence of God.

Bearing Each Other's Burdens: Fulfilling the Law of Love

Throughout the Medieval era, all four aspects of historic, biblical soul care and spiritual direction were active—sustaining, healing, reconciling, and guiding. The sustaining facet consistently followed Paul's admonition to fulfill the loving law of Christ by carrying each other's burdens (Galatians 6:2).

Heloise: Sharing Your Sorrows

Such is certainly the case with one of the most celebrated couples of all time—Heloise (1100-1163) and Abelard. They were two well-educated people, brought together by their passion, then separated by the vengeance of Heloise's uncle. Though they were married, his actions forced them to spend their lives apart for decades, connecting only through written correspondence.

It is in this context that Heloise has much to teach us about sustaining. Receiving a letter from Abelard in which he detailed his ongoing suffering, she communicated how natural it is to hurt. "No one, I think, could read or hear it dry-eyed; my own sorrows are renewed by the detail in which you have told it…"[18]

She then offered one of history's clearest statements that shared sorrow is endurable sorrow. "And so in the name of Christ, who is still giving you some protection for his service, we beseech you to write as often as you think fit to us who are his handmaids and yours, with news of the perils in which you are still storm-tossed. We are all that are left you, so at least you should let us *share your sorrow or your joy*."[19]

Heloise also provided the biblical theology and relational logic behind shared sorrow. "It is always some consolation in sorrow to feel *that it is shared, and any burden laid on several is carried more lightly or removed*."[20]

Abelard described how the process of sustaining by joint burden bearing leads to healing. "Meanwhile thanks be to God who has filled all your hearts with anxiety for my desperate, unceasing perils, and made you share in my affliction; may divine mercy protect me through the support of your prayers and quickly crush Satan beneath our feet."[21] Their empathetic care empowered Abelard to envision the defeat of Satan and his lying, condemning, despairing narrative.

Hadewijch: Giving Permission to Grieve

Just as Heloise merged sustaining and healing, so also did Hadewijch of Brabant (1200-1270). Biographical information about her is scant. We do know that she belonged to a women's movement of her day—the Beguines—who chose a life of poverty, study, meditation, manual work, and teaching. Their purpose was to live in common and to exhort one another to a good life.[22]

Hadewijch became the leader of one such community only to be rejected and exiled by most of her former followers. She humbly pled with them to sustain her breaking heart. "But I, unhappy as I am, ask this, with love, from all of you—who should offer me comfort in my pains, solace in my sad exile, and peace and sweetness."[23]

Ever the spiritual mentor, in her pain she sustained and healed a sister who is in agony on behalf of Hadewijch. She started by giving her permission to grieve. "Therefore I well understand that you cannot easily leave off grieving over my disgrace." She continued by providing this sister with healing perspective. "But be aware, dear child, that this is an alien grief. Think about it yourself; if you believe with all your heart that I am loved by God, and he is doing his work in me, secretly or openly, and that he renews his old wonders in me, you must also be aware that these are doings of Love..."[24]

Hadewijch encouraged her grieving friend to receive soul care from the ultimate Sustainer and Healer. "God be with you! And may he give you consolation with the veritable consolation of himself, with which he suffices to himself and to all creatures according to their being and their desserts."[25] God, in His infinite wisdom and love, knows exactly what every hurting person needs. He awaits our humble asking.

Mechthild: Painting Pictures of Divine Consolation

Mechthild of Madeburg (1207-1283) offers historical insight into biblical sufferology. Like Hadewijch, she was a member of the Beguine lay women's movement of the thirteenth century. Struggling with lifelong depression, she confided her deepest conflicts, longings, and experiences to her spiritual friend, Heinrich of Halle. He urged her to write of her spiritual battles and her beautiful love for Christ, which she did in *The Flowing Light of the Godhead.*[26]

As with many women soul care-givers, Mechthild spoke and wrote using not only words and ideas, but also images and pictures. Speaking of sustaining consolation, she penned, "Our Lord held two golden chalices in his hands that were both full of living wine. In his left hand was the red wine of suffering, and in his right hand the white wine of sublime consolation. Then our Lord spoke: 'Blessed are those who drink this red wine. Although I give both out of divine love, the white wine is nobler in itself; but noblest of all are those who drink both the white and the red.'"[27]

Her words are poetically reminiscent of the Apostle Paul who longed both for the fellowship of Christ's suffering (Philippians 3:10) and for the comfort of His consoling love (Philippians 2:1-2). Mechthild and Paul both teach us that if we are in Christ, then we are in Him for the whole experience—the suffering and the glory, the pain and the consolation (Romans 8:17-18).

Mechthild also taught that if we are to offer consolation, then we must be the type of Christian who habitually and humbly turns to God for comfort. Speaking to spiritual directors about the pressure of being a spiritual director, she said we should perform our duty "with great humility, turn immediately to prayer, and let God console you." Then God will empower the spiritual director's heart for ministry. "You should so transform your heart in God's holy love that you love in a special way each and every brother or sister entrusted to you in all his needs. In all their difficulties you should show your subordinates and brothers loving cheerfulness or kind concern and compassion."[28] This is exactly Paul's message in 2 Corinthians 1:4, where he tells us that if we go to the God of *all* comfort with *all* of our troubles, He then equips us so that we can comfort *anyone* in *any* trouble with the comfort we have received from God.

Encouraging an Eternal Perspective: Beholding the Mirror of Eternity

As the previous section demonstrates, it is impossible to draw a definitive line between sustaining and healing. In real life, they bleed together. Christian women of the Medieval period knew how to bring Christ's healing to bleeding hearts.

Clare: Offering Timely, Timeless Counsel

Clare of Assisi (1193-1253) is a primary example of one who encouraged hurting people to embrace an eternal perspective. Lady Clare, as she was known, was born of nobility in Assisi, twelve years after her mentor, Francis of Assisi. With Francis, Clare shared a tenacious faith in God as both all-powerful and all-generous, whose love could be seen in every aspect of life.[29] Surely she required such a mindset given that for twenty-eight years she was ill and confined to her bed.

And how did Clare derive and share such clarity? From the Scriptures. For instance, for years she wrote letters of consolation and direction to Agnes of Prague. In one letter alone, Clare alluded to or quoted twenty verses.[30]

Such a biblical outlook supernaturally led to an eternal viewpoint. A hard life of unrelenting sacrifice was bearing down upon Agnes. Clare heartened her. "What a great laudable exchange: to leave the things of time for those of eternity, to choose the things of heaven for the goods of earth, to receive the hundred-fold in place on one, and to possess a blessed and eternal life."[31] Every soul physician should be so wise as to help people beaten down by life to consider the great laudable exchange. It will be worth it all—one day.

Clare continued her line of reasoning in a second letter to Agnes, even entitling her missive "Concerning the Strong Perseverance in a Good Proposal." Here Clare pointed Agnes toward resilience in suffering by looking to Christ *and* to eternity. "Look upon Him Who became contemptible for you, and follow Him, making yourself contemptible in the world for Him."[32] In a world where we are promised that all who live godly will be persecuted (2 Timothy 3:12), Clare's advice is timely.

It is also timeless. "Place your mind before the mirror of eternity! Place your soul in the brilliance of glory! Place your heart in the figure of the divine substance! And transform your whole being into the image of the Godhead Itself through contemplation!"[33] Again, her words of counsel mirror those of the Apostle Paul. "Therefore we do not lose heart. Though outwardly we are wasting away, yet inwardly we are being renewed day by day. For our light and momentary troubles are achieving for us an eternal glory that far outweighs them all. So we fix our eyes not on what is seen, but on what is unseen. For what is seen is temporary, but what is unseen is eternal" (2 Corinthians 4:16-18).

Angela de Foligno: Applying Scripture to Life's Hurts

Unlike many of the women we have studied, Angela de Foligno (1248-1309) entered the world of spiritual friendship late in life. Born into a wealthy family, she married at a young age and enjoyed an extravagant and worldly life until age thirty-seven when she converted to Christ. When her husband passed, she embraced a new life of poverty and prayer as a lay woman.[34]

On her deathbed, Angela thanked God for the ministry He allowed her to have. "It pleased the divine goodness to place in my care, under my solicitude, all his sons and daughters."[35] Her solicitude included a brilliant blending of sustaining and healing, of hearing the story of worldly hurt and sharing the story of heavenly hope.

Speaking to a group undergoing severe hardships, Angela explained that, "the tribulations of this world mean eternal consolations."[36] Elaborating further, she offered sustaining and healing counsel. "Concerning the tribulations which you are suffering, I extend to you my heartfelt sympathy and envy. When you are afflicted and tested within and without, it is most certainly a sign that you are among the loved ones of the Beloved."[37] What intriguing encouragement—extending sympathy (sustaining) and envy (healing). Angela communicated awareness of their deep pain, but also appreciation for their deep honor of suffering for Christ as the Bride of Christ.

Angela directed her suffering friends not only to Christ's love, but also to His example. "Consider the pain of the suffering Christ and it will be a remedy for all your suffering. The Son of God was afflicted by evil for our benefit."[38] Like so much of the healing soul care of this era, Angela paraphrased and relevantly applied Scripture to life. Ponder how her quote encapsulates Hebrews 12:3. "Consider him who endured such opposition from sinful men, so that you will not grow weary and lose heart."

Also in common with her compatriots, Angela offered principles of biblical sufferology. "There are three things which these most holy, and misunderstood, tribulations accomplish in the soul. First, they make the soul turn to God, or if it has already done so, they prompt it to greater conversion and closer adherence to him. Second, tribulations make the soul grow. When rain comes on well-prepared soil, it germinates and bears fruit; so, likewise, when tribulations come, the soul grows in virtue. Third, tribulations purify, comfort, and quiet the soul, and give it peace and tranquility."[39] Imagine how those powerful, pertinent words empowered these suffering saints to persevere.

As potent as those words are, Angela knew that the ultimate hope for peace in persecution would not come through insight alone, but through dependent relationship with Christ. "O my sons, where can a creature find rest or peace if not in him who is the sovereign rest and peace, the sovereign source of peacefulness and tranquility for our souls?"[40] It's possible to hope—when we put our hope in God.

Confronting Out of Concern for Change: Granting Tastes of Holy Love

Women of the Medieval period offered reconciling and guiding spiritual direction just as readily as they bestowed sustaining and healing soul care. In the historic tradition, their reconciling counsel dealt with both the horrors of sin and the wonders of grace.

Clare: Reaffirming Human Love and Divine Grace

Clare is emblematic of this sense of balance. In *The Rule of Saint Clare*, designed to guide her community of women, she first addressed the importance of establishing a close, humble relationship with the sisters. "The Abbess is to be so familiar with them that they can speak and act toward her as ladies do with their servant. For that is the way it should be, that the Abbess be the servant of all the sisters."[41]

With these words, Clare reminded us of the counsel of Proverbs 27:6a, "Wounds from a friend can be trusted." Clare's words also reflect Paul's instructions. "Brothers, if someone is caught in a sin, you who are spiritual should restore him gently. But watch yourself, or you also may be tempted" (Galatians 6:1).

Once this meek, intimate relationship is established, then the abbess can effectively "admonish and visit her sisters, and humbly and charitably correct them, not commanding them anything which would be against their soul…"[42] As she speaks the truth in love, the abbess "must beware not to become angry or disturbed on account of anyone's sin: for anger and disturbance prevent charity in oneself and in others."[43]

Of course, it is not biblically appropriate to stop at confronting sin. Biblical counselors stress Christ's amazing grace. Once sin has been confronted, "the other sister, mindful of that word of the Lord: *If you do not forgive from the heart, neither will your heavenly Father forgive you* (Mt. 6:15; 18:35), should generously pardon her sister every wrong she has done her."[44]

In the spirit of James 5:16, we are to confess our sins to each other and pray for each other so that we may be healed. In the spirit of 2 Corinthians 2:7-8, once a sister or brother has repented we "ought to forgive and comfort him, so that he will not be overwhelmed by excessive sorrow. I urge you, therefore, to reaffirm your love for him." Why? "In order that Satan might not outwit us. For we are not unaware of his schemes" (2 Corinthians 2:11). Satan plots to overwhelm us with worldly sorrow leading to condemnation and despair. We participate in defeating his ruse by reaffirming our love and God's forgiveness.

Mechthild: Communicating "It's Diabolical to Sin"

Previously we introduced the phrase "it's horrible to sin" to convey the first aspect of the reconciling process. Mechthild pointedly heightened that language. "Some people who are learned say it is human to sin. In every temptation of my sinful body, in every movement of my heart, in every bit of knowledge of my senses, and in the whole nobility of my soul, I could never find anything else but that *it is diabolical that one commit a sin.* Whether the sin be small or great, the devil is always its companion."[45]

Mechthild developed her conviction by exposing the devil's craftiness, the core of his temptation, and the essence of human sin. She began with the big picture. "I have seen a city, its name is eternal hate. It was built in the deepest abyss from all kinds of stones of huge capital sins. Pride was the first stone, as it manifest in the case of Lucifer."[46] In listing pride as the original sin, Mechthild followed a long line of biblical interpretation.

Also adhering to biblical application, she saw Satan as the False Seducer seeking to woo the believer's soul away from God, seeking to win the Christian's love and affection. "I want now what I have always wanted—to put my chair next to his [God's]. Indeed, I would like to drive him from the chair of your soul, if I could, and sit down on it..."[47]

What a frightening and amazing depiction of the eternal love triangle in which Satan strives to captivate our hearts. Paul speaks similar words about Satan in 2 Corinthians 11:2-3. "I am jealous for you with a godly jealousy. I promised you to one husband, to Christ, so that I might present you as a pure virgin to him. But I am afraid that just as Eve was deceived by the serpent's cunning, your minds may somehow be led astray from your sincere and pure devotion to Christ."

Mechthild and Paul thus remind us that our sinning spiritual friend is not our enemy—Satan is. God calls us to "gently instruct" those we reconcile "in the hope that God will grant them repentance leading them to a knowledge of the truth, and that they will come to their senses and escape from the trap of the devil, who has taken them captive to do his will" (2 Timothy 2:25b-26).

Gertrude of Helfta: Surrounding Sinning Souls with Affectionate Sympathy

Gertrude of Helfta (1256-1302) ministered in the same renowned community as Mechthild. We know little about her life, but from her writings (*The Herald of Divine Love*) we know that she was well read in the Scriptures and the church fathers, especially Augustine.[48]

A later redactor inserted sections into her writings that assist us in seeing Gertrude's heart of zeal for righteousness and love for people as she practiced the art of reconciling. "She formed in her zeal such gracious words of love and wisdom that the hardest hearts were softened by her words and the most perverse of her hearers, if they had but a spark of piety, conceived the will, or at least the desire, to amend their lives."[49]

When her words did spark godly sorrow, Gertrude granted grace. "If she saw that a soul was moved to compunction by her advice, she surrounded it with such affectionate compassion and such tender love that her heart seemed to melt in her efforts to console it. And she procured this consolation less by her words than by the outpouring of her desires and her fervent prayers to God."[50]

Hers is an important practice that we often miss in our tendency to make hard and fast divisions between sustaining and reconciling. We think of empathy primarily related to entering the suffering of another person—when they have been sinned against. But Gertrude rightly expressed empathy by entering the sinning of another person—when they are facing the horrors of *their own sin*. Like the Puritans after her, Gertrude could both load the conscience with guilt, and also lighten the conscience with grace—via empathy.

Perhaps the reason she empathized so deeply was because she cared so intensely for God's glory and her spiritual friends' good. "When she saw some defect in the soul of another, she longed for the person to correct it; if she did not see any improvement, she was inconsolable until she was able to bring this about, at least in some measure, by her prayers to God, her exhortations, or the help of another person."[51] Gertrude used a variety of methods to prompt repentance: words, exhortations, prayer, and others within the Body of Christ.

Of course, she also prioritized God's Word related specifically to the person and situation. "When she found in Holy Scripture certain passages which she thought would be of use, if they seemed to her to be too difficult for persons of lesser intelligence, she would translate them into simpler language so that they might be of greater profit to their readers."[52]

Empowering Christians to Live Like Christ: Sharing the "Why" and the "How" of Growth in Grace

In current Christian counseling models, sometimes counselors make the assumption that if a Christian has deeply repented and humbly received Christ's gracious forgiveness, then that person will, by osmosis, continue the growth in grace process. Biblically and historically, there is a different understanding—growth in grace is an active process involving the Word of God, the Spirit of God, and the people of God (including, but not limited to, spiritual directors). Such is certainly the case in the guiding ministry of women spiritual directors of the Medieval period.

The Why of Growth in Grace: Emphasizing Our *Capax Dei*

According to these Medieval women, the human personality has a *capax Dei*: a capacity for God. We are, at our core, spiritual beings. This capacity soars above, beyond, and deeper than all other motivators and longings in the human soul (Psalm 42:1-2). God designed us with an insatiable longing for Him and what is most vital about us is our vitality for God (Philippians 3:8).[53] For example, after scores of pages, one can boil down Mechthild's book *The Flowing Light of the Godhead* to the moving story of God's heart, the human heart, and Satan's cunning enterprise to interfere with the tie that binds them.[54]

Because the Spirit regenerated our God-designed *capax Dei* at salvation, female spiritual directors like Mechthild realized that the motivation to grow in grace was already "in there." The Apostle Paul put it this way. "For this reason I remind you to fan into flame the gift of God, which is in you through the laying on of my hands. For

God did not give us a spirit of timidity, but a spirit of power, of love and of self-discipline" (2 Timothy 1:6-7).

Further, these women spiritual directors understood *relational motivation*. Our Trinitarian God Who exists forever in the perfect oneness of Father, Son, and Holy Spirit (John 1, 17) created us in His image to relate spiritually to Him and socially to one another (Genesis 2:18).[55] This is why Jesus summarized the entire Old Testament with the commands to love the Lord our God with our whole being and to love our neighbor as ourselves (Matthew 22:35-40).

Summarizing Clare's life and ministry, Armstrong noted that "the genius of Clare's perception of the spiritual life can be seen" in how she penetrated "the marvelous mystery of the Revelation of God Who reveals Himself as a Community of Love. There can be little doubt that the enclosed life of San Damiano struggled on a daily basis to express that Unity of God."[56]

Thus for Clare, Mechthild, and the other representative women of this era, guiding commenced with the conviction that it's supernatural to love. They taught that the Christian is motivated to grow in grace—defined by ever-deepening relationship with God and others—by the realization that God designed our souls to reflect His relational nature. This mindset prevented their guiding from becoming focused on legalistic rule-keeping and self-effort (Colossians 2:16-23).

Instead, they concentrated their guiding on helping regenerated people to know that they had been "raised with Christ," so they would "set your minds on things above," because they had "put on the new self, which is being renewed in knowledge in the image of its Creator" (Colossians 3:1, 2, 10). Their guiding goal was love. "And over all these virtues put on love, which binds them all together in perfect unity" (Colossians 3:14).

The How of Growth in Grace: Drawing Out Spiritual Resources

Since Clare accentuated our regenerated relationality, she practiced the soul physician guiding art of stirring up spiritual qualities by extolling them wherever she saw them actively used. With her spiritual disciple, Agnes, she commended her for "the fame of your holy conduct and irreproachable life…"[57] Instead of focusing on failures, Clare highlighted already existing strengths, in essence communicating, "It's in there supernaturally, do more of the same!"

Clare then connected these regenerated relational capacities with Agnes' relational longing for Christ. First she praised Agnes for her great Moses-like sacrifice in refusing the riches of the world for the love of Christ. Then she encouraged her to remain pure in her love for Christ. "Whose power is stronger, Whose generosity is more abundant, Whose appearance is more beautiful, Whose love more tender, Whose courtesy more gracious. In Whose embrace you are already caught up…"[58]

These Medieval spiritual guides also recognized our regenerated rational (thinking) and volitional (choosing) capacities. They understood that these capacities, too, needed to be stirred up. Speaking of one cause of spiritual immaturity, Hadewijch pinpointed our false beliefs. "This is why we are still unenlightened in our thinking, unstable in all our being, uncertain in our reasoning and understanding. This is why we suffer so, poor wretched exiled beggars… and there would be no need for this, were it not that all our thinking is false…"[59] Hadewijch understood that we pursue what we perceive is pleasing. Renewed minds perceive that God is most pleasing and thus choose to pursue Him passionately.

When we pursue Christ, we volitionally commit to living like Christ. Hadewijch said exactly that as she continued her explanation for lack of growth in grace. "And how false it [our thinking] is we show plainly when we do not live with Christ as he lived, do not abandon all as He did… If we look at what we do, we can see that this is true: whenever we can, we strive for our own ease."[60] If we love God, then we will love and do God's will as Christ did by living like Christ lived.

This was not pie-in-the-sky thinking. For Hadewijch it was eminently practical. If we love Christ, we will want to reflect Christ, and if we want to reflect the inner character of Christ, then we will reflect the daily life of Christ. "For it is man's obligation to practice virtues, not in order to obtain consideration, or joy, or wealth, or rank, or any enjoyment in heaven or on earth, but solely out of homage to the incomparable sublimity of God, who created our nature to this end and made it for his own honor and praise, and for our bliss in eternal glory. This is the way on which the Son of God took the lead, and of which he himself gave us knowledge and understanding when he lived as Man."[61] To become like Christ, we volitionally commit to practicing the spiritual disciplines and the virtues of the Christian life just as Christ did while on earth.

Listening to the Silenced Voices

When we listen to the silenced voices of Medieval women sacred friends we hear a message that consistently mingles truth and love. This message is instructive for us today. Like us, they lived in an era with two extremes: mysticism and scholasticism. The mystics tended to focus on the *relational*: affections, the heart, experiential understanding, spiritual theology, and contemplation (meditation). The scholastics tended to emphasize the *rational*: cognitions, the head, mental understanding, academic theology, and examination (study).

Then and now, those on either side of the spectrum tend to castigate those on the other side—frequently throwing out the proverbial "baby with the bath water." They quote one another out of context, make charges that are little more than "false guilt by false association," and they tend to see only what they are looking for— the supposed faults in "the other view."

However, biblical Christianity has always integrated the life of the soul and the life of the mind—affections and beliefs, the head and the heart, experience and reason, knowing God (tasting and seeing that He is good) and knowing about God (doctrinal purity). The biblically balanced approach is neither mysticism nor scholasticism. Mysticism degrades into a shallow, self-centered focus on experience apart from truth and feelings without core beliefs. Scholasticism collapses into a cold-hearted, Pharisaical emphasis on judgmentalism, sin-spotting, and "discernment" without grace. True biblical soul care and spiritual direction have always combined an unremitting concern for changing lives with Christ's changeless truth—integrating head and heart, Scripture and soul.

Learning Together from Our Great Cloud of Witnesses

1. According to this chapter, women soul physicians of this era tended to combine head and heart, relationship and rationality, perhaps more than men of this era.
    a. Why might this be?
    b. What can we learn from this?

2. From Hildegard we learned that courageous counseling does not mean the absence of fear, but the sustaining presence of God. How could this awareness impact your counseling ministry?

3. Clare taught us that any burden laid on several is carried more lightly. How could the Body of Christ implement this truth?

4. Hadewijch, along with many other women in this chapter, merged sustaining and healing. How could you blend these two more effectively in your spiritual friendships?

5. From Mechthild we learned how to paint pictures of Divine consolation.
    a. How well do you use images and pictures to convey biblical truth?
    b. Who does this well in your life? What impact does it have on you?

6. Clare offered timely and timeless counsel—relating God's eternal Word to the specifics of relationships today. Share examples of times in your life and/or ministry where you have blended today's earthly story and heaven's eternal story.

7. From Angela de Foligno we learned how to apply Scripture to life's hurts.
    a. Specifically, what could you apply from her ministry?
    b. Who does this well with you and how does it impact you?

8. In reconciling, we learned from Clare how to reaffirm human love and Divine grace, from Mechthild how to communicate that it's diabolical to sin, and from Gertrude how to surround sinning souls with affectionate sympathy. In your life and ministry, which do you need most? Why?

9. In guiding, we learned the "why and the "how" of growth in grace. How could you apply to your life and ministry emphasizing our *capax Dei* (the why) and drawing out spiritual resources (the how)?

CHAPTER SEVEN

ALL SHALL BE WELL:
UNCHAINED VOICES

"Just because I am a woman, must I therefore believe that I must not tell you about the goodness of God" (Julian of Norwich).[1]
"Great was the holy conversation that the anchoress [Julian of Norwich] and this creature [Margery Kempe] had through talking of the love of our Lord Jesus Christ for the many days that they were together" (Margery Kempe, speaking of her spiritual director—Julian of Norwich).[2]

*E*very society needs models. The women who dedicated themselves to God during the late Middle Ages fulfilled the social function of heroines of the faith who set the example as prayer warriors, counselors, and teachers.[3] These women wrote letters of spiritual consolation, penned letters of spiritual confrontation, and taught kings and paupers alike. The unchained voices of these untrained lay women empowered Christians to believe that even in the Dark Ages one day God would make all things well.

The faith they sustained was a more personal faith then in the preceding era. Earlier Medieval Christianity had previously imagined Christ as a remote Hero who conquered Satan to save souls seized due to sin. "In this struggle, human beings were little more than spectators."[4]

The conception of Christ as divine Warrior did not disappear in the late Middle Ages, "but alongside it there grew up a different emphasis on Christ as suffering man, arousing compassion in his fellow human beings."[5] Women spiritual directors like Julian of Norwich and Catherine of Siena saw Christ's incarnation as the means of salvation *and* as a means of drawing human love towards God.

Julian of Norwich: Embraced by the Love of God

We know very little about Julian of Norwich's (1342-1416) background, not even her real name. We do know that she was the first female writer in English and that on May 8, 1373, when seriously ill, she received a series of "showings" which she perceived to be signs from God. Recovering from her illness, Julian spent many years pondering the significance of these experiences.[6]

Later in life she lived as an anchoress at St. Julian's Church in Norwich from which she adopted her name and became a famous spiritual adviser. As an anchoress, Julian entered into an enclosed solitary life in a fixed place (anchored) in order to pursue growth in grace. Though living in solitude, she provided spiritual counsel to others, including Margery Kempe who called her Dame Julian.[7] After a lifetime of providing spiritual care and pondering the spiritual life, Julian penned a short and a long text of *Showings* (also called *Revelations of Divine Love*) in which she sought to interpret her experiences through the grid of Scripture.

Interestingly, her style of writing contrasts greatly with the men of her day. Male writers had been trained in disputation to emphasize opposition, combativeness, and triumph or defeat in argumentation. Theirs was the intellectual counterpart to the military training that produced knights. Thus, in a disputation, you uphold one view only by opposing another, "unhorsing your opponent as if in a joust."[8]

This disputative, adversarial quality is quite lacking in Julian's writings, as is the case generally with the women spiritual writers of this era. People writing today about soul care, spiritual direction, and biblical counseling have much to learn from Julian's model. Currently, many in these fields seem to focus on warfare, building walls, and destroying bridges. Reconciling, learning from others, and bridge building seldom occur. Fellow Christians are not enemies on the battlefield to destroy or opponents on the sports field to defeat.

Sustaining Focus: Comfort Experienced in Contemplating God's Comfort

Just as Julian focuses on building bridges of human reconciliation in her writings, so she centers her sustaining ministry on helping people to understand the reconciling heart of God. In salvation, God acts as a *Judge* justifying and forgiving us, as a *Creator and Physician* regenerating and healing us, as a *Champion and Warrior* redeeming and empowering us, and as a *Father* reconciling and comforting us.[9] While aware of each of these aspects of God's salvation grace, Julian emphasizes God's fatherly reconciliation.

She uses the old English word *homelyhede* with the full relational resonance of *home* to speak of God's friendliness, goodness, comfort, familiarity, closeness, intimacy, and accessibility.[10] For her readers and her disciples, Julian highlights the image of God as One who "is everything that is good and comforting and helpful. He is our clothing, wrapping and enveloping us for love, embracing us and guiding us in all things, hanging about us in tender love, so that he can never leave us.... He is everything that is good for us."[11] God's all-embracing goodness that swathes us in grace is central to Julian's vision of the spiritual life.

In fact, she states that the purpose of her writings was to help Christians to "eagerly, attentively, lovingly, and humbly contemplate God, who in his gracious love and in his eternal goodness" reveals Himself to us in order "to comfort us all."[12] She writes out of her own soul comfort. "I wanted it to comfort them all as it did me.... And what comforted me most... was that our Lord is so familiar and courteous. And that is what gave me most happiness and the strongest sense of spiritual safety."[13]

Like all effective soul care-givers, Julian first finds her own comfort in the comfort of God, then she shares with others from the overflow (2 Corinthians 1:3-7).

Healing Perspective: Encouragement Found in Knowing God Our Affectionate Sovereign

Julian wraps her sustaining counsel about comforting in the cocoon of healing wisdom about suffering. "God wishes us to know that he safely protects us in both joy and sorrow equally, and he loves us as much in sorrow as in joy.... But God gives us joy generously when he so wishes, and sometimes allows us sorrow, and both come from love."[14] In her sufferology, people first face suffering through a God-perspective—seeing Him as their Father of affectionate sovereignty.

To this biblical strategy, Julian insists upon an eternal perspective. "So it is God's will that we should hold on to gladness with all our might, for bliss lasts eternally, and pain passes and shall vanish completely."[15]

However, hers was no mere "rational-emotive therapy." Julian undergirds mind renewal with relational intimacy. Speaking in words akin to Psalm 73:25a ("Whom have I in heaven but you?"), Julian explains, "I was satisfied by no heaven but Jesus, who will be my bliss when I am there. And it has always been a comfort to me that I chose Jesus for my heaven in all this time of suffering and sorrow."[16]

In many ways, Julian's ministry involves the daily application of Ephesians 3:14-21. There Paul prays that believers would be strengthened through the Spirit in their inner being and through Christ dwelling in their hearts through faith. It is a faith that is rooted and established in love so that Christians "may have power, together will all the saints, to grasp how wide and long and high and deep is the love of Christ, and to know this love that surpasses knowledge—that you may be filled to the measure of all the fullness of God" (Ephesians 3:18-19).

In her ministry, Julian is addressing the question, "How do we help one another to experience Ephesians 3:15-25? How do we, *together*, experientially grasp the infinite, multi-dimensionality of God's love?" Julian understands that without knowing God's love, suffering and doubt will defeat faith and hope. "And we are troubled by them [suffering] because we do not recognize love."[17]

She astutely exposes the core problem in her day and in ours. "Love is nearest to us all. And this is the knowledge of which we are most ignorant; for many men and women believe that God is almighty and has power to do everything, and that he is all wisdom and knows how to do everything, but that he is all love and is willing to do everything—there they stop. And this ignorance is what hinders those who most love God."[18] She summarizes well her philosophy of healing: "love makes God's power and wisdom very gentle to us…"[19]

Hers is another case of feminine soul care contrasted with masculine soul care. For some male theologians, such as John Calvin, holiness must be the primary property of God that floods our minds and controls our thoughts about God. For Julian, love is the paramount attribute. This speaks to the necessity of *both* male *and* female interpretations of Scripture. Combined, we learn that our God is always, in infinite integration, the God of *holy love*. Only by intimate relationship with our God of loving holiness can we survive in and thrive above earthly suffering.

Caring Connection: Empathy Sourced in Christ

Our Father of holy love mediates His empathic care to us through Christ and Christians. For Julian, Christ is the source of Christian empathy. "Then I saw that whenever a man feels kind compassion with love for his fellow Christian, it is Christ within him."[20]

Since Christ is the final font of Christian empathy, Julian wants believers to comprehend His depth of care for them in salvation and in suffering. To handle earthly suffering, we must start with the eternal story. "Jesus wishes us to consider the delight which the Holy Trinity feels in our salvation, and wishes us to delight as much, through his grace, while we are on earth."[21]

In no way does this suggest that Julian ignores the problem of sin and suffering. In fact, she longs to understand the mystery of why God allows sin and suffering. Though finding no easy, earthly answer, she repeatedly clings to the message that all shall be well. "He supports us willingly and sweetly, by his words, and says, 'But all shall be well, and all manner of things shall be well.'"[22] On earth, we rest in Christ's promise that all shall be well. In heaven, one day, "He will make openly known to us in heaven; in which knowledge we shall truly see the reason why he allowed sin to exist; and seeing this we shall rejoice eternally in our Lord God."[23]

That we must take this on faith, and that we often struggle mightily now while living by sight, Julian makes plain. "Deeds are done which appear so evil to us and people suffer such terrible evils that it does not seem as though any good will ever come of them; and we consider this, sorrowing and grieving over it so that we cannot find peace in the blessed contemplation of God as we should do; and this is why: our reasoning powers are so blind now, so humble and so simple, that we cannot know the high, marvelous wisdom, the might and the goodness of the Holy Trinity."[24]

Julian is candid. Some things—many things—make no sense... today... by sight. However, today by faith, and one day by sight, all will make sense and all shall be well.

The only pathway to believe this now is to believe that where sin abounds, grace superabounds (Romans 5:20). Julian asks, "Ah, my good Lord, how could all be well, given the great harm that has been done to humankind by sin?" To which she perceives Christ answering that Adam's sin was indeed "the greatest harm that ever was done, or ever shall be." But we must "consider the glorious atonement; for this atonement is incomparably more pleasing to God and more glorious in saving mankind than Adam's sin was ever harmful."[25]

For Julian these were not esoteric debates unrelated to daily life. Rather, there is great daily benefit in this eternal awareness. "Since I [Christ] have turned the greatest possible harm into good, it is my will that you should know from this that I shall turn all lesser evils into good."[26]

How powerful, practical, and scriptural. It is the same message Paul communicates in 1 Corinthians 15 and 2 Corinthians 1. In 1 Corinthians 15, Paul explores the eternal benefits of Christ's *past* resurrection and our *future* resurrection. Typically, we are so amazed by those twin benefits that we forget the *present* benefit of the resurrection. Paul does not in 2 Corinthians 1:8-9. Speaking of his daily casket experiences where he despaired of life and felt the sentence of death, Paul shares that this occurred so that he might not rely on himself, but on the God who *continually* raises the dead. In the midst of our daily mini-casket experiences of life's losses and crosses, by faith we can experience daily mini-resurrection experiences.

Reconciling Wisdom: Forgiveness Bathed in Grace

The fact that Julian emphasizes how all things shall be well should not be interpreted to mean that she deemphasizes the horrors of sin.

Instead, like the Apostle Paul, Julian sees sin in light of God's grace and mercy. "Or do you show contempt for the riches of his kindness, tolerance and patience, not realizing that God's kindness leads you toward repentance?" (Romans 2:4).

It is God's lovingkindness that leads Him to expose our sin. "It is a supreme favour from our kind Lord, that he should watch over us so tenderly while we are in a state of sin; and furthermore he secretly touches our inner hearts and shows us our sin by the pure, sweet light of mercy and grace."[27]

The problem is, we don't perceive God's exposure through His loving eyes. Rather, through our eyes "when we see how filthy we are, then we think that God must be angry with us for our sins…"[28] Satan tempts us to be like Adam and Eve and sew our own self-sufficient fig leaves in a vain attempt to cover our nakedness and hide our shame. But God's way is for the Spirit to lead us to repentance and wholehearted, humble reliance upon Christ's grace.

When we follow God's manner of responding to sin's exposure, our entire image of God and relationship to God alters. "And then our kind Lord reveals himself, very joyfully and looking very pleased, with a friendly welcome, as though the soul had been in pain and in prison, sweetly saying this: 'My darling, I am glad you have come to me. I have always been with you in all your misery and now you can see how much I love you and we are united in bliss.' This is how sins are forgiven through mercy and grace and our souls gloriously received in joy, just as they will be when they come to heaven…"[29]

As with suffering, as with resurrection, so with sin and forgiveness—the assurance of our final glorification in heaven must impact our ongoing sanctification on earth. In heaven, all tears of suffering shall be wiped away. Therefore, we can persevere during earthly suffering. So also, in heaven, all scars of sin shall be cleansed by the blood of the Lamb. Therefore, like the Prodigal, we can joyfully return home to God today knowing that God graciously receives and lovingly embraces all His repentant prodigal children.

Catherine of Siena: Embracing Others through the Love of God

Their situations were drastically different. Julian of Norwich was an anchorite bound to one place, while Catherine of Siena (1347-1380) moved in remarkably wide circles. Yet their ministries overlapped. They both found that their plunge into relationship with God also plunged them into deep relationships with others.

On March 25, 1347, in Siena, Italy, a prosperous wool-dyer, Giacomo di Benincasa, and his wife, Lapa, welcomed their twenty-third child, Catherine, into the world. Her father's family belonged to the lower middle-class of tradesmen and notaries, known as "the Party of the Twelve," which ruled the Republic of Siena from 1355 to 1368. Her mother was the daughter of a local poet.[30]

Catherine's spiritual journey began at age six when she had a powerful vision of Christ. Even at that young age she devoted herself to prayer, meditation on Scripture, and spiritual disciplines. At age eighteen she received the Dominican habit. By age twenty-one Catherine began ministering to the sick in homes and hospitals. Her public activity gained her notice as did her evident spiritual depth, and people flocked to her for counsel. She began to dispatch letters of spiritual counsel to women and men in every condition of life. Amazingly, Catherine did not learn to write until the end of her life. She dictated her books and letters, sometimes reciting three documents to three secretaries at the same time. During much of her life Catherine endured excruciating physical pain.[31]

Sustaining Empathy: Drinking the Bitter Medicine

Catherine models her ministry after her caring Savior Whom she pictures as a sympathetic soul Physician. In the words of God the Father, "The coming of the great Physician, that is to say, of My only begotten Son, cured this invalid, He drinking this bitter medicine, which man could not drink on account of his great weakness, like a foster-mother who takes medicine instead of her suckling, because she is grown up and strong, and the child is not fit to endure its bitterness. He was man's foster-mother, enduring with the greatness and strength of Deity united with your nature, the bitter medicine of the painful death of the Cross, to give life to you little ones debilitated by guilt."[32]

This is a striking feminine metaphor in which Catherine pictures Christ like a mother who takes the bitter medicine for her infant who can not tolerate it. "This is how far the empathy of God is willing to go for us—taking our medicine on the cross."[33]

What Christ modeled on the cross, Christians throughout church history have also exemplified, as Catherine describes. "They made themselves infirm, being whole and without infirmity... being strong they made themselves weak... And so with love they knew how to be all things to all men, and to give to each one his nourishment.... They put themselves in the midst of the thorns of tribulation, and exposed themselves to every peril with true patience... With tears and sweat they anointed the wounds of their neighbor."[34] Ministry, for Catherine, is not some exalted office of legitimized status and official power. Rather, she perceives ministry as humble, sacrificial, empathetic service.

Catherine's concept of empathy is not simply an academic exploration of how Christ and other Christians practiced it. Her letters of spiritual consolation ooze compassion. In a letter written to Frate Bartolomeo Dominici, Catherine uses motherly imagery to convey her incarnational care. "Tell Frate Simone, my son in Christ Jesus, that a son is never afraid to go to his mother. No, he even runs to her, especially when he feels hurt. His mother takes him in her arms, holds him tight to her breast, and nurses him. Though I am a sorry mother, I will always carry him at the breast of charity."[35]

Catherine's "weeping with those who weep" does not mean that she "babies" people. Instead, she urges sufferers to refuse to quit, to reject retreat. Catherine demonstrates this aspect of her soul care in her letter to Madonna Mitarella, wife of Senator Ludovico di Masseo da Mogliano of Siena. This letter is associated with an uprising that occurred in Siena in March 1373, when the senator attempted to restore order by sentencing noble and plebeian criminals alike to execution. In the rioting, Ludovico's life was threatened, as well as the safety of his family. Madonna Mitarella wrote a letter to Catherine expressing her terror, to which Catherine responds.

You wrote me that because of what has happened to the senator (and you had apparently been very afraid of this), you are placing your faith and confidence only in the prayers of God's servants. I beg you then, in the name of God and of our gentlest love Jesus Christ, to stand firm in this sweet holy faith. Oh sweet life-giving faith! If you persevere in that faith, sadness will never overtake your heart. For sadness comes only from putting our trust in creatures. But creatures are frail lifeless things that sooner or later fail, and our heart can never find rest except in what is stable and secure. When we set our heart on other people it is not set on anything stable, for a human being is alive today and tomorrow is dead. So if we wish to have peace we must rest our heart and soul with faith and love in Christ crucified. Only then will our soul find complete happiness.[36]

We find in this letter not only aspects of sustaining, but also Catherine's Christian personality theory. We are, according to Catherine, worshipping beings who must trust something. In our sinfulness we tend toward trusting the creature instead of the Creator. But our soul's final happiness (contentment, satisfaction, hope, security) is found only in God-trust.

We find a powerful example of how Catherine sustains both in words and actions in her letter to Frate Raimondo da Capula, in which she recounts her having fulfilled a request from Niccolo di Tolodo to attend his execution. She begins with a moving description of their encounter. "I went to visit the one you know and he was so comforted and consoled that he confessed his sins and prepared himself very well. He made me promise for love of God that when the time came for the execution I would be with him. This I promised and did."[37]

Having helped Niccolo to prepare his heart for eternity, Catherine fulfills her promise by spending his last moments on earth with him. "In the morning, before the bell, I went to him and he was greatly consoled.… His will was in accord with and submissive to God's will. His only fear now was of not being strong at the final moment. But God's measureless and burning goodness tricked him, creating in him such affection and love through his love for me in God that he could not do without God! He said, 'Stay with me; don't leave me alone. That way I can't help but be all right, and I'll die happy!'"[38]

Catherine continues with an intimate description of Niccolo's final minutes.

> His head was resting on my breast. I sensed an intense joy, a fragrance of his blood—and it wasn't separate from the fragrance of my own, which I am waiting to shed for my gentle Spouse Jesus.… I waited for him at the place of execution. I waited there in continual prayer… Then he arrived like a meek lamb, and when he saw me he began to laugh and wanted me to make the sign of the cross on him. When he had received the sign I said, "Down for the wedding, my dear brother, for soon you will be in everlasting life!"[39]

Emboldened with this amazing image of his eternal bliss with Christ, Niccolo enters eternity consoled and confident. "He knelt down very meekly; I placed his neck on the block and bent down and reminded him of the blood of the Lamb. His mouth said nothing but 'Gesu!' and 'Caterina!' and as he said this, I received his head into my hands, saying, 'I will!' with my eyes fixed on divine Goodness."[40]

We talk about "climbing in the casket." Catherine *becomes* the casket—the receptacle for Niccolo's lifeless body—but only after being the vessel for the sustaining of his eternal soul. How forcefully this account illustrates the truth, even to the point of death by beheading, that "shared sorrow is endurable sorrow."

Healing Encouragement: Seeing with Spiritual Eyes

Catherine's healing ministry offers hope in the midst of difficulty. She does not attempt to diminish difficulties, but helps sufferers to see tribulation through God's eyes. Like most historic soul care-givers, Catherine first develops a biblical sufferology.

She begins by envisioning God's explanation for the existence of evil and suffering. "I send people troubles in this world so that they may know that their goal is not this life, and that these things are imperfect and passing. I am their goal, and I want them to want me, and in this spirit they should accept such things."[41] God places *His* goal before ours, because He knows how distorted our goals are. We strive for circumstantial ease and emotional happiness. God purposes for His name to be glorified as we find our full satisfaction in Him.

God uses suffering providentially. "O my dearest daughter, as I have told you so often, I want to be merciful to the world and provide for my reasoning creatures' every need. But the foolish take for death what I give for life, and are thus cruel to themselves."[42] Death—mini-casket experiences—is God's medicine of choice for our arrogant self-sufficiency. Suffering is medicinal, even when the pill we must swallow is bitter.

As with sustaining, in healing Catherine does not stop at academic theology. She uses her biblical convictions as the foundation for her practical letters of spiritual consolation. In a letter believed to be to one of her many biological brothers, she employs spiritual conversations and scriptural explorations to help him to find hope's healing.

"Take heart, take heart, dearest brother, and don't falter under God's discipline. Trust that when human aid fails, divine help is at hand. God will provide for you. Recall how Job lost his possessions, his children, his health; only his wife was left him, and she was a constant torment!" Here Catherine relates Job's level one suffering to her brother's external circumstances.[43]

She continues by connecting Job's level two suffering to her brother's doubts. "Patient Job was never confounded. No, always exercising the virtue of holy patience, he would say, 'God gave it to me and God has taken it away from me. Blessed be God's name!' I want you to do the same, dearest brother. Be a lover of virtue, with holy patience and frequent confession to help you bear your sufferings. I tell you, God will show his kindness and mercy, and will repay you for every burden you have borne for his love. Keep living in God's holy and tender love.'"[44] Though some might disagree with Catherine's assessment that Job was never confounded, still we see how Catherine applies Job's perseverance to urge her brother to similar resilience.

In another letter of spiritual consolation, she makes practical her theology of suffering. Catherine longs for the recipient of her letter to develop a God-perspective—one highlighting the generous goodness of God. "For God's love for his creatures was so strong that it moved him to draw us out of himself and give us his own image and likeness—just so we might experience and enjoy him, and share in his eternal beauty."[45]

As with Julian, Catherine does not stop with the love of God. She also insists that we grasp the holy character and the holy purposes of God, including in times of suffering. "He did not make us animals without memory or understanding, but gave us memory to hold fast his benefits, and understanding to comprehend his supreme eternal will—his will that seeks nothing else but that we be made holy. And he gave us our will to love that will of his. The will of the Word wants us to follow him on the way of the most holy cross by enduring every pain, abuse, insult, and reproach for Christ, crucified, who is in us to strengthen us."[46]

Consider how Catherine weaves together her Christian personality theory and her healing ministry. She sees us as image bearers designed to *relate* intimately to God. God also created us with *rational* capacities to remember, think, and understand, and we must use those capacities in our battle against despair—reminding ourselves of God's goodness and of His holy purposes. We are also *volitional* beings with the ability to will—to choose, to purpose, to decide how to act and react—trusting and obeying along life's often confusing path.

Reconciling Frankness: Speaking Fearlessly to Promote the Fear of God

Catherine is not shy when it comes to helping others to confront their sins. In fact, she can be quite harsh. Others receive her bold words because she walks the talk by being harsh in her own self-confrontation.

Writing to her spiritual director, Raymund of Capua, she says, "In all possible ways, I have committed measureless faults."[47]

Criticism, too, she meets with humility. "I reprove thee, dearest... daughter... Not to answer anyone who should say anything about myself that seemed to thee less than good.... I wish both of you to reply to anyone who narrated my faults to you in this wise—that they are not telling so many that a great many more might not be told... I confess truthfully that I have found little success in myself; but I have hope in my Creator, who will make me correct myself and change my way of life."[48]

People also respond to her audacious confrontation because she "possessed the most astounding theological knowledge, which had been severely tested both by theologians of her own Order and by others who had doubted her orthodoxy."[49] Thus Catherine demonstrates what is required to be intrepid in reconciling confrontation— orthopraxy (right behavior) and orthodoxy (right belief). When we practice reconciling spiritual direction, we must first take the mote out of our own eyes (Matthew 7:1-6) by first taking our own confrontation medication (orthopraxy). And we must be students of the Word so that our confrontation comes ultimately not from us, but from the ultimate Spiritual Director (orthodoxy).

Catherine is no "respecter of persons;" she speaks bold words of confrontation to any who need them. During the Great Western Schism, she rebukes three Italian Cardinals who she believes are on the wrong side of the issue. "What made you do this? The poison of self-love, which has infected the world. This is what has made you pillars lighter than straw. You are flowers who shed no perfume, but stench that makes the whole world reek!"[50]

When Pope Gregory XI refused to return to Rome for fear of being poisoned, Catherine writes to him, "Be manly in my sight and not a timorous child."[51] Catherine not only models audacious confrontation, she exemplifies the shrewd use of imagery to provoke the mind to be responsive to biblical exposure.

She uses such powerful imagery to expose sin and to exhort change. In a letter to Biringhieri degli Arzocchi, parish priest of Asciano, Catherine writes, "Please, please be the fragrant flower you ought to be, breathing out a sweet perfume in God's gracious presence! You know well that flowers that stand too long in water give off a stench instead of fragrance. It really seems to me, father, that you and other ministers ought to be like flowers. But the water this flower has been put into is the wickedness and filth of sin and worldly wretchedness. So I beg you as lovingly and tenderly as I can to be the sort of flower that breathes out a fragrance before God and for those in your care. Be a true shepherd, ready to give your life for your sheep."[52]

In this letter, Catherine again draws on her theology of how God designed and redeemed Christians as the foundation for her exhortation to change. She believes that the Christian is a new covenant person capable of virtuous behavior. She is not asking this parish priest to be something he is not. She is not asking him to work up virtue. She is exhorting him to be what he already is in Christ.

Guiding Wisdom: Empowering Christians to Live Supernaturally

Catherine's guidance involves both offering spiritual insight to people and patiently helping them to find that insight for themselves. Her words of guidance reveal the practicality of a heavenly mindset.

> If you tell me about the great concern you must have over temporal things, I answer that things are only as temporal as we make them. I've already told you that all things come from the highest Goodness; so everything is good and perfect. I don't want you evading hard work under the plea that these things are temporal. I want you to be conscientiously concerned, with your attention directed as God would have it. Above all, have concern for your sisters' souls. Don't be slow in correcting faults. Whether significant or slight, see to it that they are punished according to each one's capacity. If a person is in a condition to carry ten pounds, don't load twenty on her, but accept from her as much as she is able to give.[53]

As this letter shows, Catherine can be bluntly practical. As the next vignette illustrates, she can also be encouragingly stimulating. "I beg you to fulfill my desire, conform yourself with Christ crucified. Elevate yourself completely above the world's traffic, as I said before. In no other way can we be conformed with Christ. Clothe, clothe yourself with Christ crucified. He is the wedding garment that will give you grace here, and afterward will afford you a place with the truly joyful at the table of everlasting life."[54]

This letter encapsulates Catherine's guiding ministry. She emphasizes the glorious finished and gracious work of Christ, while at the same time imploring people to apply that work to their own lives—faith active in love.

Like Jonathan Edwards centuries later (in *Religious Affections*), Catherine understands that victorious Christian living begins in the affections (our God-designed longing, hunger, and thirst for spiritual relationship with Him). "For just as the feet carry the body, the affections carry the soul."[55] Thus, spiritual directors understand that guiding people toward *maturity in* Christ requires helping people toward *intimacy with* Christ. "The human heart is drawn by love, as I said, and with all its powers: memory, understanding, and will."[56] We pursue what we perceive to be pleasing. We trust and obey Who we most love and adore.

It's supernatural to love maturely because love is of God. "The soul cannot live without love. She always wants to love something because love is the stuff she is made of, and through love I created her. This is why I said that it is affection that moves the understanding, saying, as it were, 'I want to love, because the food I feed on is love.'"[57]

Catherine's understanding of our original design highlights our relational affections. Her perception, therefore, of the essence of sin, is equally relational. What destroys obedience? Catherine urges us to look at the first man, Adam, to see the cause which destroyed his fidelity to the Eternal Father. "So he fell into disobedience, and from disobedience to impurity, because of pride and his desire to please a woman. For he was so concerned about pleasing and bowing to his companion... that he consented to disobey my command rather than offend her."[58] Sin is pride produced by self-love and by overmuch love for anything but God.

Adam had it backwards. He turned God's relational universe upside down. His big bang of sin was starting with himself (self-love) and then moving to Eve (desiring to please his companion above God) and putting God last, if at all, on his "to-love" list. In Catherine's theology of life, creation is relational (spiritual affections); the fall and sin are relational (prostituted affections, spiritual adultery); and redemption and sanctification are relational (relational fidelity born out of the awareness and experience of God's beauty).

The Son of God models the relational nature of the Christian life. "What was the source of this Word's obedience? His love for my honor and your salvation. And what was the source of this love? The light of his soul's clear vision of the divine Essence and eternal Trinity, for he always saw me, God eternal. This vision effected most perfectly in him that fidelity which the light of most holy faith effects imperfectly in you. Because he was faithful to me his eternal Father, he ran like one gloriously in love along the way of obedience."[59]

Christ eternally and perfectly recognizes the infinite beauty of God, and, therefore, willingly, lovingly obeys His Father's will. For Christians to mature into Christlike sanctification, they must see the beatific vision of God. Therefore, spiritual directors must guide believers into ever increasing depths of awareness of the beauty of God's holy love.

Listening to the Silenced Voices

When we listen to the silenced voices of the women of the late Middle Ages like Julian and Catherine, we hear the consistent theme of God's lovingkindness. It is God's faithful love that inspires and empowers our faithfulness.

The unchained voices of Julian and Catherine unchain us from Satan's imprisoning lies. He would have us believe that life's suffering indicates that "life is bad and so is God," and that in suffering "God is getting back at us"—in vindictive anger. Satan would also have us believe that because of our personal sin we must remain forever prodigal children, unable ever to receive again our Father's loving, forgiving embrace.

Embraced by the love of God and embracing others with and through the love of God, Julian and Catherine peer into the past, remember the future, and apply these timeless realities to the present. God's loving creation of us in His image and His grace-filled redemption of us through His Son are past mirrors that reflect His current love for us. God's future promise that all shall be well is a future mirror that reflects His present loving purposes for us. Neither suffering nor sin can ever separate us from the love of God that is in Christ Jesus. Therefore, we can live today as more than conquerors through Him who loved us, loves us, and will always love us so (Romans 8:37-39).

Learning Together from Our Great Cloud of Witnesses

1. Compare and contrast Julian of Norwich and Catherine of Siena.
   a. How are they different in theology? Similar in theology?
   b. How are they different in practice? Similar in practice?

2. What would it be like to have Julian as your soul care-giver and spiritual director?

3. What would it be like to have Catherine as your soul care-giver and spiritual director?

4. Both Julian and Catherine emphasize the love of God.
   a. Do you think this is an especially vital issue for women? Why or why not?
   b. Do you think this is an especially significant feminine contribution to our understanding of God's nature? If so, in what ways?

5. Both Julian and Catherine emphasize the relational nature of creation (the image of God in humanity), fall (sin), and redemption (salvation and sanctification).
   a. Do you think these are especially vital issues for women? Why or why not?
   b. Do you think these are especially significant feminine contributions to our understanding of the Bible and of the Christian life? If so, in what ways?

6. Of the quotes in this chapter, which ones impact you the most? How will you apply those quotes to you personal life?

7. What implications can we draw for lay spiritual friendship, pastoral ministry, and Christian counseling from the life and ministry of Julian?

8. What implications can we draw for lay spiritual friendship, pastoral ministry, and Christian counseling from the life and ministry of Catherine?

CHAPTER EIGHT

THE HIDDEN TRADITION:
THE WOMEN OF THE REFORMATION

> "The reasons for undertaking this work [*Women of the Reformation*] are several. I have always had an interest in those who have not had their due… The women constituted half of the population, and had they boycotted the movement, one may be sure that would have been the end" (Roland Bainton).[1]
> "Why then is it necessary to gossip about women? Seeing that it was not a woman who sold and betrayed Jesus, but a man, named Judas" (Marie Dentiere).[2]

*M*any readers are familiar with the names associated with the male leaders of the Reformation era. Few, however, recognize the unheralded names of the women of the Reformation. By unveiling their hidden tradition, we gain insight not only into Protestant feminine soul care and spiritual direction, but also into the roles, self-concept, value, and worth of women in the early Protestant tradition.

Women of Noble Character: Reclaiming Their Voice for God

Many of the women of the Reformation had a share in the public controversies it unleashed. Given the dynamic tensions of the day, they were not only accused of doctrinal heresy, but also of behavioral and relational sin for usurping their supposed proper role. They did not stand silently by when so indicted.

Argula von Grumbach: Refusing to Bury Her Talent

Argula von Grumbach (1490-1564) was a Bavarian noblewoman from the house of Hohenstaufen. Following in their tradition of dissent and scholarship, in the early 1520s she became a serious student of the Bible and Lutheran doctrine. In 1523, the University of Ingolstadt tried a student, Arcasius Seehofer, for his Lutheran sympathies and extracted a humiliating recantation from him. Von Grumbach took up her pen on his behalf, arguing with university and secular officials in a series of letters in which she insisted that the Bible was on his side and that she would prove it.[3]

In her letters, Argula proclaimed the importance of Scripture and her right to determine faith and practice thereby. "I beseech you for the sake of God, and exhort you by God's judgment and righteousness, to tell me in writing which of the articles written by Martin or Melanchthon you consider heretical. In German not a single one seems heretical to me."[4] She continued by quoting Luke 7, 1 Corinthians 9, Psalm 36, John 2, 8, 9, 10, 14, 16, Matthew 24, and Isaiah 40, highlighting the Word of God and illumination.

Argula then defended her source of authority and commitment to it. "I have always wanted to find out the truth. Although of late I have not been reading any [information published by the Reformers], for I have been occupied with the Bible, to which all of Luther's work is directed anyway... Ah, but what a joy it is when the spirit of God teaches us and gives us understanding, flitting from one text to the next—God be praised—so that I came to see the true, genuine light shining out. *I don't intend to bury my talent*, if the Lord gives me grace."[5]

She certainly was tempted and confronted to bury her talent. Argula's husband was fired because of her and he mistreated her as a result. Her family reviled her, others wrote against her. In a letter to her cousin, Adam von Torring, she explained, "I hear you have heard that my husband has locked me up. Not that, but he does much to persecute Christ in me. At this point I cannot obey him. We are bound to forsake father, mother, brother, sister, child, body, and life. I am distressed that our princes take the Word of God no more seriously than *a cow does a game of chess*."[6] Bury her talent she did not!

Responding to rebuke for not remaining silent, she retorted, "I am not unacquainted with the word of Paul that women should be silent in church (1 Tim. 1:2) but, when no man will or can speak, I am driven by the word of the Lord when he said, 'He who confesses me on earth, him will I confess and he who denies me, him will I deny,' (Matt. 10, Luke 9), and I take comfort in the words of the prophet Isaiah (3:12), 'I will send you children to be your princes and women to be your rulers.'"[7]

And speak she did. "When I heard what you had done to Arsacius Seehofer under terror of imprisonment and the stake, my heart trembled and my bones quaked. What have Luther and Melanchthon taught save the Word of God? You have condemned them. You have not refuted them. Where do you read in the Bible that Christ, the apostles, and the prophets imprisoned, banished, burned, or murdered anyone?"[8]

As was typical of the women of the Reformation, Argula based her confidence upon Christ and His grace, not upon herself. "I do not flinch from appearing before you, from listening to you, from discussing with you. For by the grace of God I, too, can ask questions, hear answers and read in German."[9] Here we detect Argula boldly applying to her life as a woman the Lutheran doctrine of the priesthood of all believers.

Of her, Martin Luther reported to Spalatin, "I am sending you the letters of Argula von Grumbach, Christ's disciple, that you may see how the angels rejoice over a single daughter of Adam, converted and made into a daughter of God."[10] To another friend, Luther wrote of Argula, "The Duke of Bavaria rages above measure, killing, crushing and persecuting the gospel with all his might. That most noble woman, Argula von Stauffer, is there making a valiant fight with great spirit, boldness of speech and knowledge of Christ. She deserves that all pray for Christ's victory in her.... She alone, among these monsters, carries on with firm faith, though, she admits, not without inner trembling. She is a singular instrument of Christ. I commend her to you, that Christ through this infirm vessel may confound the mighty and those who glory in their strength."[11]

Since her confidence was neither in herself nor in Luther, but in Christ, Argula added these final words. "And even if it came to pass—which God forbid—that Luther were to revoke his views, that would not worry me. I do not build on his, mine, or any person's understanding, but on the true rock, Christ himself, which the builders have rejected."[12] Thus Argula von Grumbach offered all women, and men, the biblical reminder that we base our ministry upon Jesus, the ultimate Soul Physician and Spiritual Friend.

Katherine Zell: Afflicting the Comfortable and Comforting the Afflicted

Katherine Zell (1497-1562) likewise defended her right to minister in Christ's name, though she always did so in a spirit of humility. Speaking of her relationship to her husband, she described herself as "a splinter from the rib of that blessed man Matthew Zell."[13]

Matthew Zell was a celibate Catholic priest turned married Lutheran pastor. Marrying Katherine Schult, he found a life partner who had courage and conviction. As she portrayed herself, "Ever since I was ten years old I have been a student and sort of church mother, much given to attending sermons. I have loved and frequented the company of learned men, and I conversed much with them, not about dancing, masquerades, and worldly pleasures but about the kingdom of God."[14]

Protestant leaders concurred with her self-assessment. Church historian Philip Schaff observed that the well-known Reformers of her day who frequented her home said she "conversed with them on theology so intelligently that they ranked her above many doctors."[15] The admiration and the ministry were mutual. "I honored, cherished and sheltered many great, learned men, with care, work and expense.... I listened to their conversations and preaching, I read their books and their letters *and they were glad to receive mine.*"[16]

To her ministry in her home, Katherine added a public ministry—often in defense of her husband and their ministry. When Matthew was excommunicated for marrying her, opponents of the Reformation circulated the tale that she had caught him with their maid and that, when she protested, he had thrashed her. She published a refutation, saying, "I have never had a maid.... And as for thrashing me, my husband and I have never had an unpleasant 15 minutes. We could have no greater honor than to die rejected of men and from two crosses to speak to each other words of comfort."[17]

Katherine exemplified a rare and worthy-to-be-followed balance of confronting enemies while comforting loved ones.

In the same tract, she not only refuted this particular slander, but provided a vigorous defense of her ministry. "You remind me that the Apostle Paul told women to be silent in the church. I would remind you of the word of this same apostle that in Christ there is no longer male nor female and of the prophecy of Joel: 'I will pour my spirit upon all flesh and your sons and your *daughters* will prophesy.' I do not pretend to be John the Baptist rebuking the Pharisees. I do not claim to be Nathan upbraiding David. I aspire only to be Balaam's ass, castigating his master."[18] Thus with wit and wisdom she offered shrewd biblical confrontation based upon the doctrine of the priesthood of *all* believers—male *and* female.

At her husband's funeral, Katherine assured her listeners that she did not seek to become "Doctor Katrina" as rumor had it. "I am not usurping the office of preacher or apostle. I am like the dear Mary Magdalene, who with no thought of being an apostle, came to tell the disciples that she had encountered the risen Lord."[19]

Such courageous boldness might mistakenly cause us to think that Katherine was above suffering and grieving. However, the ceaseless criticism along with her overwhelming grief after Matthew's death exposed her human neediness. Friends arranged for her to stay in the home of a pastor in Switzerland, and the renowned Reformer Martin Bucer sent a letter of introduction. "The widow of our Zell, a godly and saintly woman, comes to you that perchance she may *find some solace for her grief. She is human.* How does the heavenly Father humble those endowed with great gifts!"[20] It truly is normal, human, to hurt.

Even in her ongoing grief, Katherine ministered to others. In less than a year she was back in the parsonage in Strasbourg. To one of the displaced Protestant leaders she wrote, "I have been allowed to keep the parsonage which belongs to the parish. I take any one who comes. It is always full."[21]

Yet she was able to admit candidly that she still struggled. In a letter to two Protestant Reformers, whom she helped to hide from authorities, she apologized for what she perceived as a lack of hospitality. "I wish I could have done better for you but my Matthew has taken all my gaiety with him."[22]

Out of Katherine's grief, she was able to comfort other grieving wives, offering them both sustaining empathy and healing encouragement. At Kensingen in Breisgau, the minister was forced to leave by those enforcing the Edict of Worms against Luther and his followers. They evicted one-hundred-fifty men of the parish along with the pastor. One man was executed. The rest fled to Strasbourg where Katherine housed eighty in the parsonage and fed sixty for three weeks, while finding shelter and provisions for the rest.[23]

> Katherine penned a letter of scriptural exploration to the wives left behind.
>
> To my fellow sisters in Christ, day and night I pray God that he may increase your faith that you forget not his invincible Word. "My thoughts are not your thoughts, saith the Lord" (Isa. 55:8). "Whom I make alive I kill" (Deut. 32:39). The Lord would wean you from the world that you may rely only on him. Has he not told us that we must "forsake father and mother, wife and child"? (Luke 14:26). "He who denies me him will I deny in the presence of my father," (Matt. 10:33). "Those who would reign with me must also suffer with me" (2 Tim. 2:12).[24]

Katherine continued with healing words of spiritual conversation. "Had I been chosen to suffer as you women I would account myself happier than all the magistrates of Strasbourg at the fair with their necklaces and golden chains. Remember the word of the Lord in the prophet Isaiah (54:8) 'In overflowing wrath for a moment I hid my face from you, but with everlasting love I will have compassion on you.' 'Can a woman forget her suckling child? Even these may forget, but I will not forget you' (Isa. 49:15). Are not these golden words? Faith is not faith which is not tried. 'Blessed are those that mourn.'"[25]

Katherine did not limit her soul care ministry to other women. In 1558, though ill herself, she ministered to Felix Ambrosiaster, the chief magistrate of Strasbourg who had been diagnosed with leprosy and quarantined. Her letter to Felix depicts a sensitive awareness of his *level one external suffering*. "My dear Lord Felix, since we have known each other for a full 30 years I am moved to visit you in your long and frightful illness.… We have often talked of how you have been stricken, cut off from rank, office, from your wife and friends, from all dealings with the world which recoils from your loathsome disease and leaves you in utter loneliness."[26]

Not stopping there, Katherine's words also represent brilliant insight into his *level two internal suffering*—and how to face it with faith.

> At first you were bitter and utterly cast down till God gave you strength and patience, and now you are able to thank him that out of love he has taught you to bear the cross. Because I know that your illness weighs upon you daily and may easily cause you again to fall into despair and rebelliousness, I have gathered some passages which may make your yoke light in the spirit, though not in the flesh. I have written meditations on the 51st Psalm: "Have mercy upon me, O God, according to thy lovingkindness," and the 130th: "Out of the depths have I cried unto thee, O Lord," and then on the Lord's Prayer and the Creed."[27]

One would hope that such ministry to others would always lead to ministry from others. However, Katherine's last days were filled with strife and betrayal. Ludwig Rabus, a former resident in her home and indebted to her for spiritual counsel, preached against her, calling her a "disturber of the peace of the church."[28]

Bold to the end, Katherine responded with the light of truth. "A disturber of the peace am I? Yes indeed, of my own peace. Do you call this disturbing the peace that instead of spending my time in frivolous amusements I have visited the plague infested and carried out the dead? I have visited those in prison and under sentence of death. Often for three days and three nights I have neither eaten nor

slept. I have never mounted the pulpit, but I have done more than
any minister in visiting those in misery. Is this disturbing the peace of
the church?"[29] Like the Apostle Paul throughout 2 Corinthians, false
accusations forced her to "the foolishness of self-defense," but always
for the purpose of defending a woman's right to biblical ministry.

Her own words best summarize the nature of her lifelong ministry.
In 1534, she issued a collection of hymns that she had compiled,
publishing them in four pamphlets that sold for a penny each. Her
ministry goal was to inspire lay people of all ages, all walks of life, and
both genders toward greater spirituality.

> When I read these hymns I felt that the writer had
> the whole Bible in his heart. This is not just a hymn
> book but a lesson book of prayer and praise. When
> so many filthy songs are on the lips of men and
> women and even children I think it well that folk
> should with lusty zeal and clear voice sing the songs
> of their salvation. God is glad when the craftsman
> at his bench, the maid at the sink, the farmer at the
> plough, the dresser at the vines, the mother at the
> cradle break forth in hymns of prayer, praise and
> instruction.[30]

In all her ministry endeavors, spiritual equality in Christ
motivated Katherine Zell.

Reformation Wives: Daughters of the King of Kings

Reformation historian Roland Bainton proposes that the
Reformation had a primary effect on the role of women in society. The
dropping of monasticism in Protestant lands "made for the exaltation
of the home, the especial domain of the wife, as the sphere for exercise
of the gentler virtues of the Sermon on the Mount. In Catholic thought
these have been called the counsels of perfection to be observed by
monks. Protestantism made no distinction between the counsels to
be observed by the few and the precepts binding upon all. The entire
Christian ethic was held to be incumbent upon every believer."[31]

Ruth Tucker explained the impact of this titanic change upon marital relationships. "For the first generation of Protestants, marriage was a far more significant decision than it was in the generations that followed. Renouncing celibacy was viewed by the Catholics as giving in to the sin of lust..."[32] For the leading male Reformers, the decision whether or not to marry was thus mired in complexity, culture, and conflict. For the women who married them, the nature of their husband-wife relationship was equally multifaceted.

Idelette Calvin: The Unfading Beauty of a Gentle and Quiet Spirit

Idelette Calvin (1510-1549) met John Calvin when she and her first husband fled persecution in their native Holland. Coming to Strasbourg, they connected with Calvin's church and converted to the Reformed faith. When Idelette's husband died in a plague, Calvin conducted the funeral. He was impressed with how she had cared for her dying husband as well as for her two children. He also observed that she was an intelligent woman who was unafraid to speak her mind.[33]

Calvin communicated his idea of the ideal wife in a letter written to his friend William Farel even before he met Idelette. "But always keep in mind what I seek to find in her; for I am none of those insane lovers who embrace also the vices of those with whom they are in love, where they are smitten at first sight with a fine figure. This only is the beauty which allures me, if she is chaste, if not too fussy or fastidious, if economical, if patient, if there is hope that she will be interested about my health."[34]

Though unlike the modern ideal of romantic love, Calvin saw in Idelette the unfading beauty of her gentle and quiet spirit. She ministered soul care to her husband through her patient love, and that was exactly what Calvin needed to counter his own "impatience and irritability."[35]

Since Calvin's mother died when he was three, and he had received little love from his stepmother, Calvin had modest experience of a loving home. His best model was Martin Bucer's family life. "In his family during the entire time I saw not the least occasion of offense but only ground for edification. I never left the table without having learned something."[36]

Calvin saw Elizabeth Bucer as a good mother, a hospitable homemaker, and her husband's best critic. Idelette played a similar role. Calvin called her "the faithful helper of my ministry" and "the best companion of my life." Calvin's biographers speak of her as a woman "of some force and individuality."[37]

From the beginning, Idelette's marriage to John was filled with complications and frustrations. In addition to his pastoral ministry, Calvin was a teacher and houseparent at his own boarding house, governed by a domineering housekeeper with a sharp tongue. To make matters worse, sickness would plague them both throughout their marriage.[38]

External circumstances improved when Calvin was called back to Geneva. Idelette had become "first lady" of the parish, and she could have enjoyed a lavish lifestyle. Instead, she chose to extend her soul care ministry beyond her home. "Idelette, if she had chosen, might have passed her time in presiding over brilliant social gatherings. But like her unostentatious husband, she devoted her time and energy for the most part to the performance of charitable duties. She often visited the sick, the poor, and the humble folk. On many occasions she entertained visitors from communities who sought inspiration from her husband."[39] Like so many feminine soul care-givers before her, Idelette cared for the body as well as the soul, living out Christ's call to care for the least of these (Matthew 25:35-40).

John and Idelette endured traumatic personal grief together. Idelette became pregnant three times, but none of the children lived beyond infancy. Soon after coming to Geneva, Idelette gave birth to a boy, but baby Jacques lived only two weeks. At his birth, Idelette became quite ill. His death piled sorrow on top of her physical anguish. The next month, Calvin wrote a friend, sending greetings from his wife, who was unable even to dictate a letter due to her heartache. "The Lord has certainly inflicted a severe and bitter wound in the death of our infant son."[40] Coming from a man like Calvin, known more for his head than his heart, these words are vital reminders of the normalcy of grief for all Christians.

Working through her grief, over time Idelette became known throughout the first-generation Protestant world. "Your hospitality in the name of Christ is not unknown to anybody in Europe," wrote an acquaintance.[41]

After only nine years of marriage, Idelette succumbed to her frequent illnesses. On her deathbed, she and her husband prayed together. He witnessed and wrote of her peaceful composure, and recorded her final words of tribute to God. "She suddenly cried out in such a way that all could see that her spirit had risen far above this world. These were her words, 'O glorious resurrection! O God of Abraham and of all our fathers, the believers of all the ages have trusted on Thee and none of them have hoped in vain. And now I fix my hope on Thee.' These short statements were cried out rather than distinctly spoken. These were not lines suggested by someone else but came from her own thoughts."[42] As Idelette lived, so she died—choosing to exalt God by encouraging others.

After her death, Calvin shared his profound sorrow, offering insight into what Idelette meant to him. "I have been bereaved of the best companion of my life, who, if our lot had been harsher, would have been not only the willing sharer of exile and poverty, but even of death. While she lived she was the faithful helper of my ministry. From her I never experienced the slightest hindrance."[43]

Soul care historically and currently takes many forms. Idelette Calvin epitomized soul care in the home through loving, caring, patient empathy and encouragement, as well as soul care outside the home through holistic ministry to "the least of these."

Katherine von Bora Luther: Sticking to Christ and Ministering to Christians

Katherine von Bora is the best known of all the women of the Reformation because she was Martin Luther's wife. However, she was much more than that. Katherine was born in January, 1499, in a little village near Leipzig. Her parents enjoyed a degree of financial security and, unlike most girls her age, she received an education, studying at a Benedictine school beginning at age six. At age ten, when her mother died and her father remarried, Katherine was sent to a Cistercian convent to prepare for solemn vows, eventually taking them when she was sixteen.[44]

In the early 1520s, Luther's writings began to infiltrate monastic houses. "The sisters at Nimschen, nine of them, disquieted in conscience, sought his counsel. Luther advised escape and undertook to make the arrangements."[45] Luther turned to a highly trusted layman, Leonard Kopp, who delivered barrels of smoked herrings to the nuns. Hidden in the covered wagon, they rumbled into Wittenberg. A student there wrote to a friend, "A wagon load of vestal virgins has just come to town all more eager for marriage than for life. May God give them husbands lest worse befall."[46]

Luther felt responsible that worse should not befall. All were placed either in teaching posts, in homes, or in matrimony. Katherine spent two years working in a home while Luther sought a husband for her. Finding no match, and at her initial suggestion, Luther agreed to marry Katherine because his marriage "would please his father, rile the pope, make the angels laugh and the devils weep, and would seal his testimony."[47] She was twenty-six; he was forty-two.

Though initially a marriage of convenience, they grew to love and depend upon each other profoundly. In fact, Luther would say of her, "In domestic affairs, I defer to Katie. Otherwise I am led by the Holy Ghost."[48] When he thought her at the point of death, he pleaded, "Don't die and leave me."[49] Thirteen years after their marriage, Martin would say of Katherine, "If I should lose my Katie I would not take another wife though I were offered a queen."[50]

What was it about Katherine's character and ministry that so endeared her to Luther? She "ministered to her husband's diseases, depressions, and eccentricities."[51] Her son, later a physician, praised her as half a doctor. He could not have survived his depression, which he interpreted as satanic temptations to doubt God's forgiveness, without her sustaining and healing ministry. At night he would turn over and plead with Katherine, "Forbid me to have such temptations."[52] Based upon Luther's own methods of soul care for such depression, we can surmise that Katherine responded by ministering sustaining empathy and healing encouragement through spiritual conversations and scriptural explorations.[53]

Luther's own testimony further described Katherine's empathic care. Speaking from the experience of their marriage and parenting he wrote, "Marriage offers the greatest sphere for good works, because it rests on love—love between the husband and the wife, love of the parents for the children, whom they nourish, clothe, rear, and nurse. If a child is sick, the parents *are sick* with worry. If the husband is sick, the wife is as concerned *as if* it were herself. If it be said that marriage entails concern, worry, and trouble, that is all true, but these the Christian is not to shun."[54] Undoubtedly, Martin experienced Katherine's *as if* compassion numerous times in his battles with depression.

Katherine was unafraid to lovingly rebuke Martin. When his language was too foul, she would say, "Oh come now, that's too raw."[55] Luther's *Table Talks* also disclosed that Katherine at times prodded her husband to respond forcefully to unfair attacks and doctrinal error.[56]

As with Idelette Calvin, Katherine's ministry was not exclusively to her family. The Augustinian Cloister where Luther had lived as a monk was first loaned and then given to the couple by the Elector. It had on the first floor forty rooms with cells above. Eventually not a single room was unoccupied. A friend described the scene. "The home of Luther is occupied by a motley crowd of boys, students, girls, widows, old women, and youngsters."[57] Katherine "came to be a mistress of a household, a hostel, and a hospital."[58]

Luther recognized and appreciated her versatility and creativity. "To my dear wife Katherine von Bora, preacher, brewer, gardener, and whatsoever else she may be."[59] On other occasions he referred to her as "my kind and dear lord and master, Katy, Lutheress, doctoress, and priestess of Wittenberg." Yet again, ten years after they married, he had this description. "My lord Kate drives a team, farms, pastures, and sells cows… and between times reads the Bible."[60]

But for Katherine, reading the Bible was insufficient. She longed to apply it. "I've read enough. I've heard enough. I know enough. Would to God I lived it."[61] Such was her testimony to her dying day. Ill for three months after an accident landed her on her back in a ditch filled with icy water, Katherine died on December 20, 1550, at age fifty-one. The final words from her lips depict how she lived her entire life. "I will stick to Christ as a burr to a top coat."[62] The last words of Idelette and Katherine each communicate that they were not simply wives of Reformers, but more so daughters of the King of Kings.

Listening to the Silenced Voices

When we listen to the silenced voices of the women of the Reformation we hear the Reformation message of the priesthood of all believers. These women took seriously the doctrine that salvation in Christ made every believer a new creation (regeneration) and re-established a direct relationship between the Christian and God (reconciliation). Therefore, they believed they had the right, the responsibility, and the ability to come to the Bible directly and to use it to minister the truth in love.

All agreed on this foundational principle of direct access to God and God's Word through Christ. However, they did not believe this required uniformity of roles. Some women of this chapter maintained "more traditional roles" of "wives of great leaders" and of a ministry primarily (but never always) to and in the home. Others chose the "less traditional role" of defenders of the Reformation.

Regardless of their roles, their consciences were held captive to the Word of God. Marie Dentiere (1495-1561) captured well the essence of their message and method. Writing to Queen Marguerite of Navarre (1492-1549), she biblically defended the priesthood of all believers and the calling of women. "Do we have two gospels, one for men and the other for women? One for the educated and the other for the multitude. Are we not all one in our Savior?"[63] She continued, this time more pointedly emphasizing women's roles. "For we ought not, any more than men, hide and bury within the earth that which God has given you and revealed to us women. Although we are not permitted to preach in assemblies and public churches, nevertheless we are not prohibited from writing and advising one another, in all charity."[64]

Boldly she added, "Not only do we wish to accuse any defamers and adversaries of the truth of very great audacity and temerity, but also any of the faithful who say that women are very impudent in interpreting Scripture for one another. To them, one is lawfully able to respond that all those who are described and named in the Holy Scripture are not to be judged too temerarious."[65] Dentiere then discussed a host of women of the Old and New Testament who "are named and praised in the Holy Scriptures, not only for their good morals, deeds, bearing, and example, but for their faith and doctrine...."[66]

Her concluding words encapsulate well the attitude of the great women soul care-givers and spiritual directors of the Reformation era. "If God has given graces to some good women, revealing to them something holy and good through His Holy Scriptures, should they, for the sake of the defamers of the truth, refrain from writing down, speaking, or declaring it to each other? Ah! It would be too impudent to hide the talent which God has given us, we who ought to have the grace to persevere to the end. Amen!"[67]

Learning Together from Our Great Cloud of Witnesses

1. The doctrine of the priesthood of all believers teaches that all Christians—male and female—have direct access to God and have equal access to the Holy Spirit's teaching ministry as they study Scripture. What difference could this doctrine make in how women, in particular, see themselves as students of the Word of God?

2. Argula von Grumbach refused the temptation to bury her God-given talent.
   a. In what situations are you tempted to bury your God-given talent?
   b. What can you learn and apply from Argula's life that could help you to defeat this temptation?

3. Argula, and many of the women of the Reformation, had to grapple with teachings about "women being silent in the church."
   a. What is your biblical understanding and application of this issue?
   b. How has this chapter shaped or re-shaped your understanding and application of this issue?

4. Godly male leaders in the Reformation era gladly received Katherine Zell's ministry. How does this compare to your experience today of how male Christian leaders receive ministry from female believers?

5. Katherine Zell could be courageously bold while also admitting her humanness and neediness. How easy or hard is it for you to combine such "strength" and "weakness," such boldness and vulnerability?

6. Idelette Calvin and Katherine Luther saw themselves as "wives of great men," but more so as "daughters of the King of Kings."

How hard do you think it is today for married Christian women to emulate this dual "self-concept"?

7. Why do you think so many feminine soul care-givers, like Idelette Calvin, maintained such a holistic ministry of caring for the soul *and* body of "the least of these"?

8. Katherine Luther practiced *as if* empathy in which she took on the pain of her husband and of others. How easy or difficult is this for you to do? Why do you think that is?

9. Katherine Luther, like Idelette Calvin, ministered to and in her home, while also ministering beyond her home. How hard is this balance today for Christian women? What makes it difficult? What could make it less so?

10. Like Argula von Grumbach, Marie Dentiere refused to hide her talent. As you re-read Dentiere's quotes, what are you motivated to do with your talents?

CHAPTER NINE

THE DARK NIGHT OF THE SOUL: THE FIRE WITHIN

"The soul's desire can only be assuaged by some other soul which understands it" (Teresa of Avila to Banez).[1]

"I thank and praise our good God for the blessing He is pleased to have given us through the exchange made possible by our perfect friendship; for I assure you that if my letters enkindle in you the flame of love for the supreme Good, your very dear letters arouse the same feelings in me..." (Jane de Chantal to her brother, Andre).[2]

*F*emale soul physicians of the 1500s and 1600s such as Teresa of Avila and Jane de Chantal pursued the twin tasks of an intimate spiritual life with God and a deeply relational ministry of spiritual direction. They did so in a culture that devalued women's spirituality, as Teresa herself recorded. "The world has intimidated us... so that we may not do anything worthwhile for You in public or dare speak some truths that we lament over in secret... I do not believe, Lord, that this could be true of Your goodness and justice, for You are a just judge and not like those of the world. Since the world's judges are sons of Adam and all of them men, there is no virtue in women that they do not hold suspect."[3]

Though suppressed, Teresa never surrendered hope and always continued ministering. "Yes, indeed, the day will come, my King, when everyone will be known for what he is. I do not speak for myself... but because I see that these are times in which it would be wrong to undervalue virtuous and strong souls, even though they are women."[4] Women like Teresa and Chantal offer feminine models of spiritual care that discover the fire within even during the cold, dark night of the soul and of society.

Teresa of Avila: Espousing God's Active Love

Teresa of Avila (1515-1582) was born on March 28, 1515, during the reign of Ferdinand and Isabella in Spain. Her father, Don Alonso, married in 1505, but his first wife died in 1507, leaving him with two children. In 1511, he married his second wife, Dona Beatriz de Ahumada, who gave birth to Teresa de Ahumada. Teresa's mother died in 1528 when Teresa was thirteen.[5]

In 1531, at age sixteen, Teresa was sent by her father to be educated by the Augustinian nuns at Avila. When her health no longer allowed her to stay, she visited her uncle, Don Pedro de Cepeda, who introduced her to the *Letters of St. Jerome*, which motivated her to adopt the religious life. However, her father forbade her. Then on November 2, 1535, at the age of twenty, she stole away from her father's house to give her life to God in the Carmelite monastery of the Incarnation. After two years there, her health once again worsened. Her worried father brought her home where she lived for three years as an invalid and paralytic. Though she recovered, her health remained miserable for the rest of her life.[6]

Added to her physical struggles were constant spiritual doubts that God could ever forgive and love a person like her. Attempting to deal with her doubts, she had recourse to many spiritual directors. Through their varied ministry, Teresa slowly began to progress toward some level of personal spiritual peace.[7]

The accounts of her spiritual life contained in *The Life Written by Herself*, *The Way of Perfection*, and *The Interior Castle* form a spiritual biography comparable to the *Confessions of St. Augustine*. In these works, we learn of Teresa's lifelong spiritual experiences, of her views on the spiritual life, and of her ministry as a spiritual director by which she sought to inspire others to draw nearer to the loving heart of God.

Spiritual Direction: Speaking Well about God Out of a Life Well Lived

Though many people primarily think of Teresa for her writings on spirituality, especially *The Interior Castle*, she penned numerous letters of spiritual direction, wrote frequently about spiritual direction, trained others as spiritual directors, received lifelong spiritual direction, and provided spiritual direction to hundreds of believers. Her theory and practice of spiritual direction could fill volumes.

Early in her life, Teresa longed for a spiritual guide to no avail. When her uncle gave her a book on prayer called *The Third Spiritual Alphabet*, she used it as her spiritual guide—"taking the book for my master." Elaborating, she noted, "For during the twenty years after this period of which I am speaking, I did not find a master, I mean a confessor, who understood me, even though I looked for one. This hurt me so much that I often turned back and was even completely lost, for a master would have helped me flee from the occasions of offending God."[8]

This issue of an understanding, experienced spiritual director remained a lifelong preoccupation. Years later in a letter to Gratian, Teresa exclaimed, "Oh Jesus, how wonderful it is when two souls understand each other! They never lack anything to say and never grow weary of saying it."[9]

Further, Teresa was never content that "men of learning be simply men of learning." Her ideal was that "men of learning be also men of experience, or spiritual men."[10] On the other hand, she found great fault with unlearned (in scriptural spiritual direction) directors. "Half-learned confessors have done my soul great harm…"[11] Teresa practiced what she preached, in that she herself was well-read in Augustine, Jerome, and the Scriptures, as well as an accomplished practitioner of the spiritual life who sought to connect deeply with her disciples.

Soon after receiving the book from her uncle, Teresa became acquainted with a nun who modeled this experiential spirituality. "Beginning then to like the good and holy conversation of this nun, I was glad to hear how well she spoke about God, for she was very discreet and saintly."[12] Here we find a beautiful portrait of spiritual direction—speaking well about God out of a life well-lived. Good and godly results flowed from this good and godly relationship. "This good company began to help me to get rid of the habits that the bad company had caused and to turn my mind to the desire for eternal things…"[13]

A change of location caused Teresa's relationship with this nun to be brief. For years Teresa sought for other spiritual directors. Their lack of qualifications (scriptural learning plus life experience), her own sense of unworthiness, and spiritual warfare all combined to make her search thorny. But Teresa remained persistent. "Moreover, since His Majesty desired now to enlighten me so that I might no longer offend Him and might know my great debt to Him, this fear increased in such a way that it made me diligently seek out spiritual persons to consult."[14]

At this juncture, Satan's lies began to torment Teresa. "I didn't feel worthy to speak to them or strong enough to obey them, and this made me more fearful; it would have been a difficult thing for me to converse with them and yet be what I was."[15] Many experience the same conflict today. "My inner life is a mess. I need to talk to others to find healing and cleansing. Yet I feel too messed up and ashamed to share. I have to get better before I can talk to someone about getting better!"

After lengthy and intense spiritual warfare over spiritual direction, Teresa's mind cleared. "What a terrible mistake, God help me, that *in wanting to be good I withdrew from good!* The devil must meddle a great deal in this matter when virtue is beginning; I couldn't make the fear go away. He knows that *the complete remedy for a soul lies in consulting the friends of God.*"[16]

Finally finding these friends of God, Teresa was now able to receive spiritual direction and to perceive what helpful spiritual directors look like. Speaking about the believer's need for idiosyncratic direction (what unique counsel specifically helps an individual the most), Teresa described three qualities necessary in every spiritual director. "So it is very important that the master have prudence—I mean that he have good judgment—and experience; if besides these he has learning, so much the better."[17] As spiritual directors we need prudence (relational competence) to know what biblical counsel to apply to which persons, we need spiritual experience and maturity (Christlike character), and we need scriptural insight and learning (biblical content).

Teresa further emphasized that the person of prudence (competence), experience (character), and knowledge (content) will "love very differently than those who have not reached it" (community).[18] She labeled this "spiritual love" to contrast it with selfish love and/or sensual love. "I say once again that spiritual love seems to be imitating that love which the good lover Jesus had for us."[19] The loving spiritual director loves like the ultimate Spiritual Director.

Teresa illustrated the nature of this spiritual love or "special friendship" through the relationship Monica had with her son, Augustine. Though spiritual direction involves an intimate relationship, it does not swallow the other person. Monica made sure that Augustine walked along his "own way toward the same goal."[20]

We point people not toward us, but toward Jesus. People do not so much follow us, as we journey together following Christ. The connection leads to great attachment, but not to inappropriate dependence, and not without the ability to detach appropriately.

This spiritual love of the spiritual director is other-centered and Christ-centered. "These lovers cannot in their hearts be insincere with those they love; if they see them deviate from the path or commit some faults they immediately tell them about it."[21] Flattery and pretense have no place in a loving spiritual direction relationship, as Teresa explained further in a letter to Maria, one of her directees. "When I really love anyone, I am so anxious she should not go astray that I become unbearable… true friendship does not express itself in covering up things."[22]

To these core characteristics of competence, character, content, and community, Teresa added confidentiality or secrecy. She explained that the spiritual director "should be counseled on the importance of keeping things secret; this secrecy is fitting." This was not some theoretical abstraction for Teresa. "In this respect I am speaking as one who is suffering a bitter trial because some persons with whom I have discussed my prayer are not keeping it secret, but in consulting this one and that other, they have truly done me great harm."[23]

Having described the qualities of an expert spiritual director, Teresa warned her readers and us that "super-spiritual" Christians will claim that we need only God. "You will be immediately told that speaking to him is unnecessary, that it is enough to have God. *But a good means to having God is to speak with His friends.*"[24] Wise counsel from a wise counse*lor* who was also a wise counse*lee*.

Spiritual Friendship: Sustaining and Healing Companions on Our Spiritual Journey

While Teresa surely emphasized the value of a spiritual director who focuses on the directee's life, she equally treasured mutual spiritual friendships, explaining how priceless they are. "A great evil it is for a soul to be alone in the midst of so many dangers.... For this reason I would counsel those who practice prayer to seek, at least in the beginning, friendship and association with other persons having same interest.... I believe that they who discuss these joys and trials for the sake of this friendship with God will benefit themselves and those who hear them... Since this spiritual friendship is so extremely important... I don't know how to urge it enough."[25]

Looking on spiritual friendship as a joint journey, a spiritual pilgrimage to the fatherland, Teresa extended a vulnerable invitation to four trusted friends. "I should like the five of us who at present love each other in Christ to make a kind of pact that since others in these times gather together in secret against His Majesty to prepare wicked deeds and heresies, we might seek to gather together some time to free each other from illusions and to speak about how we might mend our ways and please God more since no one knows himself as well as others who observe him if they do so with love and concern for his progress."[26]

What does spiritual friendship take, according to Teresa? It takes a *pact*: a communicated commitment. It necessitates a *plan*: to connect by gathering together. It requires a *purpose*: to free each other from sin's deceitfulness so that we mend our ways and please God. It entails a *passion*: to know each other deeply enough and with enough care to be able to provide loving feedback leading to self-awareness. It demands a *Person*: Jesus Christ—human spiritual friendships always point to the eternal Spiritual Friend—God.

Of course, Teresa did more than write about spiritual friendship (and spiritual direction). She offered it. Speaking about a woman who was "very grieved because of the death of her husband," Teresa described this widow's despair. "Her distress had reached such an extreme that they feared for her health." Hearing of Teresa's loving ministry, "the Lord gave her a strong, irresistible desire to see me; she thought I would be able to console her."[27] Reluctantly consenting to offer this widow spiritual friendship (because Teresa felt herself unworthy), Teresa's care bore great fruit. "It pleased the Lord that that lady was so comforted she soon began to improve noticeably, and each day she found herself more at ease."[28]

What brought healing? By Teresa's accounting, it was prayer, Teresa's confidence in God's good work in this hurting widow, and relationship. "And the Lord must have done this through the many prayers good persons I knew offered..." (healing by prayer). "She was very God-fearing and so good that her abundant Christian spirit supplied for what was lacking in me.... I esteemed her very much in observing her goodness" (healing by trusting in the spiritual maturity of the one being helped). "She grew deeply fond of me" (healing by relationship, connection, community).[29]

Sympathetic identification in suffering was another mark of Teresa's spiritual friendship. "It is a wonderful thing when a sick person finds another wounded with that same sickness; how great the consolation to find you are not alone. The two become a powerful help to each other in suffering... What excellent backing they give to one another..."[30] Today, counselors call this "universality"—the sense that we are all in the same boat and that others can identify with us.

Teresa found that expressing such sympathy (sustaining) always had to precede offering perspective (healing). "In sum, I have found neither a way of consoling nor a cure for such persons other than to show them compassion in their affliction—and, indeed, compassion is felt on seeing them subject to so much misery—and not contradict their reasoning."[31] Before sharing God's eternal story of hope we must enter our friend's earthly story of hurt.

None of this is to say that Teresa eschewed spiritual conversations and scriptural explorations that encouraged spiritual friends to clothe themselves in God's perspective. "Our intellects and wills, dealing in turn now with God, become nobler and better prepared for every good. And it would be disadvantageous for us never to get out of the mire of our miseries."[32] Clearly, there is a time for tears and there is a time for hope.

Soul Physicians: Reconciling and Guiding Mentors for Our Spiritual Formation

Teresa both received and provided reconciling and guiding spiritual formation. In fact, much of her life, ministry, and writing were wrapped up in the soul physician's art of spiritual formation—growth in grace through progressive sanctification.

Her experience with "counseling and sin issues" followed the same relational emphasis we found with "counseling and suffering issues." There was no dichotomy between a caring soul care-giver and a candid spiritual director. In suffering *and* sin, the soul physician models a tender and adroit bedside manner in prescribing God's health-giving remedies.

Teresa expressed her relief that her soul physician, Diego de Cetina, offered her sympathetic care when she sought to face a litany of besetting sins. "He left me consoled and encouraged, and the Lord helped me and him to understand my situation and how I should be guided.... He guided my soul by stressing the love of God and allowed freedom and used no pressure…"[33]

Cetina's counsel was no mere "God is love; do what you please" drivel. He used trialogues and scriptural conversations to relate God's truth to Teresa's sin. "In all that he said it seemed to me, according to what was impressed upon my soul, that the Holy Spirit was speaking through him in order to heal me." Neither was Cetina reticent to expose sin. "He made me very ashamed; he guided me by means that seemed to change me completely. What a great thing it is to understand a soul!"[34] He integrated guilt and grace, a conscience loaded with the horrors of sin and one lightened with the wonders of forgiveness.

When Cetina was transferred, Teresa feared she would return to her wretchedness. "It didn't seem to me it would be possible to find another like him." Yet she did. Her new director led her toward even greater maturity. "He told me that to please God completely I must leave nothing undone; he did so also with great skill and gentleness because my soul still was not at all strong but very fragile, especially with regard to giving up some friendships I had."[35]

Some seem to think that a constant style of frank, combative disruption that takes little thought for the soul or gives little heed to empathy is what God uses to crush sin. Unfortunately, what often happens with such harsh, unsympathetic confrontation is that Satan uses it to crush souls. Empathy is not an instrument in the counselor's toolbox used in sustaining and then discarded in reconciling. It is a part of the soul physician's soul expressed in love throughout the soul care and spiritual direction relationship.

Teresa was longing for what we long for and what the Apostle Paul commanded. "Brothers, if someone is caught in a sin, you who are spiritual should restore him gently. But watch yourself, or you also may be tempted" (Galatians 6:1). She found this in many of her soul physicians, including Peter of Alcantara. "Almost from the outset I saw that he understood me through experience, which was all that I needed. For at that time I didn't understand myself or how to describe my experiences as I do now… and it was necessary that the one who understood me and explained these experiences to me should himself have experienced them."[36]

Teresa communicated the same empathetic engagement with sinful struggles in her soul physician's practice. In fact, she delighted in spiritual trials because they helped her to be a more sympathetic counselor. "I believe the Lord permitted this conflict because I had never known what it was to be unhappy with being a nun… and that I might know the great favor He had thereby granted me and the torment He had freed me from; and also so that if I should meet someone who was unhappy I wouldn't be surprised but feel compassion for her and know how to console her."[37]

In her letters and writings of spiritual confrontation, Teresa called for repentance, mortification (putting off), and vivification (putting on). "Therefore, courage, my daughters! Let's be quick to do this work and weave this little cocoon by getting rid of our self-love and self-will, our attachment to any earthly thing, and by performing deeds of... prayer, mortification, obedience, and of all the other things you know."[38]

She equally emphasized helping the repentant Christian to understand Christ's grace, including in her own life. "It seemed to me impossible, my Lord, to abandon You so completely. And since I did forsake You so many times, I cannot but fear. For when You withdrew a little from me, I fell to the ground. May You be blessed forever! Although I abandoned You, You did not abandon me so completely as not to turn to raise me up by always holding out your hand to me."[39]

Having reconciled people to see the horrors of sin and the wonders of grace, Teresa next guided people to grow in grace. Much of this comes to us through her writings in *The Interior Castle*. While not all would agree with her specific theory of spiritual growth, it is important to note that she did not stop with reconciling. Her goal was to guide the soul toward a state of rest in God's infinite love. Teresa moved her readers through seven mansions in the inner castle of the soul, teaching them her theology and practice of how to enter into intimate, loving union with Christ.

She closed her opus with this synopsis. "In sum, my Sisters, what I conclude with is that we shouldn't build castles in the air. The Lord doesn't look so much at the greatness of our works as at the love with which they are done."[40] By comparison, in Martin Luther's guidance, he highlighted faith in God becoming active in love for others (faith active in love). Teresa espoused a similar viewpoint, but it might be more accurate to describe hers as love for God becoming active in love for others (spiritual love active in social love). Comprehensively, she wrapped her sustaining, healing, reconciling, and guiding in the blanket of God's love penetrating our hearts, wooing us to love Him, and motivating us to love others.

Jane de Chantal: Live Jesus

Jane de Chantal (1572-1641) was born Jane Frances Fremyot in 1572 in France, the daughter of a lawyer, a member of the rising class. Jane married an equally wealthy baron in 1592. Nine years later her husband died, leaving her with four small children and an emerging sense of vocation—of being called to give herself fully into God's service. Struggling with grief over the sudden death of her beloved husband and confused between her spiritual desires and her daily duties, she met Frances de Sales who became her lifelong friend and spiritual director.[41]

In 1610, in Savoy, France, they co-founded a congregation for women who felt drawn to a life of religious commitment but due to family ties were unable to enter the more austere religious communities. Her work there empowered Jane to fulfill her spiritual longings to draw nearer to God and to help others to find greater intimacy with God, while still caring for her children and extended family. Like many women today, throughout her life Jane juggled many roles in her daily life and ministry.[42]

We know Jane's ministry primarily through the many letters of spiritual counsel that she penned. Writing her correspondents amid the routine of her family life and ministry commitments, she combined "bits of news, requests, informal advice, with what might be called more formal spiritual counsel.... One went to God in the context of the events in which one found oneself. Jane's letters reflect this mixture of the banal and the practical with the highest ideals of Christian life."[43] Her letters reveal her theology and her heart. Always at the center is Jesus, with the phrase "Live Jesus" opening each.

Motherly Mentoring: Adoring God in the Profound Silence of Terrible Anguish

"Live Jesus" was far more than a catchy motto or a simple salutation. To study Jane's letters is to discern her focus on how to allow Jesus to live in her and in those she directed. To live Jesus is to have one's relational (spiritual, social, self), rational, volitional, and emotional capacities animated by communion with Christ which enables connection with others. Jane's spiritual direction thus followed Paul's dictum, "I have been crucified with Christ and I no longer live, but Christ lives in me. The life I live in the body, I live by faith in the Son of God, who loved me and gave himself for me" (Galatians 2:20).

As with seemingly every female soul care-giver we have studied, Jane first sought and received care for her own soul. When Frances de Sales died in 1622, Jane contacted her brother, Andre, candidly expressing her soul's torment. "You may want to know what my heart felt on that occasion. Ah, it seems to me that it adored God in the profound silence of its terrible anguish."[44] Juxtaposing adoration of God and terrible anguish is utterly foreign to how most of us live today. We think that we glorify God during times of grief only through expressions of hope, not through open admissions of agony.

That is not to say that Jane could not and did not simultaneously experience healing and hurt. "My sorrow is greater than I could ever express and it seems as though everything serves to increase my weariness and cause me to regret. The only thing that is left to console me is to know that it is my God that has done this, or at least, has permitted this blow to fall."[45] Even here we find in Jane's response a rebuke to our pseudo-spirituality where we imagine that grief is some linear process where we move neatly *through* sorrow as we cast it aside to move directly into hope. Rather, as Jane, like the Psalmists, the Apostle Paul, and Jesus model, true faith mingles hurt and hope.

The result is entirely Pauline. Paul and Jane both modeled how to long passionately for heaven while living passionately on earth. "I am torn between the two: I desire to depart and be with Christ, which is better by far; but it is more necessary for you that I remain in the body. Convinced of this, I know that I will remain, and I will continue with all of you for your progress and joy in the faith" (Philippians 1:23-25). Similarly, Jane told her brother, "Yet I still will to remain in exile [here on earth]—yes, my dear brother, I truly do. It is a terribly difficult exile for me, this miserable life. But I want to stay here, as I said, as long as it is God's plan for me. I will let Him do with me as He wishes."[46]

Jane's response was much the same eleven years later when her daughter-in-law, Marie, died. Writing again to Andre, who was now the Archbishop of Bourges, she started by reaffirming the truth that God in His goodness sends us sorrow and joy out of the same love. Yet, even avowing this, she explained that hope does not eliminate hurt. "But how does this happen that, having this knowledge and experience, we still feel so keenly the death of those we love? I must admit, my dear Lord, that as I read the little note telling me of the death of our dearest darling daughter, I was so overcome that, had I been standing, I think I would have fallen. I can't remember that any grief ever gripped me this way."[47]

Jane was not alone in her sorrow, as Andre also loved Marie dearly. Jane shared his sorrow and granted him permission to grieve. "But when I read your letter… what a blow it was to my poor heart and how much your sorrow added to mine! It is understandable that you should feel this loss as you do.… All this has touched me more than I can say, *for whatever affects you affects me acutely.*"[48]

To her permission to grieve, she added God's permission. "My beloved and dearest Lord, our first reactions are inevitable, and our gentle Savior is not offended by them; but I hope that afterward He will fill you with a thousand delicate, holy consolations."[49] What a tender reminder of God's kindness.

Such themes continue in Jane's letters of spiritual consolation to her daughter, Francoise. Jane's third child, she married Antoine de Toulonjon, who died a few hours before the birth of their only surviving son. Eventually, Francoise moved to France with her baby and her eleven-year-old daughter to be with her mother.

However, before that move, Jane comforted her grieving daughter via letter. Understandably, Francoise was struggling with grief a year later. Jane wrote, "I was deeply moved by your letter, my darling, which tells me how keenly you are suffering. Truly, your sorrow is great, and, when looked at only in terms of this earthly life, it is overwhelming [climbing in the casket]. But if you can look beyond the ordinary and shifting events of life and consider the infinite blessings and consolations of eternity, you would find comfort in the midst of these reversals, as well as joy in the assured destiny of him for whom you mourn" [celebrating the resurrection].[50] Jane's "in-the-midst" consolation was endemic to her soul care. We "live Jesus" in the midst of real life.

Jane then wondered in her letter when we will learn to apply the reality of God's goodness to life's badness. "But, imperfect as we are, we somehow transform into poison the very medicine the Great

Physician prescribes for our healing. Let's stop behaving in such a manner. Rather, like obedient children, let's surrender ourselves lovingly to the will of our heavenly Father and cooperate with His plan to unite us intimately to Himself through suffering."[51] This is Jane's biblical sufferology. Satan tempts us to view God's healing balm as malicious poison. God's medicine of choice, as the great Soul Physician, is to use adversity to draw us to intimacy.

In all these examples of motherly mentoring, we uncover a common theme. Sustaining and healing mean that we never steal God's healing by denying the pain, by lessening the agony, or by quickening the process. We support one another in inevitable trials without interfering in the sanctification work that God inexorably accomplishes through His affectionate sovereignty.

Empowering Discipleship: Engaging God's Goodness as More Than Conquerors

Like all historical mentors, Jane integrated her sustaining and healing soul care with her reconciling and guiding spiritual direction. We find the goodness of God a constant theme in her letters of spiritual direction. As Paul declared in Romans 8:31, God is *for us*, not against us. Jane derived the same application from this truth: since God is for us, in all things we are more than conquerors (Romans 8:37). In light of these twin realities (God's goodness and our victory through Christ), spiritual directors empower their disciples to rest in God's care, confident that He who has begun a good work in them will carry it on to completion until the day of Christ (Philippians 1:6). We surrender to God and work with God as He works out our sanctification (Philippians 2:12).

We witness Jane blending all these themes in her letters to Noel Brulart, known also in Jane's writings as Commander de Sillery. Brulart came seeking Jane's direction from a background as a knight of Malta, favorite of Henri IV, and ambassador to Spain and Rome. After a period of worldly vanity, this French aristocrat committed his life to Christ and used his wealth for the good of the church.[52]

From the outset, Jane guided him through exposing the gracious qualities he exhibited. "This unpretentiousness is apparent throughout your letter. I am amazed to see the extent to which you, Sir, living in the world and busy with public affairs, have acquired that spirit."[53] In another letter, Jane expounded further. "Oh, and don't tell me so many terrible things about yourself, for, you see, I have had such an insight into your soul that I can feel only awe for what God has done in you."[54] She thus drew out the heroic narrative of the work God was *already* doing in Brulart as a way of empowering him to trust that God would continue His good work.

In a letter written one year later, Jane first affirmed Brulart's ongoing responsiveness to God's direction, and then urged him to rest in God. "But, you know, I am not saying this so that you will zealously search out ways to carry out your response. On the contrary, God wants you to temper your overeagerness by calming all this ardor, reducing it to a simple assent of your will to do good quietly—and only because it is God's will…. Resign yourself to not being able to resign yourself as completely and utterly as you would like, or as you think our Lord would like."[55]

Her counsel was idiosyncratic—to others less valiant in their spiritual pursuits, Jane was known to exhort more obedience. But to Brulart, with his scrupulosity, she slowed him down. Yes, he is to be godly for God's glory, but he must do so yielding to God's timing for his godliness. "Abandon all your desires for advancement and perfection; hand them over completely into God's hands. Leave the care of them to *Him*, and only yearn for as much perfection as He wishes to give you."[56] A "Type A" spiritual director might have driven this overly-driven "Type A" directee to spiritual exhaustion and discouragement. Jane knew better.

And she knew better because she knew that God is best. "In His goodness, He will be a thousand times more pleased to have you rest in His care, surrendered to His holy will, than to have you suffer all sorts of torments in an effort to acquire that perfection you desire so much."[57] You can almost hear Brulart's sigh of relief. Just as you can almost hear Jane whispering, "Shh. Be still. Rest. Trust. Father knows best."

Not only does Father know best; Father is best. Therefore, the best means for growth in grace and maturity in Christ is imitating Christ through an intimate relationship with Him. Jane explained to Brulart that God has "…given you a heart which, in my opinion, is fashioned after His own most sacred one. In truth, my very dear brother, your good heart is capable of touching ours by its incomparable love. Apparently, you have drawn this love from the inexhaustible love of our divine Savior…"[58]

Another aspect of her ministry to Brulart that moves counter to much "professional counseling" is the depth of friendship that she encouraged and expressed. Jane wrote about nothing being a better New Year's gift than "…your renewed expression of concern for my happiness. To me, my truly dear brother, this is a rich treasure and a protection against the ambushes of my enemies."[59] Even more familiarly she shared, "God has willed to unite my heart intimately with yours, and for this I shall ever bless His goodness."[60] So much for no "dual relationship," counselor aloofness, and distance from the counselee.

Consistently, Jane's counsel was eminently practical. When Brulart retired from his secular vocation, he found to his surprise that his family was delighted. Yet, for him it was a major transition. Jane comforted him with empathy and understanding, again on the basis of God's gentleness. "At a time of such radical change, it is impossible for nature not to be upset. But this interior peace, this unwavering dependence on God… which assure you without words that you are solidly planted where God wants you, all these are infallible signs of the reign of God in you and should give you great hope that God, in His goodness, wishes to set you on a path of integrity and simplicity of mind."[61] Following the path of historic Christian guiding, Jane assisted Brulart to make his way through the complexity of life's choices, always with an eye to God's goodness and always alert to signs of His generous direction.

Jane fused guiding and reconciling in her ministry to Brulart. Like many throughout church history, his great fervor for godliness could lead him to do violence to his soul—seeking a perfection that is true only of God. Humanely, Jane counseled him to live by grace. "Now, you know that the peak of perfection lies in our wanting to be what God wishes us to be: so, having given you a delicate constitution, He expects you to take care of it and not demand of it what He Himself, in His gentleness, does not ask for. Accept this fact. What God, in His goodness, asks of you is not this excessive zeal which has reduced you to your present condition, but a calm, peaceful uselessness, a resting near Him…"[62]

None of her talk of a gentle God implied that Jane lessened God's holiness. She simply heightened God's grace. Thus she could write to her brother, Andre, "When you have committed some fault, go to God humbly, saying to Him, 'I have sinned, my God, and I am sorry.' Then, with loving confidence, add: 'Father, pour the oil of Your bountiful mercy on my wounds, for You are my only hope; heal me.'"[63] Where sin abounds, grace superabounds.

Such counsel derives from a specific image of God, as Jane described to Andre. "With the confidence of a son, rest in the care and love which divine Providence has for you in all your needs. Look upon Providence as a child does its mother who loves him tenderly. You can be sure that God loves you incomparably more."[64] Jane de Chantal built her entire approach to soul care and spiritual direction upon her conviction that God is love and out of His love we can "Live Jesus!"

Listening to the Silenced Voices

When we listen to the silenced voices of women like Teresa of Avila and Jane de Chantal, we hear the message of God's love. Teresa espoused God's active love which we are to pursue intimately and which pursuit empowers us to love God and others. Jane championed God's tender mercy and loving grace which we are to rest in ardently and which enables us to bring others to God-rest.

In offering counsel to a spiritual director on how to succeed in leading souls, Jane called upon her to reflect on her restful, loving Jesus.

> I beg you, my dear Sister, govern your community with great expansiveness of heart: give the Sisters a holy liberty of spirit, and banish from your mind and from theirs a servile spirit of constraint. If a Sister seems to lack confidence in you, don't for that

reason show her the least coldness, but gain her trust through love and kindness.... Lead them, not with a bustling, anxious kind of concern, but with a care that is genuine, loving and gentle. I know there is no better way to succeed in leading souls. The more solicitous, open and supportive you are with them, the more you will win their hearts.... Let the Sisters know how much you enjoy being with them.[65]

Our God is a Rewarder, not a Hoarder. He is generous. Gracious. His expansiveness of heart is our discipleship model. When our hearts genuinely overflow with God's goodness, then we will succeed in leading souls.

Learning Together from Our Great Cloud of Witnesses

1. Compare and contrast Teresa of Avila and Jane de Chantal.
   a. How are they different in theology? Similar in theology?
   b. How are they different in practice? Similar in practice?

2. What would it be like to have Teresa as your soul care-giver and spiritual director?

3. What would it be like to have Jane as your soul care-giver and spiritual director?

4. What implications can we draw for lay spiritual friendship, pastoral ministry, and Christian counseling:
   a. From the life and ministry of Teresa?
   b. From the life and ministry of Jane?

5. Teresa believed that the complete remedy for a soul lies in consulting the friends of God. Do you agree or disagree? Why or why not?

6. According to Teresa, qualified spiritual directors need the "4 C's" of competence, character, content, and community.
   a. Read Romans 15:14, comparing and contrasting Paul's list of qualifications for ministry with Teresa's "4 C's."
   b. Of the "4 C's," which one do you most want to add to your ministry? Why? How?

7. For Teresa, spiritual friendship requires a pact, plan, purpose, passion, and Person (Christ). How would this "5 P" model impact modern spiritual friendships?

8. Jane practiced adoring God by candid acknowledgement of anguish. What do you make of this? How similar or dissimilar is this to your sustaining and healing practice?

9. Jane highlighted God's goodness and connected it to our being more than conquerors. How similar or dissimilar is this to your reconciling and guiding practice?

10. How might God's expansive heart impact your life and your ministry?

CHAPTER TEN

WISE SPIRITUAL GUIDES: LIVING BEAUTIFUL LIVES IN AN UGLY WORLD

> "I am waiting to be next. The door is open. Death will quickly draw the veil and make us see how near we were to God and one another, and did not sufficiently know it. Farewell vain world, and welcome true everlasting life" (Richard Baxter's eulogy to his wife, Margaret).[1]
>
> "And now here is comfort, that I have to deal with a God of mercy that will hear a poor repenting sinner; a God that will in no wise cast out those that come to him, but loves whom he loves to the end" (Margaret Baxter).[2]

We know the names Richard Baxter, Charles Wesley, and John Wesley. We are much less familiar with the spiritual writings of Margaret Baxter and Susannah Wesley. Yet, when we uncover the rich buried treasure of their soul care and spiritual direction ministries, we have to wonder why the world has not told their amazing stories sooner. These two remarkable women, though vastly different in temperament, background, and ministry, exemplify unique historic components of feminine soul care and spiritual direction.

Margaret Baxter: An Artful Soul Physician

Margaret Charlton Baxter's (1631-1681) father, Francis, was a leading justice of the peace and a wealthy man. Growing up as part of England's aristocracy, "Margaret was a frivolous, worldly minded teenager" when she arrived in Kidderminster to live with her godly widowed mother and to benefit from Richard Baxter's ministry.[3] A sermon series on conversion which Baxter preached in 1657 led her to a total commitment to Christ-centered worship and service. Richard, who was twenty years older than Margaret, was often in the home she shared with her mother and provided Margaret with ongoing spiritual direction.

Baxter omitted from his memoir of Margaret "the occasion and inducements of our marriage," so we only know that they wed after her mother passed away on September 10, 1662.[4] There followed nineteen years of happy life together, till Margaret's death.

Comfort in My Suffering: The Scourge of Scrupulosity and Melancholy

According to Richard, Margaret was obsessive about her physical and spiritual health, spending much of her adult life in fear of mental collapse, and starving herself for years for fear that overeating would precipitate cancer. While today we might "diagnose" her with various psychological maladies such as "anxiety disorder," "eating disorder," and/or "obsessive compulsive disorder," Richard chose the historically current category of "scrupulosity." She was overly conscientious about her spiritual state.

As he put it, "Her understanding was higher and clearer than other people's, but, like the treble strings of a lute, strained up to the highest, sweet, but in continual danger."[5] She "proved her sincerity by her costliest obedience. It cost her... somewhat of her trouble of body and mind; for her knife was too keen and cut the sheath. Her desires were more earnestly set on doing good than her tender mind and head could well bear."[6]

Baxter also used the common term of the day, "melancholy," to further describe her emotional struggles, and to depict her victory over them. "When we were married, her sadness and melancholy vanished: Counsel did something to it, and contentment something; and being taken up with our household affairs did somewhat. And we lived in inviolated love and mutual complacency conscious of the benefit of mutual help."[7] His prescription for overcoming "depression" is fascinating, especially given the trend today toward either/or thinking and one-size-fits-all therapy. Yes, counseling was part of her "treatment plan," but so was the spiritual discipline of learning contentment, the ministry practice of serving God and others in day-to-day life, and the benefit of a marriage of mutual love and affection.

Margaret added her own assessment of God's healing powers. Speaking of her physical recovery from a serious illness and her commensurate spiritual peace, she explained, "And now I desire to acknowledge his mercy in delivering me from this death-threatening disease, and that in answer to prayers I am here now in competent health to speak of the goodness of the Lord."[8] She then provided her biblical sufferology that defines how God in His goodness uses sickness. "I desire to acknowledge it a mercy that God should afflict me; and though I cannot with the Psalmist say, *but now I keep thy statutes*; I can say, *Before I was afflicted I went astray.* And how many great sins God has prevented by this affliction, I cannot tell; but I am sure that God has dealt very graciously with me; and I have had many comforts in my sufferings, which God has not given to many of his beloved ones."[9] Rather than grow bitter at God for her ongoing physical and emotional battles, she blessed God for using them to prune her so she could blossom for His glory.

But "sanctification *today*" does not alone summarize Margaret's sufferology. She also included in her healing narrative her *future* heavenly hope. "If I belong to God, though I suffer while I am in the body, they will be but light afflictions and but for a moment; but the everlasting Kingdom will be my inheritance. And when this life is ended, I shall reign with Christ; I shall be freed from sin and suffering and for ever rejoice with saints and angels."[10] In this Margaret followed the grand church history tradition of *remembering the future.*

Yes, of course salvation has daily implications *now*. But this is *not* all there is. God finalizes the results of our salvation in a future day, in the future heaven. That hope allows us to face life realistically now, as Margaret did. "However it fareth with his children in this house (or howling wilderness), the time will come, and is at hand, when all the children shall be separate from rebels, and be called home to dwell with their Father, their Head and Husband; and the elect shall be gathered into one. Then farewell sorrow, farewell hard heart! farewell tears and sad repentance!"[11] Some today tell us that highlighting salvation as heaven *later* is irrelevant to life *today*. Not only is that historically naïve, it is theologically and practically ignorant. As the Apostle Peter says after discussing our future rewards and judgments, "what kind of people ought you to be?" (2 Peter 3:11).

Confrontation for My Sinning: The Freshness of God's Goodness and Grace

Margaret also practiced the historical art of self-confrontation. Having received God's healing physically, she cooperated with God's Spirit in finding ongoing spiritual healing (forgiveness) and growth. Consider this covenant with God that she wrote upon her healing. "I here now renew my covenant with almighty God and resolve by his grace to endeavor to get and keep a fresh sense of his mercy on my soul, and a greater sense yet of my sin; I resolve to set myself against my sin with all my might, and not to take its part or extenuate it or keep the devil's counsel, as I have done, to the wronging of God and the wounding of my own soul."[12] Margaret perceived the horrors of her sins—they wronged God and wounded her soul. She also recognized the wonders of God's grace—it is her fresh sense of goodness that motivated her to eschew evil.

Margaret was a master in the art of devil craft. "Though the tempter be busy to make me think diminutively of this great mercy, yet I must not, but must acknowledge the greatness of it."[13] What a concise, precise account of the devil's grand scheme—to con us into thinking diminutively of God's colossal grace.

To her self-reconciling, Margaret added self-guiding. She applied her theological understanding of her personal relationship to the Trinity to the issue of progressive sanctification. "...I am already engaged by the baptismal covenant to God the Father, Son, and Holy Ghost; and to the Father as my God and chief good and only happiness; and to the Son as my Redeemer, Head, and Husband; and to the Holy Ghost as my Sanctifier and Comforter..."[14]

What difference does this intimate relationship with the Trinity make as she battled besetting sins?

All creatures… had nothing that could satisfy my
soul… which should teach me to keep my heart loose
from the creature and not over-love anything on this
side heaven. Why should my heart be fixed where
my home is not? Heaven is my home, God in Christ
is all my happiness, and where my treasure is, there
my heart should be. Come away, O my heart, from
vanity; mount heavenward, and be not dead or dull
if you would be free from trouble, and taste of real
joy and pleasure…. O my carnal heart! retire to God,
the only satisfying object. There mayest thou love
without all danger of excess![15]

Here we see a sample of the enduring Puritan tradition of avoiding
over-much-love of the creature by passionately pursuing ever-increasing-
love for the Creator, our only Satisfier, and the Lover of our soul.

No wonder the master pastor, Richard Baxter, praised his wife as
an artful soul physician.

Yes, I will say that… she was better at resolving a case
of conscience than most divines that ever I knew in
all my life. I often put cases to her which she suddenly
resolved as to convince me of some degree of oversight
in my own resolution. Insomuch that of late years, I
confess, that I was used to put all, save secret cases,
to her and hear what she could say. Abundance of
difficulties were brought me, some about restitution,
some about injuries, some about references, some
about vows, some about marriage promises, and many
such like; and she would lay all the circumstances
presently together, compare them, and give me a more
exact resolution than I could do.[16]

Under the Power of Melting Grief: Telling the Truth about Tears

We learn not only from Margaret's life, but also from her death.
Most of what we know of her we glean from her husband's memorial

to her, written one month after her death. Baxter published it as *A Breviate of the Life of Margaret, The Daughter of Francis Charlton, and Wife of Richard Baxter*. Later, John T. Wilkinson reprinted it with the beautiful title *Richard Baxter and Margaret Charlton: A Puritan Love Story*.

Baxter prefaced his memorializing with the candid admission that it was, "…written, I confess, under the power of melting grief."[17] Knowing the likely criticism for such openness, Baxter continued, "…and therefore perhaps with the less prudent judgment; but not with the less, but the more truth; for passionate weakness poureth out all, which greater prudence may conceal."[18] According to Baxter, Christians, of all people, should be the most honest about pain. In our grieving, we should not conceal the truth of tears this side of heaven.

It was not simply the shock and nearness of Margaret's death that left her husband so frank. Years later in his autobiography, Baxter expressed how his wife's death left him "in depth of grief."[19] Interestingly, the original editor of Baxter's autobiography suppressed this phrase. Fortunately, truer historians have uncovered it—for the benefit of all who dare speak the truth about sorrow.[20]

Richard Baxter understood the truth that *it's normal to hurt*— even for "full-time Christian workers." His entire biography of dear Margaret is a tear-stained tribute to the affection they shared and the sadness he endured.

Of course, Baxter also understood the truth that *it's possible to hope*—for all Christians. Listen to his mingled hurt and hope. "She is gone after many of my choice friends, who within this one year are gone to Christ, and I am following even at the door. Had I been to enjoy them only here, it would have been but a short comfort, mixed with the many troubles which all our failings and sins, and some degree of unsuitableness between the nearest and dearest, cause. But I am going after them to that blessed society where life, light, and love, and therefore, harmony, concord, and joy, are perfect and everlasting."[21]

Perhaps one reason why we practice denial is our fear that entering our grief might so consume us that we will be overwhelmed with worldly sorrow. Baxter's Christian experience reminds us that this doesn't have to be the case. We can look fallen life squarely in the eyes, admit the truth that it is a quagmire of pain and problems, and still live hopefully now *if* we also look *toward* life in our heavenly world to come.

In the last paragraph of his tribute to Margaret, Baxter succinctly combined these two realities. "Therefore in our greatest straits and sufferings, let us comfort one another with these words: *That we shall for ever be with the Lord.*"[22] Shakespeare's Romeo said, "He jests at scars, that never felt a wound." Baxter might have added, "He fears facing scars who never embraces the truth that by Christ's wounds we are healed."

Susannah Wesley: Spiritual Guide Par Excellence

We know of Margaret Baxter because of her famous husband. Susannah Wesley (1669-1742) we know because of her famous sons, John and Charles. Yet both women were wise spiritual guides in their own rights.

Susannah was the youngest daughter of twenty-five children of Dr. Samuel Annesley. A minister living in London, he trained his daughter in biblical and classical languages as well as other arts and sciences. A man ahead of his times, he noted that, "I have often thought it as one of the most barbarous of customs in the world, considering us a civilized and Christian Country, that we deny the advantages of learning to women."[23]

Susannah married Samuel Wesley, a minister in the Church of England, and moved to his rural parish at Epworth. She bore nineteen children, only nine of whom lived to adulthood. Her husband was known to be difficult to get along with because he ruled with an iron hand. As a result, parishioners and townspeople alike disliked the family. At one point he was sent to prison for failure to pay a debt owed to one of his parishioners.[24]

Of her marriage, Susannah ruefully recorded, "Since I'm willing to let him quietly enjoy his opinions, he ought not to deprive me of my little liberty of conscience.... I think we are not likely to live happily together.... It is a misfortune peculiar to our family that he and I seldom think alike."[25]

Motherly Spiritual Direction: Theological Depth and Relational Focus

Like many such marriages, their distance resulted in her focusing her feminine gifts on her children. John Wesley requested, in adulthood, a letter from his mother detailing her methodical system of child rearing. On July 24, 1732, she penned such a letter. In it she described not only her method, but her theology behind her practice. "As self-will is the root of all sin and misery, so whatever cherishes this in children insures their after wretchedness and irreligion; whatever checks and modifies it promotes their future happiness and piety."[26] Therefore, "in order to form the minds of children, the first thing to do is to conquer their will, and bring them to an obedient temper. To inform the understanding is a work of time, and must with children proceed by slow degrees, as they are able to bear it; but the subjecting the will is a thing which must be done at once, and the sooner the better; for by neglecting timely correction, they will contract a stubbornness and obstinacy which are hardly ever after conquered, and never without using such severity as would be as painful to me as to the child."[27] According to Susannah, parental spiritual discipline eschews the world's esteem which they grant for indulgence. To her, it is only the cruelest parents who permit their children to develop habits they know must be afterward broken.

Though strong in disciplining the will, Susannah equally offered forgiveness and encouragement. "If they amended, they should never be upbraided with it afterward…. Every single act of obedience… should always be commended, and frequently rewarded…. That if ever any child performed an act of obedience, or did anything with an intention to please, though the performance was not well, yet the obedience and intention should be kindly accepted, and the child with sweetness directed how to do better for the future."[28]

Additionally, her focus on the will in no way suggests that Susannah's parental spiritual guidance minimized the life of the mind. She, rare in her era, taught all of her children to read by age five. More than that, in a letter to her daughter, Susan, Susannah produced a lengthy treatise on parental spiritual instruction. "My tenderest regard is for your immortal soul, and for its spiritual happiness; which regard I cannot better express, than by endeavoring to instill into your mind those principles of knowledge and virtue that are absolutely necessary in order to your leading a good life here, which is the only thing that can infallibly secure your happiness hereafter."[29]

For Susannah, we should never derive these principles from some amalgamation of self-help tenets. Instead, for her we base all spiritual training on the chief articles of the Christian faith, taking for her groundwork the Apostles' Creed. Having introduced the necessity of laying a solid theological foundation, Susannah then exegeted each phrase of the Creed. Page after page, with theological precision, she modeled the depth of theological training, biblical teaching, and spiritual direction that every Christian mother ought to pass on to her children.[30] When Christians today question the relevance of theological depth, they need to ask and answer the question, "What factors produced the two great church leaders John and Charles Wesley?"

While the first factor was theologically precise teaching, this should not cause us to think that Susannah was content with "head knowledge." She taught her children that the Creed "briefly comprehended your duty to God, yourself, and your neighbor."[31] The purpose of biblical truth is to provide us with a renewed mind that leads to loving God and loving others. As a minister, John wrote to his mother about the definition of love. On May 14, 1727, she responded. "Suffer now a word of advice. However curious you may be in searching into the nature, or in distinguishing the properties, of the passions or virtues of human kind, for your own private satisfaction, be very cautious in giving nice distinctions in public assemblies; for it does not answer the true end of preaching, which is to mend men's lives, and not fill their heads with unprofitable speculations."[32] Clearly, we need truth—theological truth, but never truth for truth's sake, but truth for love's sake.

The first two factors that produced the two great church leaders John and Charles Wesley are theologically precise teaching and truth related to daily life relationships. Adding to these, Susannah modeled two more parental discipleship methods: spiritual conversations and spiritual narratives. After a fire destroyed their home and dispersed the family until a new home could be found, Susannah wrote to her daughter Sukey on January 13, 1710. "Since our misfortunes have separated us from each other, and we can no longer enjoy the opportunities we once had of conversing together, I can no other way discharge the duty of a parent, or comply with my inclination of doing you all the good I can, but by writing. You know very well how I love you."[33] What is the duty of a mother? To do all the good for a child she can. How does a mother fulfill her duty? By lovingly conversing about life in light of God's Word (the content of the rest of her letter).

To spiritual conversations Susannah added spiritual narratives. On October 11, 1709, she wrote to her son Samuel saying, "There is nothing I now desire to live for but to do some small service to my children; that as I have brought them into the world, I may, if it please God, be an instrument of doing good to their souls." And how would she provide her soul care ministry? "I had been for several years collecting from my little reading, but chiefly from my own observation and experience, some things which I hoped might be useful to you all. I had begun to collect and form all into a little manual, wherein I designed you should have seen what were the particular reasons which prevailed on me to believe the being of a God, and the grounds of natural religion, together with the motives that induced me to embrace the faith of Jesus Christ, under which was comprehended my own private reasons for the truth of revealed religion."[34]

What if every mother did the same? What if every mother maintained Susannah's high view of her high calling? A mother can make a great difference if her confidence in God's work in her life leads her to "dare" to produce for her family her "faith history," her "spiritual narrative."

Feminine Spiritual Direction: Doing Something More

Some may say, "So, from Susannah Wesley we learn that a woman's place is in the home?" She is not a good source for that bromide. The preeminent biographer of the Wesley family, Adam Clarke, explained that, "When Mr. Wesley was from home, Mrs. Wesley felt it her duty to keep up the worship of God in her house. She not only prayed for, but with her family. At such times she took the spiritual direction and care of the children and servants on herself; and sometimes even the neighbors shared the benefit of her instructions."[35]

Clarke provided a lengthier original account as transcribed in a letter by a Dr. Whitehead.

> During her husband's absence, Mrs. Wesley felt it her duty, as has been observed, to pay more particular attention to her children, especially on the Lord's day... She read prayers to them, and also a sermon, and conversed with them on religious and devotional subjects. Some neighbors happening to come in during these exercises, being permitted to stay, were so pleased and profited as to desire permission to come again. This was granted; a good report of the meeting became general; many requested leave to attend, and the house was soon filled more than two hundred at last attending; and many were obliged to go away for want of room.[36]

Now, lest we think Susannah faced no opposition, it is important to recognize that when she told her husband, he approved of "her zeal and good sense," but objected to the continuance of the meetings because it would look "peculiar," because of her gender, and because of his position as pastor.[37] She replied in a letter dated February 6, 1712.

To the objection that it looked peculiar, she responded that was only "because in our corrupt age the utmost care and diligence have been used to banish all discourse of God or spiritual concerns out of society, as if religion were never to appear out of the closet, and we were to be ashamed of nothing so much as professing ourselves to be Christians."[38] Susannah further observed that the problem is that people only want to hear from the pulpit and not in "common conversation" anything that is "serious, or that may any way advance the glory of God or the salvation of souls."[39]

To the objection of her gender, she countered, "That as I am a woman, so I am also mistress of a large family. And though the superior charge of the souls contained in it lies upon you, as head of the family, and as their minister; yet in your absence I cannot but look upon every soul you leave under my care as a talent committed to me, under a trust, by the great Lord of all the families of heaven and earth."[40] While her thinking may not satisfy combatants on either side of the modern dispute about the "role of women in ministry," her wisdom in navigating the culture of the day is commendable. Susannah understood that ultimately she was answerable to God. "And if I am unfaithful to him, or to you, in neglecting to improve these talents, how shall I answer unto him when he shall commend me to render an account of my stewardship?"[41]

Susannah continued in her letter by explaining to her husband that she had recently read a book about missionaries that inspired her zeal so that she prayed that "I might do something more than I do."[42] This prayer surely resonates with many of the women studied in *Sacred Friendships*. Out of their enforced voicelessness due to societal norms, they, like many women today, longed to "do something more than I do." Susannah further clarified that she then resolved to start "doing more" *with her family*. "I take such a proportion of time as I can best spare every night to discourse with each child by itself, on something that relates to its principal concerns. On Monday I talk with Molly; on Tuesday with Hetty; Wednesday with Nancy; Thursday with Jacky; Friday with Patty; Saturday with Charles; and with Emily and Sukey together, on Sunday."[43]

Then, "something more" mushroomed. "With those few neighbors who then came to me I discoursed more freely and affectionately than before. I chose the best and most awakening sermons we had, and I spent more times with them in such exercises. Since this our company has increased every night, for I dare deny none that ask admittance. Last Sunday, I believe we had above two hundred, and yet many went away for want of room."[44] The explosive results were exceedingly, abundantly above all that Susannah could ask or imagine. "But I never durst positively presume to hope that God would make use of me as an instrument in doing good; the furthest I durst go was, It may be: who can tell? With God all things are possible."[45]

As to her husband's third objection that her ministry reflected poorly on him, she answered, "Therefore, why any should reflect upon you... because your wife endeavors to draw people to the church, and to restrain them, by reading and other persuasions, from their profanation of God's most holy day, I cannot conceive. But if any should be so mad as to do it, I wish you would not regard it. For my part, I value no censure on this account. I have long since shook hands with the world, and I heartily wish I had never given them more reason to speak against me."[46] We see in her words a mild rebuke for her husband's fear of what people think.

Mr. Wesley "felt the power and the wisdom by which she spoke, and cordially gave his approbation to her conduct."[47] Though he gave his blessing for her to continue, others complained to him. He then wrote again to Susannah desiring her to discontinue the meetings. On February 25, 1712, she wrote back. She now replaced her previously gentle admonishment with more forceful words. "I shall not inquire how it was possible that you should be prevailed on by the senseless clamors of two or three of the worst of your parish, to condemn what you so lately approved."[48]

She then outlined the illogic, the mistaken theology, the false guilt by false association, the jealousy, and the false labeling behind the few objectors, while also noting that the vast majority in the congregation not only approved, but benefited from the meetings. In summary, she said to her husband, "Now, I beseech you, weigh all these things in an impartial balance: on the one side, the honor of almighty God, the doing much good to many souls, and the friendship of the best among whom we live; on the other, (if folly, impiety, and vanity may abide in the scale against so ponderous a weight,) the senseless objections of a few scandalous persons, laughing at us, and censuring us as precise and hypocritical; and when you have duly considered all things, let me have your positive determination."[49]

Humbly bold to the end, she concluded with this forceful request. "If you do, after all, think fit to dissolve this assembly, do not tell me that you desire me to do it, for that will not satisfy my conscience; but send me your positive command, in such full and express terms as may absolve me from all guilt and punishment, for neglecting this opportunity of doing good, when you and I shall appear before the great and awful tribunal of our LORD JESUS CHRIST."[50]

Dr. Whitehead summarized the entire account. "Though I find no further record of these transactions, yet I take it for granted that this letter was decisive, and Mrs. Wesley's meetings continued till her husband returned to Epworth."[51]

As Richard Baxter praised his wife as a skilled soul physician, so Adam Clarke, in his biography, acclaimed Susannah Wesley as an expert spiritual director. "The good sense, piety, observation, and experience of Mrs. Wesley, qualified her to be a wise counselor in almost every affair in life, and a sound spiritual director in most things that concerned the salvation of the soul. Her sons, while at Oxford, continued to profit by her advices and directions, as they had done while more immediately under her care."[52]

Soul Care in Life and in Death: On the Borders of Eternity

We would be mistaken to assume that Susannah Wesley provided spiritual direction without commensurate soul care. True, in her humility and honesty, she felt at times unfit to offer sustaining and healing counsel. John Wesley wrote his mother concerning affliction and the best method of profiting from it. On July 26, 1727, she responded, "It is certainly true that I have had large experience of what the world calls adverse fortune. But I have not made those improvements in piety and virtue, under the discipline of Providence, that I ought to have done; therefore I humbly conceive myself to be unfit for an assistant to another in affliction, since I have so ill performed my own duty."[53] Though she was perhaps overly self-deprecating, her words do remind us of the truth that the best preparation for soul care is taking our own soul care issues to the great Soul Physicians.

That Susannah was overly deferential about her soul care abilities is easy to discern given the records we have of her care for hurting people. When an unnamed female friend was afflicted in body and depressed in spirit, Susannah described to another female acquaintance how she empathized with her. "I heartily sympathize with the young lady in her affliction, and wish it was in my power to speak a word in season, that might alleviate the trouble of her mind, which has such an influence on the weakness of her body."[54]

Of course, Susannah realized that human comfort carries only so much weight. So she pointed this sufferer to her caring Savior. "It is with relation to our manifold wants and weaknesses, and the discouragements and despondencies consequent thereupon, that the blessed Jesus hath undertaken to be our great high priest, physician, advocate, and Saviour.... His deep compassion supposes our misery; and his assistance, and the supplies of his grace, imply our wants, and the disadvantages we labor under."[55]

After sustaining this hurting young woman by helping her to see that her illness was normal and not due to her sin, Susannah then shared healing care by persuading her to see Christ's goodness. "And here, madam, let me beseech you to join with me in admiring and adoring the infinite and incomprehensible love of God to fallen man, which he hath been pleased to manifest to us in the redemption of the world by our Lord Jesus Christ."[56] Understanding that there are no spiritual quick fixes, including in spiritual conversations, she invited ongoing connection. "I shall be very glad to hear often from you."[57] Given her many duties in the home and in her neighborhood ministry, it is remarkable what an open heart Susannah demonstrated.

To her son, Charles, who had been struggling with his faith, she wrote empathetically on October 19, 1738, "It is with much pleasure I find your mind somewhat easier than formerly, and I heartily thank God for it. The spirit of man may sustain his infirmity,—but a wounded spirit who can bear? If this hath been your case, it has been sad indeed."[58]

Humble as she was, Susannah could receive soul care just as easily as she dispensed it. Writing to Charles on December 27, 1739, she shared about a recent visit from his brother, John. "You cannot more desire to see me, than I do to see you. Your brother... has just been with me, and much revived my spirit. Indeed, I have often found that he never speaks in my hearing without my receiving some spiritual benefit."[59] She increased her vulnerable openness when she admitted, "But, my dear Charles, still I want either him or you; for indeed, in the most literal sense, I am become a little child, and want continual succor. 'As iron sharpeneth iron, so doth the countenance of a man his friend.' I feel much comfort and support form religious conversation when I can obtain it."[60]

She could equally accept care from non-family members. "I have been prevented from finishing my letter. I complained I had none to converse with me on spiritual things; but for these several days I have had the conversation of many good Christians, who have refreshed in some measure my fainting spirits."[61]

Perhaps there is no life event where soul care is more necessary than the end of life. John gave the following account of his mother's last moments as she began her ascent to heaven. "I left Bristol on the evening of Sunday, July 18, 1742, and on Tuesday came to London. I found my mother on the borders of eternity; but she had no doubts nor fear, nor any desire but as soon as God should call, 'to depart and be with Christ.'"[62] How we live on the borders of eternity says much about how we have lived up to that point. It also speaks either comfort or despair to our loved ones.

On Sunday, August 1, 1742, John writes of his mother's funeral and shares Susannah's grave inscription.

> Here lies the body of Mrs. Susannah Wesley,
> the youngest and last surviving daughter of Dr.
> Samuel Annesley.
>
> In sure and steadfast hope to rise
> And claim her mansion in the skies,
> A Christian here her flesh laid down
> The cross exchanging for a crown.
>
> True daughter of affliction, she,
> Inured to pain and misery,
> Mourn'd a long night of griefs and fears,
> A legal night of seventy years:
> The Father then reveal'd his Son,
> Him in the broken bread made known;
> She knew and felt her sins forgiven,
> And found the earnest of her heaven.

Meet for the fellowship above,
She heard the call, 'Arise, my love,'
'I come,' her dying looks replied,
And lamblike, as her Lord, she died.[63]

Susannah Wesley could die "lamblike" and could die granting comfort to her mourning children because of her conviction that God is our supreme good. Seven years before her death, on November 27, 1735, a few months after her husband's death, she shared that experiential truth with John. "God is Being itself! The I AM! And therefore must necessarily be the supreme Good! He is so infinitely blessed, that every perception of his blissful presence imparts a vital gladness to the heart. Every degree of approach toward him is, in the same proportion, a degree of happiness."[64] In this last letter she ever penned, she offered spiritual consolation based upon spiritual communion with God. Truly this was a fitting legacy to her life.

Listening to the Silenced Voices

When we listen to the silenced voices of wise spiritual guides like Margaret Baxter and Susannah Wesley, we hear the message of feminine empowerment. Margaret, by her temperament, never seemed destined to influence others powerfully. Susannah, by her marriage to a husband who ruled like a despot, never seemed likely to be a leader on the spiritual care journey. And neither woman lived in a cultural era that encouraged her spiritual propensities to flourish.

Yet, flourish they did. Why? The unique common denominator linking Margaret and Susannah was their conviction that God was their total happiness and their supreme good.

While they at times struggled with self-doubt and were doubted by others, their faith in God's loveliness and in His love for them empowered them to live loving lives in an unloving world. Because they refused to diminish God's infinite beauty, they lived beautiful lives in an ugly world.

Learning Together from Our Great Cloud of Witnesses

1. Compare and contrast Margaret Baxter and Susannah Wesley.
   a. How are they different in theology? Similar in theology?
   b. How are they different in practice? Similar in practice?

2. What would it be like:
   a. To have Margaret as your soul care-giver and spiritual director?
   b. To have Susannah as your soul care-giver and spiritual director?

3. From Margaret's life, what principles can we draw for overcoming scrupulosity and melancholy?

4. Margaret's biblical sufferology highlighted the relevance *today* of our *future* heavenly hope. What do we lose in biblical counseling if we forget to *remember the future*?

5. Margaret exposes the devil's grand scheme to con us into thinking diminutively of God's colossal grace. How can knowing this plot influence how we live and minister?

6. Richard Baxter told the truth about tears. When you are under the power of melting grief, how do you typically respond? What can you learn from Richard's candor over Margaret's death?

7. Susannah's parental spiritual guidance blended theological depth *and* relational focus. How would our parental discipleship counseling change if we shared her balance?

8. Susannah crafted a personal faith history/spiritual narrative that traced and defended why she believed in Christ.
   a. What is your personal narrative of faith in Christ?
   b. Will you dare to produce and share your personal spiritual narrative? Why or why not?

9. Susannah also dared to "do something more." What "more" is God calling you to do? When, where, and how will you begin?

10. Margaret and Susannah shared the conviction that God was their total happiness and their supreme good. This empowered them to live beautiful, loving lives in an ugly, unloving world. How are you developing and applying the conviction that God is *your* total happiness and supreme good?

CHAPTER ELEVEN

THE FRIENDSHIP OF WOMEN:
CONSOLERS OF SOULS

"The Puritans were too honest to dilute the vinegar of life" (Harriet Beecher Stowe).[1]

"In sickness and in health, through good report and evil, she was ever his [Charles H. Spurgeon] support and it would be difficult to find anywhere another woman who, in spite of adverse circumstances and conditions, ill-health and infirmity, did such monumental work for God and man as Susannah Spurgeon" (Charles Ray, Susannah Spurgeon's biographer).[2]

*M*ost people today do not recognize the names Sarah Edwards and Susannah Spurgeon. With Sarah, a glimmer of acknowledgement may arise when they connect her to her more famous husband, Puritan pastor, theologian, and author of *Sinners in the Hands of an Angry God*, Jonathan Edwards. Yet her letters, testimonials to her character and ministry, and her husband's accounts of her spiritual experience all combine to depict an accomplished spiritual friend, a godly woman, a devoted wife, and a compassionate mother.

With Susannah, some awareness may appear when people connect her to her more famous husband, Baptist pastor, theologian, and author, Charles Haddon Spurgeon. Yet her letters, her own ministries, her writings, and her husband's writings all testify to her spiritual depth and her skillfulness as a consoler of souls.

Sarah Edwards: Always Conversing with and about God

Sarah Edwards (1710-1758) exuded the "charm, practicality, and tact" of her great-grandfather, pastor Thomas Hooker, who founded the Connecticut colony.[3] She was born into the wealthy family of James and Mary Pierrepont in 1710 in New Haven, Connecticut. Her father was one of the founders of Yale, and her mother came from an even more distinguished family. Her cultured parents oversaw her education, where she learned both the book knowledge and the practical skills that a woman needed in the American colonies. Even as a young teenager, Sarah was already a marvel. Master of Divinity student Jonathan Edwards mused about her:

> They say there is a young lady in New Haven who is beloved of that almighty Being, who made and rules the world, and that there are certain seasons in which this great Being, in some way or other invisible, comes to her and fills her mind with exceeding sweet delight; and that she hardly cares for anything except to meditate on him.... She has a strange sweetness in her mind, and sweetness of temper, uncommon purity in her affections; is most just and praiseworthy in all her actions; and you could not persuade her to do anything thought wrong or sinful, if you would give her all the world, lest she should offend this great Being. She is of wonderful sweetness, calmness and universal benevolence of mind. She will sometimes go about, singing sweetly, from place to place, and seems to be always full of joy and pleasure; and no one knows for what. She loves to be alone, and to wander in the fields and on the mountains, and seems to have someone invisible always conversing with her.[4]

After three years of friendship and courtship, Jonathan and Sarah married on Friday, July 28, 1727. She was seventeen; he was twenty-four. Age was not the only significant difference. "It is remarkable that these two survived their courtship. Moody, socially bumbling, barricaded behind the stateliness of the very shy, Edwards was totally unlike the girl who fatefully caught his eye. She was a vibrant brunette, with erect posture and burnished manners. She was skillful at small talk—he had no talent for it at all. She was blithe—he given to black patches of introspection."[5]

Survive they did—happily married for thirty-one years until parted by death in 1758. Evangelist George Whitefield of England, after a lengthy stay in their home, noted that "a sweeter couple I have not seen."[6] So moved was Whitefield that he resolved to get married when he returned home (which he did one year later). Likewise, theologian Samuel Hopkins, who visited their home frequently, admired "the great harmony and mutual love and esteem that subsisted between them."[7]

Spiritual Conversations: Talking Feelingly and Solidly of the Things of God

Settling in Northampton, Massachusetts, Jonathan was first assistant pastor to his grandfather, Solomon Stoddard, and then full pastor from 1729 to 1750. Sarah's relationship to Jonathan was a core part of his recovery from a three-year bout with spiritual depression. Three months after their marriage he was able to write, "'Tis just about three years, that I have been for the most part in a low, sunk estate and condition, miserably senseless to what I used to be, about spiritual things."[8] What was it about Sarah's style of relating that contributed so mightily to Jonathan's spiritual healing?

George Whitefield commented about her that she "talked feelingly and solidly of the Things of God."[9] What a stunning portrait of spiritual conversations. In her, truth and love kissed. She combined passion (feelingly) and doctrine (solidly) in her spiritual friendships, including with her struggling husband. The practice was mutual. Most days he would ride or walk with her, and he carefully guarded his evenings to be with her and their growing family. He considered whatever matter Sarah was concerned about to be worthy of his full attention at any moment.[10]

Those who knew Sarah left a unified report that she had a "way of putting people at ease,… the combined result of goodness and intelligence," and her "genius was her ability to tune in on the feelings of other people."[11] Sarah practiced her Christian spirituality in stark contrast to the false stereotype of Puritan Christian living. According to an eyewitness account, "her religion had nothing gloomy or forbidding in its character. Unusual as it was in degree, it was eminently the religion of joy."[12] As Sarah joyfully lived the truth in love, Jonathan gradually found victory over his lengthy battle with despondency.

Sarah put to good use with her children her keen ears for hearing people's hearts and her earnest tongue for speaking to their souls. Hopkins, who stayed in their home often, described her discipline (reconciling) and discipleship (guiding) of her eleven children. "She had an excellent way of governing her children. She knew how to make them regard and obey her cheerfully, without loud, angry works… in speaking to them, used mild, gentle, and pleasant words. If any correction was needful, it was not her manner to give it in a passion."[13] How far this is from the false typecasting given to Puritan parenting!

Hopkins continued his sketch. "And in her directions or reproofs, in any matters of importance, she would address herself to the reason of her children, that they might not only know her inclination and will, but at the same time be convinced of the reasonableness of it."[14] For Sarah, obedience was never, "Because I said so!" In all her discipline and discipleship, she saw herself as training the heart for God. "Her system of discipline was begun at a very early age and it was her rule to resist the first as well as every subsequent exhibition of temper or disobedience in the child… wisely reflecting that until a child will obey his parents, he can never be brought to obey God."[15] In this, Sarah put into practice Jonathan's theology: "Every family ought to be a little church."[16]

But Sarah did not limit her ministry of spiritual conversations to her husband and children. After one of his frequent stays in their home, Hopkins observed:

> She was remarkable for her kindness to her friends and visitants, who resorted to Mr. Edwards. She would spare no pains to make them welcome, and provide for their convenience and comfort; and she was peculiarly kind to strangers who came to her

house. She would take such kind and special notice of such, and so soon get acquainted with them, as it were, and show such regard and concern for their comfort, and so kindly offer what she thought they needed, as to discover she knew the heart of a stranger, and well understood how to do it good, and so as to oblige them to feel, in some measure, as if they were at home.[17]

Here we witness the purposeful discovery of the feelings of others that resulted in heart-to-heart connection which made others feel at home and affectionately loved.

According to Hopkins, Sarah also delighted in spiritual conversations with spiritual friends. "She was eminent for her piety and experimental religion. Religious conversation was much her delight, and this she promoted in all companies… and her discourse showed her understanding in divine things…" Those who loved to converse about God "were her peculiar friends and intimates, to whom she would open her mind freely, and tell them the exercises of her own heart, and what God had done for her soul, for their encouragement and excitement in the ways of God."[18] As a noble spiritual friend, Sarah opened her heart to empower others to experience greater intimacy with the ultimate Spiritual Friend.

Candid Communication: Earnestly Wrestling with Self, Others, and God

What Hopkins shared as true with Sarah and others, he personally experienced during a winter-long stay in their home. It came at a time when his soul also felt the coldness of winter. "I was very gloomy and was most of the time retired in my chamber." Perceiving his state, "After some days, Mrs. Edwards came into my chamber, and said, 'As I was now become one of the family for a season, she felt herself interested in my welfare; and as she observed that I appeared gloomy and dejected, she hoped I would not think she intruded, by her desiring to know, and asking me what was the occasion of it,' or to that purpose."[19] Gently she invited Hopkins to open his wintry heart to the warmth of her caring concern.

His heart melted, and he accepted Sarah's invitation. "I told her the freedom she used was agreeable to me; that the occasion... was the state in which I considered myself. I was in a Christless, graceless state, and had been under a degree of conviction and concern for myself, for a number of months. I had got no relief, and my case, instead of growing better, appeared to grow worse." Rather than judging him, Sarah consoled him. "Upon which we entered into a free conversation; and on the whole she told me, that she had peculiar exercises [in prayer] respecting me, since I had been in the family; that she trusted I should receive light and comfort, and doubted not that God intended yet to do great things by me."[20] How right she was. Hopkins eventually studied under Jonathan and later became an influential abolitionist pastor.

Perhaps Sarah was able to accept Hopkins' candor because she also practiced truthfulness in her own struggles. She did not hide from Jonathan her ongoing battles with depression. In his work *Some Thoughts Concerning the Present Revival of Religion*, written in 1742, Jonathan records that Sarah had always been prone to "many ups and downs" and "a vapory habit of body, and often subject to melancholy, and at times almost overborne by it."[21] In her own version, Sarah described two especially troublesome situations that often caused her to teeter on the brink of despondency. First was "the ill treatment of the town." Being the minister's wife, she was subject to carping criticisms of the congregation and community, which she could not bear. The second, and even more vexing feeling, was her inability to stand any "ill will of my husband."[22]

As she "worked through" these issues, she diagnosed herself as being overly concerned with what others thought of her. Her struggle with the esteem of others came to a head when Jonathan commented that "he thought I had failed in some measure in a point of prudence, in some conversation I had with Mr. Williams of Headley"[23] (Chester Williams, a pastor and a distant cousin). Sarah became mortified by Jonathan's criticism, taking it and her resulting resentment as evidence of her lack of sufficient sanctification.

Rather than surrender hope, Sarah made the courageous choice to wrestle with herself and God. Being honest with herself about her response to Jonathan's comment, she remarked, "It seemed to bereave me of the quietness and calm of mind not to have the good opinion of my husband."[24] Feeling very uneasy and unhappy, she stepped on the mat with God. "I thought I very much needed help from God.... I had for some time been earnestly wrestling with God."[25]

The God she called out to and wrestled with, came and embraced her. The next day, while contemplating her longing to address God as Father and Christ as Husband, she was overcome. "God the Father, and the Lord Jesus Christ, seemed as distinct persons, both manifesting their inconceivable loveliness, and mildness, and gentleness, and their great immutable love to me." The peace that followed "was altogether inexpressible." At the same time, she explained that "I felt compassion and love for all mankind, and a deep abasement of soul, under a sense of my own unworthiness."[26]

This was no passing feeling. The next Wednesday while at a church service, she felt led "to converse with those who were near me, in a very earnest manner." She then exhorted men as well as women witnessing her experience of God's love. The next morning in another meeting, she felt herself "entirely swallowed up in God" and was totally overcome with "a ravishing sense of the unspeakable joys of the upper world." That night she spent "the sweetest night I ever had in my life" as though "to float or swim, in these bright, sweet beams of the love of Christ." Each minute seemed part of eternity, "worth more than all the outward comfort and pleasure, which I had enjoyed in my whole life."[27]

Jonathan Edwards' preeminent modern biographer, George Marsden, explained that Sarah's path to deepened sanctification aligned perfectly with Jonathan's emphasis on our religious affections and relational longings. Speaking of Calvinists in general and Edwards in particular, he noted, "Some of the most effective sermons, including some of Jonathan's, urged men as well as women to think of themselves as 'virgins' preparing for Christ, 'the Bridegroom.'" Edwards urged believers to accept "this intimate eternal covenant" and "be ravished with the love of Christ and filled with the Spirit."[28] Sarah Edwards applied these eternal truths of God as our Father and Christ as our Groom to her daily struggles to wean herself from the esteem of people by feasting on God's intimate love for her.

Life, as it will, repeatedly tried to steal Sarah's joy. When, after twenty-one years of pastoral ministry in Northampton, the congregation fired Jonathan at age forty-six, he fell into a pit of depression. "I am now thrown upon the wide ocean of the world and know not what will become of me and my numerous and chargeable family." He felt he was "fitted for no other business but study."[29] Suffering deeply, he tried to control his outward demeanor. There are, he wrote, "but few that know the heart of a minister under my circumstances."[30]

Sarah knew. She remained "the resting place of Jonathan's soul."[31] In the security of her love, he had a tangible expression of God's love and light. As her daughter, Esther, remarked, "You can't conceive how everything alters when Mother is away. All is dark as Egypt."[32] Through her help, and God's, Jonathan's hope revived and he moved to a new ministry in Stockbridge in June 1751.

Their ministry there continued until 1758, when he accepted the presidency at Princeton. However, after only a few weeks he died of smallpox. On his deathbed he consoled his family. "Give my kindest love to my dear wife and tell her that the uncommon union that has so long subsisted between us has been of such a nature as I trust is spiritual and therefore will continue forever. And I hope she will be supported under so great a trial and submit cheerfully to the will of God. And as to my children, you are now like to be left fatherless, which I hope will be an inducement to you to seek a Father who will never fail you." Just before he died he told one of his daughters at his bedside, "Trust in God and you do not need to be afraid." Hopkins reported of her that she "had those invisible supports that enabled her to trust in God."[33]

Sarah wrote to one of her children two weeks after her husband's death, "My very dear child: What shall I say? A holy and good God has covered us with a dark cloud.... He has made me adore His goodness that we had him so long, but my God lives, and He has my heart."[34] Sarah, the grieving wife, testified and clung to the goodness of God in the valley of the shadow of death.

Her own ability to grieve as those who have hope enabled Sarah to inspire others. When her daughter Mary lost her first child and was preparing to deliver another baby, she urged Mary to "hope in a good God, who is able to carry you through all that is before you."[35] To the very end, Sarah Edwards excelled at conversing with and about God.

Susannah Spurgeon: Consoler of Souls

Susannah Thompson Spurgeon (1832-1903) was born on January 15, 1832, and spent most of her days in London. With her parents she attended New Park Street Chapel where she heard a sermon on Romans 10:8 and "was first aroused to a sense of her own personal need of a Savior."[36] She recalled, "From that service, I date the dawning of the true light in my soul. The Lord said to me, through his servant, 'Give me thy heart,' and, constrained by his love, that night witnessed my solemn resolution of entire surrender to himself."[37]

On Sunday, December 18, 1853, Charles Hadden Spurgeon, then nineteen, preached for the first time in the pulpit of New Park Street Chapel. Being a country boy, he did not look the part and Susannah settled down to hear him with prejudicial thoughts racing through her mind. However, looking back years later, she could perceive the providential hand of God. "Ah! How little I then thought that my eyes looked on him who was to be my life's beloved; how little I dreamed of the honour God was preparing for me in the near future! It is a mercy that our lives are not left for us to plan, but that our Father chooses for us; else might we sometimes turn away from our best blessings, and put from us the choicest and loveliest gifts of his providence."[38]

In hindsight, Susannah diagnosed her spiritual condition. "For, if the whole truth be told, I was not at all fascinated by the young orator's eloquence, while his countrified manner and speech excited more regret than reverence. Alas, for my vain and foolish heart! I was not spiritually minded enough to understand his earnest presentation of the gospel and his powerful pleading with sinners—but the huge black satin stock, the long badly-trimmed hair, and the blue pocket handkerchief with white spots which he himself has so graphically described—these attracted most of my attention and I fear awakened some feelings of amusement."[39]

A Pilgrim's Progress: Following Mr. Greatheart

She was not to remain in such an unspiritual condition. "Gradually I became alarmed at my back-sliding state and then, by a great effort, I sought spiritual help and guidance from Mr. William Olney… who was an active worker in the Sunday School at new Park Street, and a true Mr. Greatheart and comforter of young pilgrims."[40]

What an awe-inspiring name from *The Pilgrim's Progress* for a counselor: Mr. Greatheart, the comforter of young pilgrims. Far too often biblical counselors become "Mr. Meanheart, the confronter of evil pilgrims." Of course, confrontation is needed in all our lives. However, what Susannah and all of us need is comfort and confrontation from Greathearts who know the Great Soul Physician, who know the great story of grace abounding to the chief of sinners, and who know how to direct young pilgrims to journey on that greater narrative.

Susannah found a second Mr. Greatheart. "One day I was greatly surprised to receive from Mr. Spurgeon an illustrated copy of *The Pilgrim's Progress*, in which he had written the inscription 'Miss Thompson, with desires for her progress in the blessed pilgrimage, from C. H. Spurgeon, April 20th 1854.'"[41]

Pastor Spurgeon continued to minister to his future wife. She described, "I do not think that my beloved had any thought concerning me than to help a struggling soul heavenward; but I was greatly impressed by his concern for me, and the book became very precious as well as helpful. By degrees, though with much trembling, I told him of my state before God; and he gently led me, by his preaching, and by his conversations, through the power of the Holy Spirit to the cross of Christ for the peace and pardon my weary soul was longing for."[42]

His ministry to Susannah exemplified so many aspects of historic soul care. He counseled out of concern, with gently leading, and with patience as she by degrees opened up. He counseled through the pulpit

ministry of the Word *and* through the personal ministry of the Word—
unfortunately, a rare combination today. He counseled empowered by
the Spirit with an eye always to the cross of Christ (God's glory) *and* to
the peace and pardon of her weary soul (for her good).

Later, after they were engaged, Susannah applied for baptism
and he asked her to write her testimony. Responding to her longings
to experience God more deeply and her sense of spiritual dryness,
Charles provided spiritual advice for her spiritual despondency. "Oh!
I could weep for joy (as I certainly am doing now), to think that my
beloved can so well testify to a work of grace in her soul. I knew you
were *really* a child of God, but I did not think you had been led in
such a path. I see my Master has been ploughing deep and it is the
deep-sown seed, struggling with the clods, which now makes your
bosom heave with distress."[43]

Having summarized her plight and provided his diagnosis, Pastor
Spurgeon offered his spiritual prescription. "If I know anything of
spiritual symptoms, I think I know a cure for you. Your position is
not the sphere for earnest labour for Christ. You have done all you
could in more ways than one; but you are not brought into actual
contact either with the saints or with the sinful, sick or miserable,
whom you could serve. Active service brings with it warmth and this
tends to remove doubting, for our works thus become evidences of
our calling and election."[44]

Charles understood that individual spiritual disciplines, as valuable
as they are, can never be our sole method for soul care. To them we
must add fellowship (actual contact with the saints), ambassadorship
(evangelistic contact with the sinful), and stewardship (ministry to
the physically sick and emotionally distressed). Too often modern
counselors with their extensive training in the therapeutic methods of
"talk therapy" believe that what occurs *in* the session is most curative.
Spurgeon realized that what occurs *between* meetings is much more
therapeutic.

This is not to say that Charles demeaned self-awareness and
personal insight. Concluding his letter, he applauded his fiancée.
"Up to the time I saw your note [her baptismal salvation testimony],
I could not imagine that you had seen such great sights and were so

thoroughly versed in soul-knowledge."[45]

Life and Death Are in the Power of the Tongue: Weathering the Gale

Susannah put her soul-knowledge to good and godly use in her ministry to others—especially to her husband. Pastor Spurgeon faced vicious criticism throughout his ministry and it often led to severe bouts of self-doubt and spiritual depression. Susannah's biographer, Charles Ray, in *The Life of Susannah Spurgeon*, published in the year of her death, extolled her life-giving words. "When the storms of abuse and slander broke on her loved one's head, she might well have been crushed and broken, but she bore up and by her words of comfort, her strong affection and her piety and faith, helped him to weather the gale."[46]

Early in his ministry, Spurgeon's preaching became so famous that his church could not hold the crowds. So his congregation rented the Surrey Music House. The first night some hooligans yelled, "Fire!" Some in the crowd fled in panic, with seven dying and dozens injured. Spurgeon urged everyone to stay while he continued to preach, unaware that several people had already been crushed to death. Moments later, another panic arose. This time Spurgeon fainted and had to be carried away.

Experiencing guilt, and battered in the local press, Spurgeon plunged into depression. Susannah recorded their resultant mutual despair. "I wanted to be alone, that I might cry to God in this hour of darkness and death! When my beloved was brought home he looked a wreck of his former self—an hour's agony of mind had changed his whole appearance and bearing. The night that ensued was one of weeping and wailing and indescribable sorrow. He refused to be comforted. I thought the morning would never break; and when it did come it brought no relief."[47]

The ensuing days were no better, as Susannah recounted. "The Lord has mercifully blotted out from my mind most of the details of the time of grief which followed when my beloved's anguish was so deep and violent that reason seemed to totter in her throne, and we sometimes feared he would never preach again. It was truly 'the valley of the shadow of death' through which we then walked; and, like poor Christian, we here 'sighed bitterly' for the pathway was so dark that oft times when we lifted up our foot to set forward, we knew not where or upon what we should set it next."[48]

Friends took Pastor Spurgeon to the country town of Croydon where he stayed in the house of Mr. Winsor, one of his deacons, with Mrs. Spurgeon and their one-month-old twin baby boys. Mrs. Spurgeon's biographer wrote, "It was hoped that the rest and change of scene would aid in the restoration of his mental equilibrium, and although at first his spirit seemed to be imprisoned in darkness, light at last broke in."[49]

Susannah shared her account of her husband's recovery. "We had been walking together as usual, he restless and anguished; I sorrowful and amazed, wondering what the end of these things would be; when at the foot of the steps which gave access to the house, he stopped suddenly, and turned to me, and, with the old sweet light in his eyes (ah! how grievous had been its absence!), he said, 'Dearest, how foolish I have been! Why! what does it matter what becomes of me, if the Lord shall but be glorified? And he repeated with earnestness and intense emphasis Philippians 2:9-11.'"[50] By an amazing inner working of the Holy Spirit, Spurgeon was able to take his eyes off his own agony, placing them instead on God's glory.

Though Spurgeon began to recover his mental and spiritual equilibrium, upon his return to London critics wrote even more critical articles about him and his ministry. Spurgeon collected every critical article into a book, on the cover of which he wrote the title *Fact, Fiction and Facetiae.*

Of these, Susannah reflected years later: "At the time of their publication what a grievous affliction these slanders were to me. My heart alternatively sorrowed over him and flamed with indignation against his detractors."[51] Every ministry spouse can relate.

Caring deeply for her husband, Susannah set about the task of ministering to his soul. For a long time I wondered how I could set continual comfort before his eyes, till, at last, I hit upon the expedient of having the following verses printed in large old English type and enclosed in a pretty Oxford frame: "Blessed are ye when men shall revile you and persecute you and shall say all manner of evil against you falsely for my sake. Rejoice and be exceeding glad: for great is your reward in heaven: for so persecuted they the prophets which were before you"—Matthew 5:11-12. The text was hung up in our own room and was read over by the dear preacher every morning, fulfilling its purpose most blessedly, for it strengthened his heart and enabled him to buckle on the invisible armor, whereby he could calmly walk among men, unruffled by their calumnies, and concerned only for their best and highest interests.[52]

Amazing. What men meant for evil, God wove into good—through the good counsel of God's good Word and a good spiritual director—Susannah Spurgeon.

Earth's Sorrows Transformed into Heavenly Joy: Escaping from the Dungeons Beneath the Castle of Despair

Of course, recovery from this event did not insulate Susannah and Charles from life's crosses and losses. Both of them battled depression. Charles' description of his depression is perhaps one of the most heartbreaking ever recorded. "There are dungeons beneath the Castle of Despair."[53] No wonder Susannah posted Isaiah 48:10 on the wall of their bedroom. "I have chosen thee in the furnace of affliction."[54]

It seems the prophet Isaiah was Susannah's constant traveling companion. In her book *Morning Devotions* she referred to Isaiah often, frequently mingling earth's hurts and heaven's healing. Reflecting on Isaiah 25:8 ("The Lord God will wipe away tears from off all faces"), she invited her readers to "Come, all you sorrowful, mourning souls and see what a fair pearl of promise your God has brought to light for you, out of the very depths of the sea of your affliction."[55]

Susannah next presented a remarkable image for meditation. "I have sometimes wondered whether that glorious arch, encircling the very throne of God, can be typical of the transformation of earth's sorrows into heavenly joys—a lovely symbol of the shining of God's pardoning love upon the rain of tears from mortal eyes, for sin, and suffering, and death."[56] Like so many feminine soul care-givers before her, Susannah pointed us to the truth that all shall be well. "And with what inconceivable tenderness shall the bitter tears caused by *bereavement* be wiped away when we get home! Here the deep waters of our sorrow seem to be assuaged for a little while, only to burst forth again with greater power to deluge our hearts with the memory of past anguish; but how completely will all traces of grief vanish there!"[57]

While pointing forward, Susannah, again like her feminine predecessors in the faith, looked for present empowerment. Hers was no "heavenly escapism." Referencing Isaiah 54:10 ("My kindness shall not depart from me"), she reminded her readers of current consolation. "Sometimes we like to think of the consolation that awaits us in heaven, when our warfare is accomplished, and our iniquity is pardoned; but here, in this precious word, we have comfort and help for the daily life and strife of earth."[58]

Susannah faced the ultimate test of her faith when her beloved C. H. died on January 31, 1892. Any grieving spouse can relate to the frankness of her response, written soon after his passing. "Oh! my husband, my husband, every moment of my now desolate life I wonder how I can live without thee! The heart that for so many years has been filled and satisfied with thy love must needs be very empty and stricken now that thou art gone!"[59]

Outliving him by a dozen years, Susannah resisted grieving as those who have no hope. Six years later she was able to write, "Ah! my husband, the blessed earthly ties which we welcomed so rapturously are dissolved now, and death has hidden thee from my mortal eyes; but not even death can divide thee from me or sever the one love which united our hearts so closely. I feel it living and growing still, and I believe it will find its full and spiritual development only when we shall meet in the glory-land and worship together before the throne!"[60]

Susannah's own pending death brought one final opportunity to apply God's words of hope. In the summer of 1903, she had a severe attack of pneumonia from which she never recovered. She was confined to bed, and her sons visited her almost daily "to comfort and cheer her in the closing days of her life."[61] The comfort was mutual. "Though he slay me, yet will I trust in him," she said feebly, then quoted the lines, "His love in times past forbids me to think; He'll leave me at last in trouble to sink."[62]

On October 7, she gave her parting blessing to her son Thomas. "The blessing, the double blessing, of your father's God be upon you and upon your brother. Good-bye, Tom; the Lord bless you for ever and ever! Amen." When very near the end, she clasped her hands together and exclaimed, "Blessed Jesus! Blessed Jesus! I can see the King in his glory!"[63] Susannah Spurgeon passed away peacefully at 8:30 a.m. on Thursday, October 22, 1903. Though dead, however, her life yet speaks.

Listening to the Silenced Voices

When we listen to the silenced voices of women like Sarah Edwards and Susannah Spurgeon, we hear the message of feminine encouragement. Both women evince gentle strength that encourages—plants the seeds of courageous resilience into the soil of souls ready to wilt.

Neither woman would likely enjoy such commendation, for both repeatedly focused their consoling ministry on Christ, not on self. As they faced death—their own and that of their loved ones—with eyes looking heavenward, so they faced the many mini-casket experiences of life with palms extended humbly upward. It was from the courage they found via their intimate walk with God that they offered encouragement to their fellow pilgrims on their journey home. Sarah and Susannah were Mrs. Greathearts.

Learning Together from Our Great Cloud of Witnesses

1. Compare and contrast Sarah Edwards and Susannah Spurgeon.
   a. How are they different in personality? Similar in personality?
   b. How are they different in practice? Similar in practice?

2. What would it be like:
   a. To have Sarah as your soul care-giver and spiritual director?
   b. To have Susannah as your soul care-giver and spiritual director?

3. What principles for spiritual conversations can we draw from Sarah Edwards' practice of talking feelingly and solidly of the things of God?

4. Sarah Edwards, like all the Puritans, was too honest to dilute the vinegar of life. What application can you draw for your life from Sarah's candid communication style of earnestly wrestling with herself, others, and God?

5. Sarah and Jonathan Edwards both believed that Christians (male and female) should apply to their lives the images of God as Father and Christ as Husband.
   a. What do you think of their counsel?
   b. How could you apply their counsel to your life and ministry today?

6. Susannah Spurgeon offers us the image of a counselor as "Mr. Greatheart: the comforter of young pilgrims."
   a. To what extent does this describe your counseling ministry today?
   b. How could you further integrate the essence of this image into your ministry?

7. Susannah's account of her husband's ministry offers many exemplars: concern, gentle leading, patience, the pulpit ministry of

the Word, the personal ministry of the Word, Spirit-empowerment, cross-focused, and person-centered. Which of these would you most like to integrate further into your ministry? Why? How?

8. What can we learn about sustaining and healing from Susannah's ability to speak life words to help others to "weather the gale"?

9. Both Sarah and Susannah refused to grieve as those who have no hope. Personally, pastorally, and professionally, what can you learn from their joint examples?

Chapter Twelve

Voices of Healing: African American Women of Faith

"Man would die but not hope sustain him" (Florence Spearing Randolph).[1]
"The Negro has a history which God intends shall never be blotted out though his Caucasian brother would try to rob him of it, and bring him about a problem. Let us cease to talk about problems, or wonder about opportunity but rather be ready for the opportunity when it comes" (Florence Spearing Randolph).[2]

*A*frican American sisters of the spirit like Elizabeth Keckley, who ministered to the grieving Mrs. Lincoln, and Octavia Albert, who ministered to the soul-wounds of ex-enslaved African Americans, vividly demonstrate how to move beyond suffering to healing hope. Their courageous, hope-based spiritual care is a small sampler, an appetizer, if you will, of a great breadth of wisdom for soul care and spiritual direction contained in the history of women in the African American church.

While space allows just this sampler, history is replete with powerful and empowering examples of African American feminine sustaining, healing, reconciling, and guiding.[3] Though some have tried to silence their voices, their speaking of God's truth in love with hope can still be heard by those with ears to hear and hearts to learn.

Elizabeth Keckley: A Voice of Hope

Picture the scene. It's Civil War America. Women have no right to vote. Across the south, blacks have no rights whatsoever. President

Lincoln is assassinated. His widow, Mary Lincoln, is devastated. To whom does she turn?

To a black woman. To Elizabeth Keckley.

In the story of her life, *Behind the Scenes, or Thirty Years a Slave and Four Years in the White House*, Elizabeth (1818-1907) explained, "...I have been intimately associated with that lady [Mrs. Lincoln] in the most eventful periods of her life. I have been her confidante... I have written with the utmost frankness in regard to her—have exposed her faults as well as given her credit for honest motives."[4]

Given the inauspicious beginnings of Elizabeth's life story, her spiritual friendship with Mary Lincoln is staggering. "My life has been an eventful one. I was born a slave—was the child of slave parents—therefore I came upon the earth free in God-like thought, but fettered in action."[5]

How did a black woman of that cultural era become confidante to the slain President's wife? Elizabeth expressed her understanding with Christian humility. "God rules the universe. I was a feeble instrument in His hands..."[6]

All Silver in Heaven: Acquainted with Grief

Like her Savior, Elizabeth was a woman of sorrow acquainted with grief, and thus was able to bring sustaining and healing spiritual care to Mrs. Lincoln. Though enslaved, her first few years were at least spent in the love of her intact family. However, soon her father was sold to another slaver and the golden dream faded. Elizabeth poignantly recalled, "The announcement fell upon the little circle in that rude log cabin like a thunderbolt. I can remember the scene as if it were but yesterday;—how my father cried out against the cruel separation; his last kiss; his wild straining of my mother to his bosom; the solemn prayer to Heaven; the tears and sobs—the fearful anguish of broken hearts. The last kiss, the last goodbye; and he, my father, was gone, gone forever."[7]

Elizabeth's earthly despair was all-encompassing; her longing for heaven all-embracing. "The shadow eclipsed the sunshine, and love brought despair. The parting was eternal. The cloud had no silver lining, but I trust that it will be all silver in heaven."[8]

As was typically the case in slavery, Elizabeth's family was not given permission to grieve or the opportunity to hope. "Deep as was the distress of my mother in parting with my father, her sorrow did not screen her from insult. My old mistress said to her: 'Stop your nonsense; there is no necessity for you putting on airs. Your husband is not the only slave that has been sold from his family, and you are not the only one that has had to part.'"[9] To these unfeeling words, Elizabeth's mother made no reply. "She turned away in stoical silence, with a curl of that loathing scorn upon her lips which swelled in her heart. My father and my mother never met again in this world."[10]

When she was fourteen, Elizabeth went to live with her master's oldest son, a Presbyterian minister, married to "a helpless wife, a girl that he had married in the humble walks of life. She was morbidly sensitive…"[11] When Elizabeth was eighteen, a Mr. Bingham, a village schoolmaster and member of her master's church, said he would whip her naked. She refused. He subdued her. Tied her. Stripped her dress. Whipped her. "I could not sleep, for I was suffering mental as well as bodily torture. My spirit rebelled against the unjustness that had been inflicted upon me, and though I tried to smother my anger and to forgive those who had been so cruel to me, it was impossible."[12]

He again tried to conquer her, striking her with savage blows. "As I stood bleeding before him, nearly exhausted with his efforts, he burst into tears, and declared that it would be a sin to beat me any more. My suffering at last subdued his hard heart; he asked my forgiveness, and afterwards was an altered man."[13] In her future ministry in the White House, Elizabeth would need her indomitable spirit in the face of unspeakable suffering.

Great Hearts Sorrowing: Permission to Grieve

Years later, through a series of sovereign appointments, Elizabeth found herself in the role of dressmaker for the President's wife. More than that, she found herself in the relationship of sacred friend to the President's wife—Mary Todd Lincoln.

Over time, the emotional, turbulent Mary Lincoln came to love and even need "Lizabeth," as she called her. The need exploded when Mrs. Lincoln's son, Willie, became ill. "He was very sick," Elizabeth reported, "and I was summoned to his bedside. It was sad to see the poor boy suffer. Always of a delicate constitution, he could not resist the strong inroads of disease." According to Elizabeth, "He was his mother's favorite child, and she doted on him. It grieved her heart sorely to see him suffer."[14]

Willie worsened, lingering a few days, and then died. "God called the beautiful spirit home, and the house of joy was turned into the house of mourning." Elizabeth was there when President Lincoln arrived. "I never saw a man so bowed down with grief. He came to the bed, lifted the cover from the face of his child, gazed at it long and earnestly, murmuring, 'My poor boy, he was too good for this earth. God has called him home. I know that he is much better off in heaven, but then we loved him so. It is hard, hard to have him die!'"[15]

The scene continued. "Great sobs choked his utterance. He buried his head in his hands, and his tall frame was convulsed with emotion. I stood at the foot of the bed, my eyes full of tears, looking at the man in silent, awe-stricken wonder. His grief unnerved him, and made him a weak, passive child. I did not dream that his rugged nature could be so moved. I shall never forget those solemn moments— genius and greatness weeping over love's idol lost. There is a grandeur as well as a simplicity about the picture that will never fade."[16]

Mrs. Lincoln's grief was inconsolable. "The pale face of her dead boy threw her into convulsions. Around him love's tendrils had been twined, and now that he was dressed for the tomb, it was like tearing the tendrils out of the heart by their roots. Willie, she often said, if spared by Providence, would be the hope and stay of her old age. But Providence had not spared him. The light faded from his eyes, and the death-dew had gathered on his brow."[17] Mrs. Lincoln was so completely overwhelmed with sorrow that she did not attend her son's funeral.

Elizabeth could empathize with a grieving mother's broken heart. "Previous to this I had lost my son. Leaving Wilberforce, he went to the battlefield with the three months troops, and was killed in Missouri—found his grave on the battlefield where the gallant General Lyon fell. It was a sad blow to me, and the kind womanly letter that Mrs. Lincoln wrote to me when she heard of my bereavement was full of golden words of comfort."[18]

Clearly, all were given permission to grieve. Speaking of President Lincoln and all the President's men, Elizabeth described the funeral scene. "And there sat the man, with a burden on his brain at which the world marvels—bent now with the load at both heart and brain—staggering under a blow like the taking from him of his child! His men of power sat around him—McClellan, with a moist eye when he bowed to the prayer, as I could see from where I stood; and Chase and Seward, with their austere features at work; and senators, and ambassadors, and soldiers, all struggling with their tears—*great hearts sorrowing with the President as a stricken man and a brother.*"[19]

The permission to grieve extended over time, as it should. "For two years after Willie's death the White House was the scene of no fashionable display. The memory of the dead boy was duly respected. In some things Mrs. Lincoln was an altered woman."[20]

From Elizabeth's perspective, President Lincoln grieved as one who had found Christian hope. "Mr. Lincoln was reading that divine comforter, Job. He read with Christian eagerness, and the courage and hope that he derived from the inspired pages made him a new man."[21] Here Elizabeth recorded a profound Presidential example of scriptural exploration bringing hope to the hurting. In her words, "What a sublime picture was this! A ruler of a mighty nation going to the pages of the Bible with simple Christian earnestness for comfort and courage, and finding both in the darkest hours of a nation's calamity. Ponder it, O ye scoffers at God's Holy Word, and then hang your heads for very shame!"[22]

A Tornado of Sorrow: Light beyond the Dark, Mysterious Shadows of Death

Just a few years later, at 11 o'clock at night, Elizabeth awoke to the news that Mr. Lincoln had been shot. In the confusion of the night, she finally learned that the President was dead. Her first thought was of Mrs. Lincoln. "I wanted to go to Mrs. Lincoln, as I pictured her wild with grief; but then I did not know where to find her...."[23]

Mrs. Lincoln was overcome. Mrs. Secretary Wells asked Mrs. Lincoln who could comfort her. "Is there no one, Mrs. Lincoln, that you desire to have with you in this terrible affliction?" Mrs. Lincoln responded, "Yes, send for Elizabeth Keckley. I want her just as soon as she can be brought here."[24]

Bringing her in, Mrs. Wells excused herself and Elizabeth was left alone with Mrs. Lincoln. "She was nearly exhausted with grief, and when she became a little quiet, I asked and received permission to go into the Guests' Room, where the body of the President lay in state."[25]

Returning to Mrs. Lincoln's room, Elizabeth reported, "I found her in a paroxysm of grief. Robert was bending over his mother with tender affection, and little Tad was crouched at the foot of the bed with a world of agony in his young face. I shall never forget the scene—the wails of a broken heart, the unearthly shrieks, the terrible convulsions, the wild, tempestuous outbursts of grief from the soul."[26]

How did Elizabeth respond? "I bathed Mrs. Lincoln's head with cold water, and soothed the terrible tornado as best I could. Tad's grief at his father's death was as great as the grief of his mother, but her terrible outbursts awed the boy into silence."[27]

In those days, of all people, a formerly enslaved black woman was the one human being on the face of the earth who could comfort the President's widow. And how? With her empathy. With her silence. With her physical presence. With her loving companionship.

"Every room in the White House was darkened, and every one spoke in subdued tones, and moved about with muffled tread. The very atmosphere breathed of the great sorrow which weighed heavily upon each heart. Mrs. Lincoln never left her room... She denied admittance to almost every one, and I was her only companion, except her children, in the days of her great sorrow."[28]

Mrs. Lincoln's testimony says it all. "Lizabeth, you are my best and kindest friend, and I love you as my best friend."[29]

Elizabeth Keckley not only understood how to offer sustaining comfort. She also recognized how to impart healing hope. "At the grave, at least, we should be permitted to lay our burden down, that a new world, a world of brightness, may open to us. The light that is denied us here should grow into a flood of effulgence beyond the dark, mysterious shadows of death."[30]

The hope-giving spiritual friendship between "Lizzy" Keckley and Mary Lincoln continued for a lifetime. The widowed Mrs. Lincoln needed it desperately. Elizabeth described Mrs. Lincoln in these post-White House years. "A few words as regards the disposition and habits of Mrs. Lincoln. She is no longer the sprightly body she was when her very presence illumed the White House with gayety. Now she is sad and sedate, seeking seclusion, and maintaining communication merely with her most intimate personal friends."[31]

Lizzy, or Lizzie, as Mary affectionately called her in letter after letter, was her most intimate of friends—a friendship continued by letters until Mrs. Lincoln passed away. Unfortunately, history records only the letters written to Elizabeth from Lincoln. But even these provide more than a glimpse into the openness of this sacred friendship, and the trust and safety that an otherwise mistrusting Mrs. Lincoln felt because of Elizabeth's care for her soul.

Writing on Sunday morning, October 6, 1867, the still-grieving Mrs. Lincoln opened her heart wide to Lizzy. "My Dear Lizzie: I am writing this morning with a broken heart after a sleepless night of great mental suffering.... Pray for me that this cup of affliction may pass from me, or be sanctified to me. I weep whilst I am writing. I pray for death this morning. Only my darling Taddie prevents my taking my life.... Your friend, M. L."[32]

One week later, Mary cried out again for Elizabeth's friendship. "Oh! That I could see you. Write me, dear Lizzie, if only a line.... I am always so anxious to hear from you, I am feeling so *friendless* in the world. I remain always your affectionate friend. M. L." It is obvious from these lines that Elizabeth provided sustaining and healing soul care. It is equally clear that she was Mary Lincoln's source of reconciling and guiding spiritual direction from the following words. "Write me my dear friend, your candid opinion about everything. I wish to be made better off..."[33] Lincoln offered a great purpose statement for spiritual direction—helping others to be better off—spiritually, socially, mentally, emotionally.

The next month, on November 9 and 15, 1867, Mary expressed further appreciation for the depth of connection that she shared with Lizzy. "How hard it is that I cannot see and talk with you in this time of great, *great* trouble. I feel as if I had not a friend in the world save yourself. I sometimes wish myself out of this world of sorrow and care...."[34]

"Your last letter has been received, and believe me, I duly appreciate your great interest in my affairs. I hope the day *may* arrive when I can return your kindness in *more* than words."[35]

The widow's sadness was unrelenting. Her need for her best friend's enduring presence was equally indefatigable. "Chicago, November 24. Why, why was not *I* taken when my darling husband was called from my side? I have been allowed no rest by those who, in my desolation, should have protected me. How dearly I should love to see you *this very sad day*."[36] What is a soul care-giver? She is someone like Elizabeth Keckley who can be trusted to provide unremitting rest, protection, and presence in the saddest days of life on fallen planet earth.

Octavia Rogers Albert: A Voice for the Voiceless

She lived a mere thirty-seven years, yet in *The House of Bondage* Octavia Rogers Albert (1853-1890) chronicled two-hundred-fifty years of African American history. Like no one before her or since, male or female, she provided a voice for voiceless ex-enslaved African Americans. Her writing offers the immediacy of first-person accounts mediated by her sensitive interviews and empathic conversations, and recognizes the insufficiency of secondary sources. "None but those who resided in the South during the time of slavery can realize the terrible punishments that were visited upon the slaves.... The half was never told concerning this race that was in bondage nearly two hundred and fifty years."[37]

Octavia's lifelong mission was to unpack the personal narratives of those whose "home" was the "house of bondage." When Colonel Douglass Wilson derided himself for telling his experiences of enslavement and of military service in the Civil War, Octavia insisted that he testify. "I believe we should not only treasure these things, but should transmit them to our children's children. That's what the Lord commanded Israel to do in reference to their deliverance from Egyptian bondage, and I verily believe that the same is his will concerning us and our bondage and deliverance in this country."[38]

Her resolve was steely. She wrote to give God glory by giving African Americans a voice to answer the question, "Who shall return to tell Egypt the story?"[39] The hymn (*Sound the Loud Timbrel O'er Egypt's Dark Sea*) that concludes her narrative of former slaves "summarizes her theme that abolition was the triumph of God's will over evil and that those who have been delivered must return to tell the story."[40]

Octavia did not write as an aloof observer. Born on December 24, 1853, in Oglethorpe, Georgia, of slave parentage, she faced firsthand the horrors and humiliation of enslavement. While still living in Oglethorpe she joined the African Methodist Episcopal Church, which was led by the legendary Bishop Henry McNeal Turner, whose ministry grounded her in her lifelong Christian faith. After Emancipation, she studied at Atlanta University. Her first teaching job was in Montezuma, Georgia, where, on October 21, 1874, at age twenty-one, she married another teacher at the school, the Rev. A. E. P. Albert, D.D., who later became an ordained minister in the Methodist Episcopal Church.

Soon after their marriage, the Alberts moved to Houma, Louisiana, where Octavia began conducting her interviews with men and women once enslaved. She apparently suffered an untimely death, the circumstances of which are unknown. The preface to her book, authored by her husband and their only child, Laura, implies that she died in 1890.

Throbbing with Sympathy: An Ear to Hear, a Mouthpiece to Speak

According to historian John Blassingame, Octavia Albert was one of the few well-trained and one of the most interesting interviewers in the country during the Reconstruction era.[41] She combined academic excellence with sympathetic brilliance. That combination, important to researchers today, was vitally meaningful to the ex-slaves who shared their stories with her. As the educated "First Lady" (pastor's wife) of an African American church, she represented to them a figure of compassion, accomplishment, and status. So it is no surprise that when she moved to Louisiana her home became a gathering place for former slaves. "There she offered them food, read them scriptures, taught them to read and write, and encouraged them to talk about themselves and their slave experiences."[42]

Her decision to offer them a listening ear and to be their mouthpiece surprised even her interviewees. Among those Octavia ministered to, Charlotte Brooks was preeminent. Octavia told Charlotte that she greatly enjoyed their conversations, had listened to every word of her "past unhappy life" in the cane fields of Louisiana, and that "I desire to write it in your own words." Charlotte bluntly expressed her shock that any human would identify with her. "La, me, child! I never thought any body would care enough for me to tell of my trials and sorrows in this world! None but Jesus knows what I have passed through."[43] And not just anyone—but the "First Lady" valued "Aunt Charlotte" by dispensing the sustaining grace of listening to her story of suffering. As "Jesus with skin on her," Octavia's ministry was life changing.

Octavia recorded her own perceptions of her soul care of Charlotte. "It was in the fall of 1879 that I met Charlotte Brooks. She was brought from the State of Virginia and sold in the State of Louisiana many years before the war. I have spent hours with her listening to her telling of her sad life of bondage in the cane-fields of Louisiana."[44] If one picture is worth 1,000 words, then this one example is worth 1,000 pages of training in sustaining. Spend hours listening to people tell their sad story of suffering. Our quick-fix, solution-focused, speak-first culture desperately needs to develop the relational competency of sustained listening.

Of course, listening without feeling is worthless. Octavia combined both. "Poor Charlotte Brooks! I can never forget how her eyes were filled with tears when she would speak of all her children: 'Gone, and no one to care for me!'"[45] Octavia then wept with Charlotte. "I must say that she caused tears to flow from my eyes many a day while relating her hardships."[46] Octavia taught us that it is not enough to listen (as foundational as that is); it is not enough to feel for another; we also must *communicate our compassion.*

Octavia did so not only via her shed tears, but also through her expressed commiseration. "Aunt Charlotte, my heart throbs with sympathy, and my eyes are filled with tears, whenever I hear you tell of the trials of yourself and others. I've read and heard very often of the hard punishments of the slaves in the South; but the half was never told."[47] Charlotte's response indicated that Octavia had heard her accurately. "No, half of it aint been told. I could sit right here and tell you the trials and tribulations I have had to go through with my three marsters here in Louisiana, and it would be dark before I got half through with my own; but if I tried to tell of the sorrows of others, what I have seen here in Louisiana since I have been here, it would take me all the week, I reckon."[48]

Imagine Aunt Charlotte not thinking that anyone would ever want to listen, but Jesus. Thinking no one would ever care, no one would ever record her words, much less hear them. Then having this college-educated pastor's wife weeping with her. Identifying with her.

Keeping the Faith: Hope Inspired through Inspired Scripture

Sustaining enables suffering people to survive. Healing and guiding encourage and empower sufferers to move beyond the suffering—to thrive. Healing and guiding never ignore, deny, or minimize affliction; they always heroically, resiliently empower believers to keep the faith (healing) and to live out that faith active in love (guiding).

Octavia challenged her suffering spiritual friends to live their Christian faith by recognizing the common bond they shared with captive Israel of old. Her work emphasized the unshakable faith of slaves who survived and thrived despite their captivity, their ridicule, and the hypocrisy of their masters.[49] Though urging them to be longsuffering, Octavia never encouraged them to be passive.

Her husband and daughter, in their original preface to *The House of Bondage*, clearly saw Octavia's twin goals of sustaining (surviving) and healing/guiding (thriving). "An only daughter unites with the writer [Octavia's husband] in sending out these pages penned by a precious and devoted mother and wife, whose angelic spirit is constantly seen herein…" Having honored Octavia's character, her daughter proceeds to venerate her ministry. "…and whose subtle and holy influence seems to continue to guide and protect both [daughter and husband] in the path over which they since have had to travel without the presence and cheer of her inspiring countenance."[50]

Octavia inspired hope through inspired Scripture. Often it involved spiritual conversations through guiding questions that drew out Aunt Charlotte's embedded faith. Having listened to Charlotte's testimony of repentance and faith in Christ, Octavia asked her "whether she felt lonely in this unfriendly world." Charlotte answered, "No, my dear; how can a child of God feel lonesome? My heavenly Father took care of me in slave-time. He led me all the way along, and now he has set me free, and I am free both in soul and body."[51]

At other times, Octavia's counsel was more direct as she used scriptural exploration and Bible reading to encourage Aunt Charlotte and others. Charlotte was nearly blind by the time she met Octavia, and thus harbored no hopes of learning to read. On one occasion, while discussing the hope-giving nature of Scripture, Octavia read Job 19:25-27 ("I know my redeemer lives"). "Thank you, too, for it" Charlotte exclaimed in response.[52]

What stands out in Octavia's use of spiritual conversations and scriptural explorations is her remarkable knack for selecting the right topic and/or passage for the right person at the right moment. When Aunt Charlotte shared about the inhumane, brutal treatment she received at the hands of her white masters, Octavia responded by reading the hymn *All the Way My Savior Leads Me*. Charlotte replied immediately. "O, bless the Lord for the chance of hearing those word! *They suit my case*. I want to sing that very hymn in glory."[53] To "suit the case" of another is to connect, to speak timely words, appropriate for the person and the situation. In this, Octavia followed the inspired counsel of the Apostle Paul. "Do not let any unwholesome talk come out of your mouths, but only what is helpful for building others up according to their needs, that it may benefit those who listen" (Ephesians 4:29).

Octavia was equally adept at using Scripture, hymns, spirituals, and even Christian literature to minister healing soul care and guiding spiritual direction. Aunt Charlotte disclosed how they sang the spiritual *My God Delivered Daniel* and then said that "it seemed the more trials

I had the more I could pray." Octavia responded, "Aunt Charlotte, you remind me of Pilgrim's Progress." In the ensuing conversation, she compared Charlotte to John Bunyan (the author of *Pilgrim's Progress*) who, like Charlotte, remained faithful to God even when persecuted for his faith. Charlotte, identifying with Bunyan, noted, "But that's the time a true child of God prays, when he gets in trouble."[54]

Octavia also skillfully used imagery in her biblical counseling ministry. After discussing living for this life or living for eternity, she summarized her practical theology. "This world is our dressing-room, and if we are not dressed up and prepared to meet God when we die we can never enter the promised land; for there is no preparation beyond the grave. The Bible tells us, 'Whatsoever a man soweth, that shall he also reap.'"[55]

Her ministry certainly wasn't all talk. More than anything, Octavia loved to draw out, stir up, and honor Aunt Charlotte's faith. Discussing the evils of slavery and the goodness of God, Charlotte displayed her own astute theology. "You see, my child, God will take care of his people. He will hear us when we cry." Octavia then fanned Charlotte's faith into flames. "Aunt Charlotte, it really makes me feel happy to hear you express your faith in the goodness of God."[56]

Octavia ministered to many ex-enslaved Christians. In talking to Aunt Lorendo about her husband's (Uncle John Goodwin) health, Lorendo noted that John would never be physically well due to the cruel treatment he endured. Expressing her faith and hope, Lorendo said to Octavia, "I trust we both will rest by and by." Octavia replied, "Yes, Aunt Lorendo, the Bible promises that there is 'rest for the people of God.' And it affords us joy to know that although we have trials and tribulations here we who prove faithful till death shall enter that 'rest prepared for the people of God.'"[57]

Toppling the House of Bondage: Frank Confrontation of Corporate Sin

If Octavia's ministry stopped here, then some might rightly complain that while she should be commended for sustaining, healing, and guiding African American Christians, she should be questioned for not confronting (reconciling) American slave-owners. However,

Octavia let no one "off the hook." Hers was not only a message of the "sweet bye and bye." While highlighting future heavenly hope for those who had little realistic earthly expectations to cling to, she also forcefully and frankly addressed the earthly arena from God's perspective.

In fact, her book itself was a salvo in the battle for the truth. From the 1860s to the 1890s, there were two competing narratives of American slavery. One, propagated by whites, told the story of idyllic southern plantations where paternalistic Christian slave owners cared for, fed, and employed uneducated, untrained blacks. Octavia Albert's work protested this "misrepresentation of both the recent slave past and the present condition of the former slaves.... Her plan for reform rested upon a sober recognition of this shameful heritage and upon each individual's prayerful acceptance of responsibility for its legacies and its lessons."[58]

Since slavery had flourished in a "Christian nation," how could true Christians, Octavia demanded, "as heralds of Jesus, sit quietly by and see the needs of seven millions or more of human souls crying in the valley of sin and sorrow and not give a listening ear to them?"[59]

She waited no longer than page one to speak the truth in love. "Consider that here in this Bible land, where we have the light, where the Gospel was preached Sunday after Sunday in all portions of the South, and where ministers read from the pulpit that God has made of one blood all nations of men, etc., that nevertheless with the knowledge and teachings of the word of God, the slaves were reduced to a level with the brute."[60]

Hardly finished, she immediately added, "There are millions of souls now crowned around the throne of God who have washed their robes white and are praising God, although they spent their lives in sorrow, but who will rise up in judgment and condemn this Christian nation."[61]

To support factually her admonitions and exhortations, Octavia consistently recorded firsthand testimony to the abject cruelty and anti-Christian nature of slavery. For instance, Aunt Charlotte shared, "The white people thought in slave-time we poor darkies had no soul, and they separated us like dogs. So many colored people are dead from grieving at the separation of their children that was sold away from them."[62] Octavia repeated such reports numerous times from copious voices throughout *The House of Bondage*.

Speaking specifically about Christian slave owners, Aunt Charlotte and Octavia both marveled at the mystery. "But how could they have good religion and keep us poor darkies in bondage and beat us half to death?"[63] asked Charlotte. To which Octavia attempted a reply.

> Well, Aunt Charlotte, I am hardly able to answer you satisfactorily, I must confess, for when I pause and think over the hard punishments of the slaves by the whites, many of whom professed to be Christians, I am filled with amazement. Religion fills our souls with love for God and humanity. The Bible moreover says, "We know we have passed from death unto life, because we love the brethren." And you know as a rule there were comparatively few colored people during the period of slavery, or even now, but what are members of some Christian denomination. So they were their brethren through Christ.[64]

Later, while speaking of divisions within the Methodist church over slavery, Aunt Charlotte offered her astute analysis. "It seems to me every Christian that honors God in the pardoning of their sins ought to agree to everything that is holy and good. How could any Christian man believe it was right to sell and buy us poor colored people just like we was sheep?"[65]

Octavia, not content to expose only the Methodist hypocrisy, decried supposed Christians who practice racial prejudice. "Do you preach that Jesus tasted death for *every man?* How strange that here in the South the Methodist Church and the Baptist Church seem ready and willing to send missionaries to other countries, and are not willing to extend a helping hand to these needy souls who have served them so long and faithfully! Behold your 'brethren in black' at your doors; arise and let them in. And the least you do for Jesus will be precious in his sight."[66] Repeatedly, Octavia utilized theological truth and biblical teaching to confront relevantly and righteously a sinning nation and a sinful church.

Octavia also attacked the lie that blacks were lacking in industry, intelligence, and ability. Her compatriot in this battle was Colonel Douglass Wilson, "a colored man of considerable prominence, not only in Louisiana, but in the nation."[67] Having recounted several examples of black successes even against countless obstacles during Reconstruction, Wilson shared, "If our people did so well when only a few years removed from the house of bondage, wherein they were not permitted to learn to read and write under penalty of death or something next to it, what may we not expect of them with the advances they have since made and are making?"[68] He continued:

> One thing, however, I can tell you without fear of successful contradiction, and that is that no people similarly situated have ever made the progress in every department of life that our people have made, since the world began. Why, just think of it! Twenty-seven years ago we did not own a foot of land... not even a name. We had no marriage-tie, not a legal family... But today we have two millions of our children in school, we have about eighteen thousand colored professors and teachers, twenty thousand young men and women in schools of higher grade, two hundred newspapers, over two million members in the Methodist and Baptist Churches alone, and we own over three million dollars' worth of property in this Southern country.[69]

Colonel Wilson ended with a vision that, in hindsight, seems astonishing. "My plan is for us to stay right in this country with the white people, and to be so scattered in and among them that they can't hurt one of us without hurting some of their own number.... God's plan seems to be to pattern this country after heaven. He is bringing here all nations, kindreds, and tongues of people and mixing them into one homogeneous whole; and I do not believe that we should seek to frustrate his plan by any vain attempts to colonize ourselves in any corner to ourselves."[70]

Octavia concluded with these words of hope and inspiration. "Let us all thank God and rejoice that the unearthly institution has been swept away forever in a sea of blood never to rise again."[71] And then she left her empowered readers reflecting on the words of *Sound the Loud Timbrel O'er Egypt's Dark Sea.*

> Sound the loud timbrel o'er Egypt's dark sea;
> Jehovah has triumphed, his people are free!
> Sing, for the pride of this tyrant is broken,
> His chariots, his horsemen, all splendid and brave—
> How void was their boast, for the Lord hath but spoken
> And chariot and horsemen are sunk in the wave.
> Sound the loud timbrel o'er Egypt's dark sea;
> Jehovah has triumphed, his people are free!
>
> Praise to the Conqueror, praise to the Lord!
> His Word was our arrow, his breath was our sword.
> Who shall return to tell Egypt the story
> Of those she sent forth in the hour of her pride?
> For the Lord hath looked out from his pillar of glory,
> And all the brave thousands are dashed in the tide.
> Sound the loud timbrel o'er Egypt's dark sea;
> Jehovah has triumphed, his people are free![72]

Listening to the Silenced Voices

When we listen to the silenced voices of African American women like Elizabeth Keckley and Octavia Albert, we hear the voice of enduring hope. Elizabeth modeled lasting, stable, hope-giving sacred friendship to the nation's grieving First Lady. Octavia, a First Lady herself, offered the nation uncompromising hope if they would face the truth of a sinful, shameful past, and come clean with God and one another.

Both women remind us of another courageous African American women of this era, Florence Spearing Randolph (1866-1951)—

Christian, educator, minister, writer, and national leader of the Women's Temperance Union. She preached persistent hope. "If we would make this life what it should be, a foretaste of the heavenly, we must encourage a hopeful disposition; for with such a disposition the head and heart are set to work, and one is animated to do his or her utmost. And by continually pushing and assuring, a seeming impossibility is made to give way."[73] This life is a preview of heaven and we survive and thrive only with the resilient mindset of heavenly hope that empowers us to persist in today's war against evil wherever we uncover it.

She preached audacious hope. "History proves that every great man or woman in the world who has climbed the steep stairs of fame, and made a mark in the world was first inspired by hope, 'auspicious hope.' Though many of them were poor, they realized that life was action, life was duty, that God had given existence with full power and opportunity to improve it and be happy; or to despise the gift and be miserable. Life is a mission, or journey, and it is important that we do our utmost to make the journey a successful one."[74]

Elizabeth Keckley, Octavia Rogers Albert, and Florence Spearing Randolph together provide the voice of hope by reminding African American Christians, and all believers, that life is a spiritual journey, an adventure with God as our guide. God has given us minds to remember the narratives of past victories that inspire us today on our path. And He has created us with volitional freedom to choose life instead of death, to follow the road of faith toward the destiny of hope through a life of love.

Learning Together from Our Great Cloud of Witnesses

1. You've learned from three representative sisters of the Spirit of the African American church: Elizabeth Keckley, Octavia Rogers Albert, and Florence Spearing Randolph.
   a. What impact could knowledge of African American sisters like these three women have upon Americans? African Americans? African American females?
   b. Why do you think the history of African American females like these is so infrequently highlighted? What could be done to reverse this pattern?

2. Permission to grieve, or the lack thereof, was a theme in Elizabeth Keckley's ministry.
   a. In your life, when have people failed to grant you permission to grieve? What impact did it have upon your healing? Why do Christians often fail to allow one another to grieve?
   b. In your life, when have others granted you permission to grieve? How has this assisted you along the path of healing? How can the Christian community better model the biblical principle of grieving as those who have hope?

3. Elizabeth Keckley entered the vortex of Mrs. Lincoln's "tornado of sorrow" and brought her light in the darkness. What can you apply in your ministry from how Elizabeth did so?

4. Elizabeth Keckley was a soul care-giver who could be trusted to provide unremitting rest, protection, and presence in the saddest days of life. How would your spiritual friends rate you on those areas of soul care? What could you do to grow in those areas?

5. Octavia Albert consistently offered empathetic listening, communicated compassion, and expressed commiseration.
   a. Of these competencies, which would you like to work on the most? Why? How?

b. Share an example of when you offered one or more of these
    sustaining "gifts" and how it positively impacted your spiritual
    friend.

6. Octavia Albert adeptly used spiritual conversations, scriptural
    explorations, Scripture sharing, hymns, spirituals, Christian
    literature, and images to inspire hope and to motivate faith active
    in love.
    a. Of these competencies, which would you like to work on the
        most? Why? How?
    b. Share an example of when you offered one or more of these
        healing and guiding "gifts" and how it positively impacted
        your spiritual friend.

7. Octavia Albert frankly confronted corporate sin. What societal
    sin do you sense God calling you to battle against and confront?
    How and where could you begin to enter the battle?

CHAPTER THIRTEEN

Changing the World for Christ:
Ministering to the Least of These

> "...I feel a sacred call to be the helper of the helpless..." (Harriet Beecher Stowe).[1]
>
> "A large portion of the whole sum of good, which is accomplished in the world, is the result of female diligence and liberality" (James D. Knowles, Ann Judson's biographer).[2]

*G*odly and passionate Christian women are a force to be reckoned with. With the Bible as their foundation they dare to challenge the societal norms and tackle the social ills of their generation. Two such women are Ann Judson and Amelia Sieveking. Their impact was powerful and life-changing. Ann opened the door for American women to travel to dangerous foreign lands in order to share God's Word with the unsaved. Amelia declared and proved that women have a vital role to play in the spiritual and physical life of their community. They inspire us with their love and concern for the least of these, the downtrodden, the voiceless, the powerless. They amaze us with their tireless dedication to Christ, their personal sacrifices, and their compassionate interactions with the individuals they serve.

Ann Hasseltine Judson: Sacrificing All

When Ann Hasseltine (1789-1826) was a young teenage girl consumed with the pleasures of parties, balls, and the things of this world, it is unlikely she could have imagined the life that soon awaited her. But a "chance" incident began the process of change.

"One Sabbath morning... I accidentally took up Hannah More's Strictures on Female Education; and the first words that caught my eye were, *She that liveth in pleasure, is dead while she liveth.*"[3] Although troubled by these words, she kept her concerns to herself until she could no longer tolerate their weight. While visiting an aunt, Ann broke down and told her relative what was troubling her. "She urged the importance of my cherishing those feelings, and of devoting myself entirely to seeking an interest in Christ, before it should be forever too late. She told me, that if I trifled with the impressions which were evidently made by the Holy Spirit, I should be left to hardness of heart, and blindness of mind. Her words penetrated my heart, and I felt resolved to give up every thing, and seek to be reconciled to God."[4] This nameless woman reminds us that we can have eternal impact in ways we could never imagine or know this side of heaven. Ann's aunt kindly and lovingly took the time to invite Ann to share what was troubling her. She listened and then proceeded both to reconcile and guide Ann. This pivotal moment in Ann's life was the beginning of a change that impacted countless others in years to come.

Over the next few years Ann experienced ups and downs in her spiritual journey but through it all she expressed a desire to "be more extensively devoted to his glory, and the benefit of my fellow creatures."[5] In 1810, Ann met Adoniram Judson. Shortly thereafter he proposed and with his proposal came the invitation to join him on the mission field. The couple faced many hurdles toward this goal, but in February, 1812, they were married and a few days later set sail for Calcutta.[6] Thus, Ann Judson became the "first American female, who resolved to leave her friends and country, to bear the Gospel to the heathen in foreign climes."[7]

Strength for the Journey: Cultivating the Inward Life

Ann Judson's resolve to sacrifice friends, family, and country in order to bring those who were far away from God into His Kingdom is courageous, but by no means foolhardy and was not carried out in her own strength. Ann, like all devoted spiritual friends, knew that more than anything she needed an inner life that would reflect the peace and wisdom of her heavenly Father. To that end she studied the Scriptures and read other spiritual material such as commentaries. While aboard the ship that carried her and her husband to their new life among the "unreached," Ann wrote to her friend Lydia. "My dearest L.,… I have spent the most of my time, since on the water, in reading. I knew I needed a more intimate acquaintance with the sacred Scriptures; consequently, I have confined my attention almost exclusively to them. I have read the New Testament once through in course, two volumes of Scott's Commentary on the Old, Paley, Trumbull, and Dick, on the Inspiration of the Scriptures, together with Faber and Smith on the Prophecies." She also knew how beneficial this would be to other believers. "O my dear Lydia, how much enjoyment Christians lose by neglecting to study the Bible. The more we are conversant with it, the more shall we partake of the spirit of its author, and the more we shall feel that this world is not our home, and that we are rapidly hastening to another."[8] As we will see shortly, Ann did not merely lament the lost benefits to others, but she spurred on her friend with words of exhortation and encouragement to be more fully dedicated to God.

In the midst of many illnesses among the missionaries, death of friends, tumultuous travel, unfriendly populace, hostile governments, leaving their missionary board, and finding themselves all alone in a foreign land, Ann soothed her soul in worship and thanksgiving, finding her way back to trusting God. "Every thing respecting our little mission is involved in uncertainty. I find it hard to live by faith, and confide entirely in God, when the way is dark before me. But if the way were plain and easy, where would be the room for confidence in God? Instead, then, of murmuring and complaining, let me rejoice and be thankful that my heavenly Father compels me to trust in him, by removing those things, on which we are naturally inclined to lean."[9]

Sharing the Journey: Spurring One Another to Love and Good Deeds

Ann and her good friend, Lydia, grew up together, shared the frivolities of their early teen years, went to school together, and eventually devoted themselves to Christ, one of them being persuaded by the other.[10] When Ann was considering the possibility of entering the mission field she wrote to Lydia, reminding her of their initial exuberance for the Lord. Ann implored Lydia to join her in renewed commitment to Him. "Did we not frequently meet to converse about the things of the kingdom, and eagerly inquire, 'how we could most promote the glory of God?'... But where is now that engagedness for God? What have we ever done for him who has so distinguished us? O Lydia, let us weep, let us be deeply affected with our ingratitude in living no more devoted to him. O let us, dear L. now begin, and sacrifice everything that comes in competition with the glory of God, and give our whole selves to him."[11]

Ann fanned into flame the passion that had been there and invited Lydia to do the same. The reminders, the rebukes, the admonitions, and the encouragements were mutual. Repeatedly Ann said, "we" and "let us." She looked for and anticipated the continuation of an iron-sharpening-iron-relationship with Lydia. Ann gave herself fully to this relationship, not holding back her own shortcomings as she saw them. She called for mutual repentance, reminding Lydia of their past conversations and desires.

From her shipboard diary during the first leg of their missionary travels, we learn that Ann, her husband, and their companions were also engaging in mutual accountability to grow in grace. "*April 6.* Spent the evening in conversing on religious subjects, particularly the difficulty of living a holy, spiritual life. We resolved to be more watchful over the sins of our hearts, and make greater efforts to live devoted to God. O may these resolutions not be in vain; for our future usefulness depends essentially on our advancement in the divine life. At present, I feel that I am a weak Christian indeed, and if only sincere, am willing to be considered the very least in the whole church."[12] Isn't it equally true for us today, as counselors, mentors, and disciplers that "our future usefulness depends essentially on our advancement in the divine life?"

Ann had the gift of fanning into flame love and good deeds, not only with individuals, but also among groups of her Christian sisters. During an unexpected visit to the states Ann penned the following as part of an address to females in America. "Favored as we are from infancy with instruction of every kind, used as we are to view the female mind in its proper state, and accustomed as we are to feel the happy effects of female influence, our thoughts would fain turn away from the melancholy subject of female degradation, of female wretchedness. But will our feelings of pity and compassion—will those feelings which alone render the female character lovely, allow us to turn away—to dismiss the subject altogether, without making an effort to rescue—to save?"[13]

Ann included herself in her gentle exhortation to aid the unsaved women. She didn't speak as though she were better than the women she was addressing, but counted herself among them and gently drew them to the reconciling conclusion that they could and must do something to help those unfortunate women who were like themselves in many respects, but who lacked the advantages of the American women.

"No!" she said. "I think I hear your united voices echo the reply: 'Our efforts shall be joined with yours. Show us the situation of our tawny sisters the other side of the world, and though the disgusting picture break our hearts, it will fill us with gratitude to Him who has made us to differ, and excite to stronger exertion in their behalf.' Listen, then, to my tale of woe!"[14] As Ann's biographer observed, she "appeals, with eloquence and force, to the sensibilities of the female heart—to the sympathies and compassion of Christian mothers, wives and daughters."[15]

Purpose of the Journey: Demonstrating God's Love

In a letter to her sisters, Ann relayed a most poignant story about seeing her neighbor beat a female slave with a club. "My blood ran cold within me, and I could quietly see it no longer. I went up to the mistress, and in broken French, asked her to stop, and what her servant had done." Ann took a risk. In a courageous move she asked the mistress to stop beating the slave. She did not berate or threaten the woman. Instead she inquired what the slave had done to evoke such a response. "She immediately stopped, and told me that her servant was very bad, and had lately run away. I talked with her, till her anger appeared to be abated, and she concluded her punishment with flinging the club she had in her hands at the poor creature's head, which made the blood run down on her garment. The slave continued with her hands tied behind her all night."[16] Undoubtedly, Ann would have preferred to see no further harm come to the slave and have her released from shackles. However, given the violent nature of the beating, it seems quite plausible that Ann saved the slave from death.

The story does not end here. The next night Ann "saw a large chain brought into the yard, with a ring at one end, just large enough to go round her neck. On this ring were fixed two pieces of iron about an inch wide, and four inches long, which would come on each side of her face, to prevent her eating. The chain was as large and heavy as an ox chain, and reached from her neck to the ground. The ring was fastened with a lock and key. The poor creature stood trembling while they were preparing to put the chain on her." The scene became even more heinous. "The mistress' rage again kindled at seeing her, and she began beating her again, as the night before." Once more Ann could not stand by. "I went to her again, and begged she would stop. She did, but so full of anger that she could hardly speak. When she had become a little calm, I asked her if she could not forgive her servant. I told her that her servant was very bad, but that she would be very good to forgive her. She made me to understand that she would forgive her, because *I* had asked her; but she would not have her servant to think it was out of any favor to her."[17]

In this instance, as in the night before, Ann took hold of the Proverbs 15:1 principle that a gentle answer turns away wrath. Ann could not have known for certain that she was not in harm's way when approaching someone who was so completely overtaken with rage. Yet, it was her love and concern for others that took precedence over her own safety. Ann cared enough to intervene in a situation when she did not know how she would be received. She related to the mistress on the mistress' terms and presented truth in such a way that the mistress could receive it. Rather than condemn her for her horrid behavior, Ann explained how good the mistress would be to do the right thing and forgive.

Ann continued her narrative. "She told her slave that she forgave her because I requested it. The slave came, knelt and kissed my feet, and said, 'Mercy, madam,—mercy, madam,' meaning, Thank you, madam. I could scarcely forbear weeping at her gratitude. The mistress promised me the chain should not be put on her, and ordered it carried away. I have felt very happy this evening, that this poor slave can lie down and sleep, without that heavy chain."[18]

Although Ann took comfort in knowing the slave would not be harmed any more that evening, her heart grieved for the eternally important matter of the slave's spiritual condition. "But O, my dear sisters, how much more wretched is the spiritual than the temporal state of these slaves. They have none to tell them of their danger, none to lead them to that Saviour, who is equally the friend of the slave and the master."[19]

In a rather lengthy narrative to her brother, Ann described the horror they experienced as war erupted in Burma. Her husband was imprisoned, horribly mistreated, and became quite ill. She suffered through a good deal of extortion; treacherous travel, much of the time with her infant daughter and two Burmese children; and an outbreak of smallpox that was nearly fatal to many in her company, including her baby. Throughout most of that time the Lord had seen fit to spare Ann's health and she was able to care for her husband and the children. But near the end she was overcome with a native illness that was almost always fatal to foreigners.

Concerning that time, Ann noted, "When in health I could bear the various trials and vicissitudes, through which I was called to pass. But to be confined with sickness, and unable to assist those who were so dear to me, when in distress, was almost too much for me to bear; and had it not been for the consolations of religion, and an assured conviction that every additional trial was ordered by infinite love and mercy, I must have sunk under my accumulated sufferings."[20] Ann was much more able to bear her own sufferings than she was to watch others suffer, particularly when she was unable to bring about some relief. But even in those troubling times Ann was able to see life with spiritual eyes, to view life from the lens of the all-loving Father who has a purpose and a plan in all things, including suffering. While it was, no doubt, immensely troubling for her brother to be so far away and to hear of such trials, one can only imagine what an inspiration Ann's faith must have been to him.

Ann's resolve to sacrifice family, friends, and country for the cause of Christ is amazing. The extent of her ability to endure physical, emotional, and spiritual hardships is both inspiring and convicting. Her strength of character and fortitude are uncommon. She dared to do what no American woman had done up to that point and she paved the way for others to do the same, all because she loved her Savior.

Amelia Wilhelmina Sieveking: Instrument of Blessing

Amelia Sieveking (1794-1858) was the fourth of five children and the only girl.[21] By the time she was fifteen, Amelia's mother, a brother, and her father had died. Upon the death of her father the children were separated. Amelia and her governess, Miss Hösch, were placed in the care of an elderly woman, Mademoiselle Dimpfel. Also residing at the house was Dimpfel's ten-year-old niece. Amelia discovered she had a natural ability to manage children when she transformed the spoiled and ill-tempered child into one who was "perfectly respectable and obedient."[22]

Amelia later lived with a Madame Brünnemann, helping her care for her invalid son and another elderly woman.[23] By the time she was eighteen she had begun a small school, teaching six or seven of the neighbor's children.[24] From that point forward Amelia was involved in some capacity of service whether it was the expanding of her free school, living in a cholera hospital assisting doctors with the care of patients, or establishing an association for the care of the sick and poor.[25] This last endeavor was so successful in her own community that similar organizations around the country and even outside of Germany started developing and she was often sought out for her advice.[26]

Character and Content: The Foundation of a Spiritual Friend

Amelia exhibited many qualities that set her apart as an outstanding spiritual friend. She demonstrated repeatedly that God and His Word were her anchor. One incident in particular provides a clear picture of what it meant for Amelia to be centered on the Lord in all things. In the fall of 1831, cholera swept across the country and made its way to Hamburg. Amelia offered her live-in services to a cholera hospital for as long as the outbreak plagued the city. She wrote to her former governess, Minna Hösch, to let her know of her decision. "Like everything out of the common course, this step meets with very differing judgments, and while some certainly think more of it than it really deserves, many blame and some despise it... in such cases, if I once feel clear in my own mind before God, these things cannot make me doubt my decision."[27] Amelia was not swayed on this or other matters when she believed she was in God's will.

It was Amelia's consistent and cherished time with the Lord that gave her confidence in her decisions. While still serving at the hospital, Amelia wrote to her adopted mother. "I spoke yesterday of odd quarters of an hour that I meant to employ in writing to my dear mother, but I was scarcely able to find one available for this purpose. In the odd *minutes* of leisure that I sometimes have, I feel the most pressing need of turning to my God in prayer, otherwise amid all this outward turmoil I might drift away from what is the true anchorage of my life."[28] Amelia knew she was useless to anyone or any purpose without the Lord as her firm foundation. In a discussion concerning charitable work she acknowledged that, "as I learned to know my own heart, I became conscious that, even in the vocation for which I felt myself inspired, I must refrain from working in my own strength, and must give myself up to the guidance of my God."[29]

Amelia teaches us through her own experiences that right motives are the foundation behind right behavior. As a young girl she wanted to relieve the suffering of the poor. She quickly learned that their poverty was not as great in real life as she had expected it to be, but also that what she could do paled in comparison to the needs. "But what grieved me most was, that the objects of my kindness were by no means so grateful as I expected. My acts of charity gave me, indeed, some pleasure, but it was not the true, full happiness that they should afford."[30]

Eventually she did find happiness in acts of charity, but not until she took to heart Matthew 25, and felt "that it is the Lord who meets us in the persons of our poor brethren—and that when we feed the hungry, give drink to the thirsty, clothe the naked, and visit the sick, He will accept it all as done to Himself."[31] After this epiphany Amelia was able to demonstrate genuine care and concern for the poor rather than expecting them to satisfy her desires for gratitude and appreciation.

A diary entry from Amelia's early twenties gives us some insight into her approach to the role of spiritual director, a role she had with the children in her school as well as with the members of her association to help the poor and sick. "But I often long to find myself connected with some one whom I should be compelled to recognize as my superior on all sides, and who could judge me at once strictly and truthfully. I feel painfully that my aunt's endless indulgence, her undeservedly high opinion of me, exercise an injurious influence on my moral character. How shall I preserve the precious jewel of humility?"[32] What a profoundly teachable spirit we find in young Amelia.

Letters to her brother, Gustavus, and to her former governess, Minna, illustrate the value she placed on honesty in communication among spiritual friends. Gustavus sent Amelia a sermon he had written and asked for her opinion. Regarding a difference in their faith she said to her dear brother, "At first, I own, I shrank from voluntarily pointing out this difference, through a fear that it would lessen your good opinion of me. But then I reflected that so close and dear a relation as that between us two must be founded, if it is to be stable and permanent, on perfect truth and the unrestrained interchange of thought. And so here, too, I will explain myself frankly and openly."[33] While Amelia valued honesty, she also demonstrated that grace and humility make excellent accouterments to truth-telling.

Not only was Amelia able to give honest feedback, she was able and willing to receive it. She sent Minna a copy of a work that was soon to be published and it seems that Minna had expressed some differences of opinion. Amelia responded, "With regard to your remarks on my book, they are not unexpected to me, and I am very glad to find that you know me well enough to be sure that your outspokenness would not displease me."[34]

Amelia subscribed to the philosophy of leading by example. In describing the characteristics of a woman who effectively leads others in the aid to the sick and the poor she explained, "If she would excite those round her to greater activity, she must herself do more than she expects from them."[35] While Amelia was speaking specifically of how the president of a Christian society should conduct herself with her members, the principles hold true in any relationship in which we have responsibility to, and oversight of, others.

Competence and Community: The Dance of Soul Care and Spiritual Direction

As a masterful spiritual friend, Amelia adeptly moved in and out of sustaining, healing, reconciling, and guiding, adjusting her approach according to the needs of the individual and the circumstances. Amelia was one of those delightful souls who is able to establish community and connection among people from all walks of life. Whether interacting with the poor and the sick or the Queen of Denmark who had become a friend, she treated all with respect and in return received respect.

Regarding the association to help the poor and the sick, Amelia explained that "the main object of the Society can only be attained by personal intercourse with the poor at their own houses."[36] She believed that the best way to help people is to develop a connection with them and one of the best ways to do that is by caring enough literally to enter their world. Go to them instead of expecting them to come to you. "Unless we take into consideration a man's outward circumstances and conduct, we can hardly learn to estimate rightly his spiritual condition and spiritual needs, and without this knowledge we shall fall into great errors."[37]

Today we would say that this is one way to begin evaluating level one suffering. It might include illness, unemployment, living conditions, change in marital status, and more. Amelia understood that we do our friends a disservice to assume we understand them without first considering the situation in which they find themselves.

Amelia shared with the members of the society, called "visitors," that more was needed. The visitor should "lend an attentive ear to their communications." She acknowledged the challenges that can arise and prepared them for what might lie ahead. "It cannot be denied that these communications have often a wearisome prolixity, and this is particularly the case with the old and sick, when they are describing their sufferings. But is it not a relief to them to be able sometimes to pour out their complaints to a human ear? And should we not gladly afford them this trifling solace?"[38] Her climbing in the casket allowed her friend to unburden her heart and soul to a sympathetic ear. If that were all she did, then the visitor and the object of her visit would both drown in a sea of despair. Amelia directed them to set limits on such complaints. ".... only too many of our sick poor are so filled with the thoughts of their bodily condition, that if one let them go on, they would talk of nothing else. This should not be; and the more danger the sufferer is in of being crushed to the dust by the weight of his griefs, the more the visitor should exert herself to direct his thoughts to that which alone can help him, which can raise him on the wings of faith, above the sad regions of earth, to the brightness of heaven."[39] What a beautiful picture of the healing process. She directed the visitors to draw a line in the sand of defeat and to redirect the grieving person's attention to the great source of ever-present help.

Amelia knew how to speak the truth in love. It is evident that she had an agape love for the sick and the poor and yet she did not sugarcoat the realities of dealing with them. She understood the need for sustaining, but also understood that while climbing in the casket is an essential aspect of helping people, she couldn't leave them there. She consistently sought to understand the temporal and very real circumstances of people while, at the same time, maintaining a view of the eternal. She felt it her job as a spiritual friend to help redirect the gaze of the sufferer to the beauty of *The* Spiritual Friend.

Amelia also knew how to interweave the principles of reconciling and guiding into her relationships. "Works of love, done in the spirit of faith... must ever be the principal means by which a Christian visitor can win the poor to godliness; but direct religious exhortation, when prudently used, may also be a means of great good.... If we ever use sharpness in rebuke, it is where we find them trying to make a gain of godliness, and imagining to win favour with us by making a talk about religion, without troubling themselves with the reality...."[40] While the Society sought to aid the poor and the sick, Amelia would not allow it to get away with making a mockery of the faith which she held so dear. While they must confront this, she cautioned that it be done wisely.

She also noted that reconciling is not always easy. "I well know that such reprehension is one of the hardest duties of our vocation, but it must not on that account be omitted. If ever, indeed, we need wisdom from above, it is here. This wisdom only can teach us to give to our words due impressiveness, and where it must be so, due severity, without creating bitterness.... "[41]

It is interesting to observe that while Amelia talked to the visitors about reconciling the poor and the sick, she was actually offering the visitors spiritual direction through guiding. She helped them understand how they would grow in spiritual maturity as they worked with the poor and she directed them back to the source of all wisdom on which they should rely.

She explained that the wisdom from above is especially helpful during the reconciling process because it "...can keep alive in us that love and humility, which, even when we are wounding the self-love of the poor, will convince them of our real good intentions...."[42] Her desire was to "show them that we do not assume the office of a judge to condemn them, but rather that of a faithful friend, to counsel and exhort them."[43]

Listening to the Silenced Voices

When we listen to the silenced voices of women like Ann Judson and Amelia Sieveking we hear the message of powerful impact. Both these women dared to break the prescribed mold for their gender and as a result each opened doors of opportunity for women while at the same time opening the gospel to people the world wanted to ignore. For Ann it meant sacrificing all that was familiar so she could lovingly bring spiritual relief to a group of people who were very far from God.

For Amelia it meant sacrificing the norm of the day and forgoing marriage so she could bring spiritual relief to a group whose physical needs were often so great they did not take time to consider God.

One crossed an ocean and settled in a far away continent. The other lived and died in the same community to which she was born. One married. One remained single. Together they remind us of the impact women have when empowered by the Holy Spirit as they bring "heaven down to earth, making a paradise within the heart, if it cannot always succeed in doing so in the outward world."[44]

Learning Together from Our Great Cloud of Witnesses

1. Ann sacrificed everything that was familiar to her in order to demonstrate God's love to a lost people group.
   a. What have you sacrificed to fulfill God's calling in your life?
   b. In coming days, what might God be calling you to sacrifice?

2. Even in the most treacherous and difficult of circumstances Ann was able to trust God and His goodness for the outcome, whatever that might be.
   a. How are you able to do the same?
   b. In what ways are you able to impart trust in the Lord to others?

3. Ann put the will of God and the needs of others above her own comfort or desires. In what ways are you able to do the same?

4. Ann and Amelia were both devoted to knowing the Lord more intimately through prayer, Bible reading, worship, thanksgiving, and other spiritual reading. How are you deepening your relationship with the Lord so that you can be the best possible spiritual friend?

5. The Lord gave Ann a passion for missions when she was barely twenty years old. He put a burning compassion for the poor in Amelia's heart as a young girl.
   a. What passions stir within your soul?
   b. What might God be leading you to do with those passions?

6. We find in Amelia a particularly teachable spirit. She wants to be corrected and set upon the narrow path.
   a. On a scale of 1-10, how teachable would you rate yourself?
   b. What are some practical ways in which you can increase your teachability?

7. Amelia could be trusted to speak the truth even when it might be hard to say or hard for someone to hear, and she did it lovingly.

Would your friends, loved ones, co-workers, or employees say the same of you? Why or why not?

8. Amelia thought that reconciling was one of the more difficult aspects of spiritual direction. Would you agree? Why or why not?

9. Reread the quote from Amelia's letter to the Queen of Prussia. What do think of her belief that all women share one mission in common?

CHAPTER FOURTEEN

DISPENSING SOLID FOOD: THE QUIET
LIVES OF FAITHFUL NURTURERS

"You are coming to that decisive time when you will make of your life one of two things: either, as many people do, something purposeless and vague, without any strong moral discipline, useless and consequently harmful; or something beautiful, harmonious, and purposeful, sowing good seed on the earth and preparing a rich harvest for eternity" (Elisabeth Leseur).[1]

"...having devoted yourself to the Lord, you cannot choose your friends and associates without His permission. In all your social intercourse now, you have two objects in view: viz., to do good, or to get good" (Sarah Jackson).[2]

Over the millennia the majority of Christians have lived out their lives quietly and anonymously. This is no less true of the last two hundred years of Christianity. The quietness in which these believers lived, however, does not speak to their impact. A great deal of soul care and spiritual direction has occurred during the last two centuries, one person at a time, under the loving and truthful guidance of our less conspicuous sisters who have preceded us. These gracious women journeyed through life the only way they knew how, in total dependence on and adoration of the Lord. They embraced the opportunities the Lord provided them and walked alongside the spiritually younger men and women He put in their paths.

Catharine Brown: Seeing Life through Spiritual Eyes

Catharine Brown (c. 1800-1823) was born around 1800 between Raccoon and Lookout Mountains in what is now Alabama.[3] Her parents, Yau-nu-gung-yah-ski and Tsa-luh, were known to the white man as John and Sarah Brown. Both of Catharine's grandmothers were "full blooded" Cherokee. Although at least one of her grandfathers was white, both of her parents were raised among the Cherokee people in the Cherokee tradition as was Catharine.[4] When Catharine was seventeen or eighteen she became aware of the Brainard Missionary School located approximately one hundred miles from her home. The desire to attend the school welled within her and she begged her parents for permission to go. They agreed and on July 9, 1817, Catharine began her formal education.[5] It seems that Catharine was quite prolific in the writing of diaries and letters; however, all that remains is a small book written about her by Rufus Anderson who was at the time the Assistant Secretary of the American Board of Commissioners for Foreign Missions. Fortunately, Anderson had access not only to Catharine's material, but also to many individuals who knew Catharine and were more than willing to give an account of her and the impact she had on so many in such a short time.

A Reconciling Passion for Her People: Turning Souls from Darkness to Marvelous Light

Six months after entering Brainerd, Catharine "indulged a hope, that she had been pardoned and accepted, through the Lord Jesus Christ."[6] From that point forward she devoted herself to the Lord and to the things of life that concerned Him, not the least of which was the salvation of her people. Catharine had an Apostle Paul-like quality in her fervent desire for all to come to saving faith in Christ, but she especially longed for her fellow Cherokees to have life eternal with Christ. Reverend William Chamberlain tells us that "…her desires for the salvation of her people, were strong and ardent. She wept and prayed for them, in secret places, as well as in the company of her female friends at their weekly prayer-meetings."[7]

Catharine also had a natural and particular concern for her immediate family. One morning she went to the woods to have her devotions. She began to pray for her brother, David, and as she did "…she became so deeply engaged in prayer for this dear brother, that the time passed insensibly, and she remained in her sacred retreat till the sun was near setting."[8]

In a letter written from Brainerd on July 5, 1819, to Mr. and Mrs. Williams, Catharine wrote, "I hope you will pray for them, and also for me, that I may be useful to my dear people. My heart bleeds for their immortal souls. O that I might be made the means of turning many souls from darkness unto marvellous (sic) light."[9] The "them" to whom she referred were her parents whom she loved immensely.

Catharine didn't stop at praying for her family. She actively engaged them in spiritual conversations and her actions were motivated by what was best for others rather than by her own personal desires. In a letter from Mrs. Potter, a missionary who stayed with the Browns for a short time and who then housed Catharine for some time, we learn something of Catharine's character, particularly as it relates to her family and their spiritual wellness. "For sweetness of temper, meekness, gentleness, and forbearance, I never saw one, who surpassed her. To her parents she was uncommonly dutiful and affectionate. Nothing, which could contribute to their happiness, was considered a burden; and her plans were readily yielded to theirs, however great the sacrifice to her feelings. The spiritual interests of the family lay near her heart, and she sometimes spent whole evenings in conversation with them on religious subjects."[10]

Whether Catharine lived to see any of her family other than her brother, David, converted is unclear. However, we do know that both her parents and another brother, John, became Christians, no doubt due, in part, to her influence and prayers.

Walking in Meekness: Showing True Humility to All

Perhaps it was Catharine's humility that drew others to her and allowed her to enter into their lives with such impact. According to Mrs. Potter, humility "was the most conspicuous trait in her character.... She received many letters, some of which were highly complimentary; but so far from fostering pride, they always seemed to increase her humility. Once, having received a letter full of expressions of the strongest admiration of her character, she was gently cautioned against being lifted up with vanity. The tears started into her eyes, and she replied, 'I do not wish to be proud.'"[11]

Catharine spent several months with the family of Dr. Alexander A. Campbell, "a pious and esteemed physician," who wrote of Catharine, "She received very marked attentions from the visitors at my house, and many of the principal families in the town sought an acquaintance with her, appeared sensible of her worth, and esteemed her friendship highly. These attentions, so far from exciting her vanity, had the effect to humble her the more. She appeared ever to think much less highly of herself, than others thought of her. I have often been astonished to see how the flattering address and high encomiums of people of elevated standing in society, seemed to render her more distrustful of her own worth."[12]

Catharine took to heart the Lord's exhortation to clothe herself in humility (1 Peter 5:5) despite her apparent fame and popularity, and followed the Lord's example as one who was gentle and humble in heart (Matthew 11:29). The value and necessity of humility in any believer, especially in one who provides soul care and spiritual direction, cannot be missed or overlooked. Catharine modeled for us that an effective spiritual friend will, in humility, put others above self (Philippians 2:3).

The Dance of Spiritual Friendship: Living in the Rhythm of Unity

Spiritual friendships are a lot like dance. Each goes at its own pace and tempo. Each has its own music and style. Even within a single friendship, the tempo changes, the rhythm varies, and the style fluctuates. But, in the deepest and most meaningful Christ-centered relationships, hearts are knit together and the dance partners take their cue from the Master. Such is what we see as we glimpse into some of Catharine's more intimate relationships with her sisters in Christ.

In a letter to an unnamed spiritual friend Catharine wrote:

> Dear Sister in Christ,
> I thank you much for your affectionate letter. ...O my sister let us rejoice continually in our Lord and Saviour, and as we have put on Christ, not only by outward profession, but by inward and spiritual union, let us walk worthy of our high and holy

vocation, and shew the world, that there is something in true religion. And may the Lord give us strength to do his will, and to follow continually the example of our meek and lowly Jesus. I thank you for the present you sent me, which I received as a token of love. …O that I were more engaged for God, to promote his cause, among these dear children, and my people. I am going soon to visit my parents, which is an hundred miles from here, and expect to stay two months. I hope you will pray for me, that the Lord would bless my visit, and renew the hearts of my dear parents. Your sincere friend and sister in Christ.[13]

One gets the sense from Catharine's letter that the affection between her and her friend was both deep and mutual. Catharine's love for this woman, her people, her family, and most of all her Lord, flows throughout this short letter. She offered encouragement to her friend and shared her sincere feelings with her sister and asked earnestly for prayer. At the center of this friendship and sisterhood was Christ who knits unlikely hearts together.

In another letter to her dear friend Mrs. Isabella Hall, we find an even greater depth of sisterhood and fervor for the Lord. She began her letter with "My dear Sister" and continued with deep affection and encouragement. "It is with pleasure I take time this morning to assure you, that my love for you is still as great as ever. You cannot tell how painful it was to me to hear that you had been sick. But we know, that the Lord is good, and that all things will work together for good to those who love him, and put their whole trust in him. O could we see each other, how would we talk, and weep, and sing, and pray together."[14]

In the same letter, Catharine made a remarkable assessment of their separation. "But our Heavenly Father has separated us. Perhaps we loved each other more than we loved him, and did not pray to him, and praise him, and thank him, as we ought to have done. And is it not so, dear sister? Did we not neglect our duty, and grow cold and careless, when we were together? Now we are sorry, and the Lord will forgive us."[15] Catharine's brokenness emerged as she recognized and confessed that they cared more for their friendship than the Lord. She proceeded then to instill hope and offer encouragement, both essential characteristics of healing. "Still, dear sister, we can pray for each other. Think you not that our prayers often meet at the throne of grace? O then let us pray on, and never cease to pray for each other, while he lends us breath; and when we meet in heaven, we shall see him whom our soul loveth...."[16]

She concluded by spurring herself and her friend on to love and good deeds. "And now, my dear sister, may we both be faithful to our Lord, and do much in the world. And when time with us shall be no more, may we be permitted to meet in that world, where Christians will be collected to sing through eternity the song of Moses and the Lamb. From your sister"[17] What a beautiful picture of unity in Christ. Passion, honesty, unrelenting love for Christ, and ardent affection for one another radiate from this short missive. Catharine did not waste time or words as she offered her friend encouragement to press on, and reminders of God's goodness and plans even in the midst of trial. Clearly, her eyes were fixed on Jesus.

A Life Well Lived: The Final Goodbye

Catharine became gravely ill at the young age of twenty-three, only six short years after her conversion. That Catharine touched many lives with her humble love for God and people is apparent by the outpouring of love from those who rightly expected never to see her again. The number of people who came out to glimpse and touch their beloved friend one last time is evidence of a life well-lived. Again we hear from Mrs. Potter as she told us that many gathered to see their "beloved friend" one last time. "Old and young were bathed in tears, and some were obliged to use their influence to prevent a general and loud lamentation. Catharine alone was calm, while she bade farewell to those she tenderly loved."[18]

Mrs. Leech continued the narrative. "...small groups of her acquaintance were frequently seen on the road, waiting her approach. When she arrived where they were, they would hasten to the side of the litter, take her by the hand, and often walk away without speaking a word, the tears all the while rolling down their cheeks."[19]

Catharine was transported to Dr. Campbell's home where there were momentary hopes of her partial recovery. During this time she dictated one last letter to her brother, David. She reminded him how much she loved him and told him that he "must not be grieved" when he hears of her illness. "You must remember, that this world is not our home...."[20] A few weeks later, with family and friends by her side, Catharine departed from this world.[21] Catharine, as all powerful soul friends, lived her life so heavenly minded, that she was of great earthly good.

Sarah Jackson: Walking with the Young in Faith

Apart from her character, we know very little about Sarah Jackson (c. 1800-?). Apparently a seasoned and devoted follower of Christ, she wrote a series of letters to a young woman named Eugenia. These letters, regarding Eugenia's new-found faith, were originally published in the *Advocate* and *Guardian*, presumably local newspapers, perhaps in New York. They were later published in book form in 1852 by the American Female Guardian Society. Seemingly they were well received and in 1858 a fourth edition was published by the same organization.[22]

Far more important than what we don't know is what we do know. Sarah loved the Lord and desired to impart that love and how to cultivate it to her dear young friend and sister in the faith, Eugenia. Her letters abound with exemplary soul care and spiritual direction as she engaged Eugenia in the discussion of vital truths that would serve her well through the years.

Preparing for the Journey: Normalizing Setbacks and Practicing the Spiritual Disciplines

Without a doubt the most important concept Sarah shared with young Eugenia is that, "In the first place, you want to be a *Bible Christian*. Now do not look among the members of the church in order to find out what that is; go straight to the Bible."[23] In her first guiding principle, Sarah pointed Eugenia directly to the source of all wisdom and all truth, the Bible. She immediately took the focus off herself, off the world, and off all others to whom Eugenia might look as the final authority on living the Christian life.

Sarah knew it can be easy for a mentee to become attached to or dependent on a mentor or to look to older and seemingly wiser individuals within the church rather than doing the hard work of digging into Scripture for herself. Sarah thus reminded Eugenia at the onset that God's Word should be her guide above all else. With that foundation laid, she launched into specific instructions regarding Eugenia's walk with the Lord.

Sarah knew that as Eugenia began to search the Scriptures for herself she would realize, if she were honest, that she fell so very short of reflecting the image of Christ. Sarah also understood that Eugenia would need to acknowledge the truth and handle it appropriately, if she were to grow spiritually. "Now my two words of counsel are, *first*, Don't be unwilling to see the worst of yourself; *second*, Don't be discouraged at the sight."[24] Sarah knew that self examination, while necessary, can be most unpleasant. She knew that the temptation for discouragement waits patiently, looking for entry into the hearts and minds of believers. But Sarah prepared Eugenia for the likelihood that discouragement would raise its ugly head and she warned Eugenia not to become caught in its trap.

Fortunately, Sarah didn't leave her friend only with an admonition. She guided Eugenia through the process toward a practical biblical solution. "As soon as you discover any infirmity, defect, bad habit, any form of selfishness, or anything that hinders you in the Divine life, carry it at once to the Lord Jesus Christ, and ask Him to take it away. Remember that he has offered to 'supply all your need,' 'purge away all your dross,' and 'sanctify you wholly.' If you are honest, he is faithful, and all will be well."[25] While Sarah did not quote chapter and verse, it is evident that her guidance came straight from God's Word. She continued, "Never for one moment give way to *discouragement....* The best thing you can do, is, to be all the time trying to strengthen your faith. To this end, make the PROMISES your *study*. Have them all in your memory and in your heart. Keep them bright by constant use. Dwell much on the assurances of God's love, with which the Scriptures abound. Endeavor to get a full, deep persuasion of His love to you, and let your heart triumph in the wonderful fact....Dwell on these things, and then read those sweet words, '*I have loved thee with an everlasting love.*"[26] Sarah entreated Eugenia to strengthen her faith continuously and explained how to go about it. Today we would say that Sarah was teaching Eugenia about spiritual formation by employing the spiritual disciplines of Scripture memorization, meditation, prayer, confession, Bible reading, self examination, and Bible study.

To keep Eugenia from believing that Sarah's instruction was only for newer believers, Sarah offered comforting self-disclosure. "I dwell on this subject the more, because I find in my own experience there is nothing like being fully persuaded that God loves me. Realizing this, I can not help loving Him, and thus all duties are made easy, and all trials light."[27]

Active Listening: The Power of Silence

Sarah understood that communication of the best kind requires silence, and sometimes a fair amount of it. "People generally seem to think that when together they must talk all the time. Whenever a pause occurs in the conversation, they hasten to fill it up with something—no matter what. In this way a great deal is said that had much better have been left unsaid. Now, it appears to me that occasional pauses, even of considerable length, so far from being unpleasant or unsuitable, may be very serviceable...."[28] What a valuable lesson Sarah imparted to young Eugenia. Listen to conversations around you and no doubt you will find this phenomenon at work, often to the point of people talking over top of one another.

Sarah explained that silence affords "time to commune with God, and listen to the Inward Voice. If we would have the Lord direct the conversation, we should give Him time to speak, or rather give ourselves time to hear. I do not think the time is lost when there is a pause in a conference meeting, or in a social interview—certainly not among spiritual persons. It would be well for those who so eagerly fill up every gap in the conversation with whatever comes to hand, to inquire whether a few moments of 'inward recollection' might not be more profitable."[29] This is a good picture of a trialogue where Sarah's conversation not only included the people in the room, but also wisely invited the Lord to participate.

In this instruction and throughout her letters, it is evident that Sarah took to heart the grand tradition of the Titus 2 principle that exhorts older women to instruct younger women. Her letters overflow with tender and affectionate soul care and spiritual direction for Eugenia. Sarah overwhelming demonstrated her abiding love first and foremost for her Lord. This love for her Savior spilled over to Eugenia, and no doubt to others, for as she said, "One who loves God will love his fellowmen...."[30] Her command of Scripture was remarkable and a significant reminder to all of the value of reading, studying, memorizing and applying the Word of God. Indeed, Sarah saw it as essential to a vibrant relationship with the Lord and a fruitful life, lived for Him.

Elisabeth Leseur

Were it not for Elisabeth Leseur's (1866-1914) husband, Felix Leseur, the world would likely know nothing about her. Although she was in the thick of Parisian high society, a woman living in the world, and "fulfilling superbly the obligations of her state," she lived her life most unassumingly, all the while gently, but profoundly, impacting those whose hearts she touched with her devoted love for God and her unpretentious humility and love for others.[31]

She was well-read, fluent in at least three languages, and an ardent traveler. At the age of twenty-three she married Felix. The couple was childless, but Elisabeth maintained active involvement with her extended family, including her niece and nephews. She adeptly and frequently engaged people from all walks of life, believers and unbelievers alike. During her lifetime she suffered extensively through many familial deaths, her own illnesses, and Felix's unbelief and sometimes very antagonistic attitude toward Elisabeth's faith.[32] After her death in 1914, at the age of forty-eight, Felix discovered her diary and later was persuaded to publish it for the benefit of others.[33]

Cultivating Tender Respect for Others: Witnessing to an Unbelieving World

Those who are learning the art of soul care and spiritual direction commonly ask, "How do these biblical principles work with unbelievers?" A look into Elisabeth's life offers valuable answers.

Elisabeth believed that demonstrating respect for people was an important part of building meaningful relationships. This belief spilled into all her relationships, many of which were with unbelievers. "I must simply and strongly profess a faith that God has gradually created in me. But I must do this in a way that never harms or offends conviction or its absence in others."[34] After her death, a dear unbelieving friend shared with Felix that "Elisabeth had in recent years a profound influence on me and my ideas; and this was unknown to herself, for she never attempted to convert me or even to approach the question of religion. But what I saw of her was so beautiful!"[35] Elisabeth found the middle ground that allowed her to stand uncompromisingly strong in her faith while at the same time graciously allowing others to have their beliefs and ideas. It had an impact.

Historically, guiding has included drawing out strengths and envisioning power. Elisabeth was able to apply the basics of this principle to unbelievers by encouraging them to see beyond their current circumstances. Jeanne Alcan was a close social friend and a non-practicing Jew who suffered from depression.[36] In a letter to Jeanne, Elisabeth told her, "I am convinced little by little that your nature will overcome the suffering and the lethargy and that you will recover all your optimism and your liveliness."[37] Elisabeth reminded Jeanne that her nature was not one to succumb to affliction and indolence, but rather one that embraced hope.

Elisabeth then moved to what we might call counselor self-disclosure. "I have had to struggle a great deal against physical and moral depression. Right now, that is over. I have regained my self-possession, through repeated efforts, which have led me little by little to deep interior peace. Now, it seems to me that I leave this difficulty the better for it, understanding all suffering even more, and loving more deeply my family and my dear friends, of whom you are one."[38] Her self-disclosure was purposeful. There is hope. I have survived the struggle. You can, too.

Another way Elisabeth related and ministered to unbelievers was to find a tie that binds hearts together. She did this beautifully with her friend Aimee Fievet. Aimee was an intellectual unbeliever. The letters between them dialogue about Aimee's health and about their very different interpretations of reality.[39] Elisabeth drew on her own experiences to empathize with Aimee. "You are somewhat isolated and, of course, depressed; I, too, have been burdened these last months with sadness and concerns. Perhaps in connecting our trials a little, we will be able to strengthen one another in them."[40]

Longing for Spiritual Companionship: Inside the Heart of a Soul Physician

Elisabeth loved the Lord and lived to serve Him. In order for her to pour into the lives of people seeking guidance and comfort, she needed spiritual refreshment. Her primary source of this refreshment is the Lord, but she also seeks deep, meaningful, and refreshing communion with like-minded companions. For a good deal of her life, Elisabeth does not have such a companion, but her soul longs deeply for one.

> I love interior solitude with God alone; it strengthens me, and gives me light and energy again. But sometimes isolation, which is different from solitude, wears me down. I long for spiritual companionship, to bare my soul to those who are dear to me, to speak of God and immortality and the interior life and charity. But the human soul is so delicate that it must feel the same notes resonating in another of those divine instruments before it can make its own sound. The perfect union of two souls—what beautiful music that would make! With him I love best in the world, let me one day make this music, O my God![41]

God mercifully provided such a friend for Elisabeth. Sister Marie Goby was a Hospitaller sister in Beaune. The two met through a young patient of Marie's and they developed a deep and mutual spiritual friendship that continued until Elisabeth's death.[42] The depth of their affection is apparent. "These are very intimate matters that I share with you, my sister and friend; there is not another person with whom I would share them. God has placed you in my path, perhaps because he saw that in spite of his loving caresses, I still remained in spiritual isolation, and he wanted to give me the sweet consolation of a completely spiritual friendship. May God be blessed for that!"[43] Elisabeth also remembered that all good gifts are from above and she readily praised God for their friendship.

In another letter to Marie, Elisabeth reminded us that distance does not mean the demise of a spiritual friendship. "We're never really separated, since we live and work for the same beloved Master and are one with him in front of the tabernacle or at other times of prayer. And yet I experience such a deep calm, truly a consolation when I'm able to open my heart to you, fully one with you in spirit. Although we're not near one another, it is so good to know I'm united with a true spiritual sister who prays for me, and that in God there is no distance, since all hearts meet together in the heart of Jesus."[44] Sacred friendships meet at the place where two hearts beat in harmony with the love of Christ.

Listening to the Silenced Voices

When we listen to the silenced voices of women like Catharine Brown, Sarah Jackson, and Elisabeth Leseur, we hear the message of passion. In all things they sought the face of God. They not only turned their attention to their Savior, they pointed others to Him as well, not seeking glory or attention for themselves.

We also hear from their voices the message of humility. While we don't know the circumstances involving the publication of Sarah's letters, we do know that were it not for others seeing the benefit of making known the letters and diaries of Catharine and Elisabeth, we would never be aware of these women today. At the time they were ministering to others, their relationships were deeply personal and private. Felix Leseur, for instance, had been completely unaware of his wife's many spiritual friendships and the profound impact she had on others until after her death.[45]

We also very clearly hear by listening to their silenced voices that God's Word is relevant for all time, all people, everywhere. Whether we live in the Alabama wilderness or Parisian high society, are single or married, young or old, well-educated or not, Christ changes lives with His changeless truth. And the art of soul care and spiritual direction always plays a vital role in loving Christian community. These three godly women paint for us a beautiful picture of Christ's command to love the Lord with all your heart, soul, strength, and mind, and to love others as yourself.

Learning Together from Our Great Cloud of Witnesses

1. Catharine demonstrated remarkable dedication and sacrifice for the hope of the salvation of those dear to her. What can you learn about sacrificing your time or turning your attention to such great depths of concern for the unsaved?

2. Catharine assessed her relationships in light of their impact on her relationship with the Lord. What can you learn from her example?

3. Sarah invested in the spiritual development of Eugenia. In whom are you investing? How?

4. Take a moment to evaluate your conversations.
   a. Do you take advantage of silence or are you quick to speak when there is a pause?
   b. Why do you suppose so many sacred friends have a dislike for silence?

5. Elisabeth had a deep yearning for intimate spiritual companionship. Do you have a Sister Marie in your life?
   a. If so, who? In what ways are your hearts knit together?
   b. If not, is that something you desire? How do you soothe your soul during times of isolation?

6. What practical lessons will you take away from Catharine, Sarah, and Elisabeth?

7. What are your favorite quotes from these women and why?

CHAPTER FIFTEEN

ANGELS IN THE FIRESTORM:
DISPENSERS OF GRACE AND TRUTH

> "If all of us do our part faithfully, God is faithful to fulfill His promises, and will send us the help we need at this time" (Pandita Ramabai).[1]
>
> "Many times I thought I could never overcome this pain; but the Lord gave me strength to go on" (Sabina Wurbrand, co-founder of the Voice of the Martyrs).[2]

*I*n the world's darkest hours, the Lord brings forth a flicker of light. And though the light may originate from an unlikely source and at first glance may seem insignificant, it begins to chase away the darkness one small shadow at a time. Like a line of candles being lit one from the other, the light leaves a noticeable trail. Laura Haviland and Betsie ten Boom are two such lights who shone brightly during terribly dark days.

Laura said no to slavery in America, sacrificing her time and money and risking her life, in order to help slaves experience the freedom that belongs to all men, women, and children. She comforted the frightened, gave hope to the dying, and stood her ground against those who supported slavery. She was particularly spirited with men and women who claimed to be Christians but at the same time found no fault with slavery and its attending abuses.

Betsie ten Boom refused to succumb to hatred while being held in Nazi prison camps for aiding Jews in their escape from the Nazi regime. When others, including her sister, Corrie, saw the prison guards as heinous monsters, Betsie saw hurting human beings who could be taught to love. She brought peace and consideration for others to the teeming barracks in which she lived her last months and where she led many to the threshold of God's Kingdom.

Laura Smith Haviland: Changing Hearts and Minds

Laura Haviland (1808-1898) spent the first seven years of her life in Canada. Her parents moved the family to New York where, ten years later, Laura met and married her husband Charles Haviland. Not long after they married Laura and Charles moved to the Michigan Territory, joining her family who had settled there earlier. Although they had been active members of the Quaker church for many years, the Haviland and Smith families became disillusioned with the Quakers' inactivity against slavery. They left the Quaker church and became Wesleyan Methodists. Shortly after that they opened a school for indigent children and by 1837 the family opened the Raisin Institute, a school that accepted "colored" children.[3]

Laura was no stranger to death and sorrow. A terrible disease hit their small town of Raisin and within six weeks Laura lost her husband, both parents, her sister, and her youngest child to the outbreak.[4] Laura was also extremely ill during that time, but the Lord was not finished with her and spared her life. Hardship quickly followed sorrow as she was left with seven children to care for in an era when women were not believed to be capable of managing their own affairs. Despite her personal troubles she soon became a significant part of the Underground Railroad.

Softening Hearts: Standing Firmly on God's Word

In the years leading up to the Civil War, the subject of slavery evoked strong opinions and dangerous tempers. However, that didn't keep the petite mother of eight from graciously, yet firmly, speaking out against the appalling institution.

In a conversation, an amiable pro-slavery acquaintance told Laura that he would most certainly turn in runaway slaves in order to obtain the reward money. To this Laura replied, "I am astonished to hear this from one who professes to be a follower of the Lord Jesus, a part of whose mission was to unbind the heavy burdens and let the oppressed go free. It is pain to me to hear you advance the sentiments you do in the presence of your children; and a class-leader in the Methodist Protestant Church. I can not henceforward acknowledge you as a brother in Christ." The man responded that she was the "most uncharitable person" he had ever met and proceeded to inform her that her remark had hurt his feelings more than anything she had said in "presenting (her) radical position."[5]

Laura still did not yield. "I do hope and pray that the enlightening influences of the Holy Spirit may lead to a far different view from your present one. I am grieved to hear this from one who is looked upon as a leader to the Lamb of God, who shed his blood for the whole universe of man, regardless of color or nation."[6] He then invited her back to his house later that evening because he wanted to address several additional arguments from Scripture to support his view.

Laura agreed to his request but said that she would be in prayer about it throughout the day and asked the same of him to which he agreed. At the appointed time, Laura arrived at the man's home, but nothing was spoken of the intended subject for the first hour, at which time Laura inquired about the scriptural arguments he wanted to discuss with her. "He replied that he had thought of but little else during the whole day; but on the whole doubted whether his reasons would stand the test, and declined saying any thing farther in defense of the position he had advanced. A few weeks later he died of cholera. I called on his widow, who said he died a happy soul, and he often spoke of his confidence in me as an honest-hearted Christian, and she never heard him speak disparagingly of the colored people after the long conversation we had on that subject."[7]

Turning Enemies into Friends: Truth-telling with Respect

It may be easier to speak hard truth to people we know, than to people we don't, but Laura did not let that deter her. While she was teaching in a school for black children in Ohio, a group of Irish men and women regularly pronounced systematic curses on Laura for her connection with the black students. Laura looked for an opportunity to speak with them; however, they were frequently drunk so she waited patiently for the right moment. Eventually, she found her opportunity and respectfully approached a small group of women. "I have long desired to talk with you, as I am confident you do not understand me in teaching this colored school. I have felt it my duty to aid the most neglected class of people." She talked to them about prejudices and reminded them that some were prejudiced against the Irish. "People are too apt to despise other nations and classes of men. All this is wrong; God made us all as it pleased him, and it is not for us to find fault with our Heavenly Father, who loves all the human family alike. As we acknowledge the fatherhood of God, we should also acknowledge the brotherhood of man in all nations and classes."[8]

One of the men said to another, "In faith, Pat, that's good doctrine." "Yes, indade, that's the doctrine Father Mathew prached, ye know." "Jamie, that's all right," said another. As the conversation ensued various members of the group asked Laura questions regarding rumors they had heard about her. Laura patiently answered them, quickly dispelling the many untruths. The group was so won over by Laura that they dared to tell her that some of their company had planned to burn down the school house and give her "a dressin' of tar an' fithers" but the "praste forbid it." Remarkably the primary instigator came to his door and said to Laura, "Indade, missus, we didn't know ye; an' now we'll fight for ye, an' we are sorry we didn't know ye for so long."[9]

She concluded the story. "When I left them I shook hands with them all, for by the time our conversation closed about all their little community had convened, and I took occasion to speak highly of Father Mathew, the great temperance reformer of Ireland; and my little congregation pronounced as strong blessings upon me as they had curses. Even my systematic curser was among my best friends after that, and my scholars, as well as myself, were treated with the utmost respect ever after...."[10]

Nourishing the Soul with Comfort: Compassion for the Hurting

Laura just as easily comforted the brokenhearted and despairing soul as she confronted the obstinate one. Speaking of a slave who was frantic over the impending sale of one of her children, Laura said she "...looked upon that poor, crushed spirit, the most frantic with grief of any person I ever saw…." She reminded the woman that she had the freedom to approach a loving God. "Now go to Jesus; he will do great things for you. You lose confidence in your friends, you lose confidence in yourself; but go to the Lord Jesus, and believe he will direct you, and he will do it. Let prayer be thy constant work, then faith will increase—that will not fail." Laura simultaneously provided the woman with comfort and the gentle exhortation to keep her eyes fixed on Jesus. Laura concluded, "At these few words she became calm…."[11]

Laura was quick to lavish her motherly compassion and guidance on any of the downtrodden who crossed her path. While in Toledo she called on a woman to seek financial help for a sick man. A young woman standing nearby heard the story and also gave some money. Later that day Laura tried to find out who the young woman was and discovered that she was an "inmate of a house of ill-fame." The girl didn't want Laura to know where she was living because she believed Laura would never speak to her if she knew the truth.

Laura sent word to the girl that she would like to meet her at the girl's house. "I found her sitting in the parlor waiting for me. As I took her by the hand, placing the other on her head, I said, 'My dear girl, you are an unhappy child.' And she burst into a flood of tears…." Once the girl was able to compose herself, she relayed her story to Laura who then gave her a plan of escape from the dreadful situation in which she found herself. "As we parted she leaned her head upon my shoulder, with fast dropping tears, and said, 'I shall always thank you for acting the part of a mother in helping me away from this horrible place'"[12]

Comfort for the Dying: Paving the Way to Eternity

Perhaps Laura's tragic personal encounters with death prepared her for ministry to the dying. Her own loved ones who left this earth before her were followers of Jesus and she desired to help others join them in God's Kingdom.

At the request of a dying man's mother, Laura visited his sickbed. Previously the dying man had refused to speak to a minister or any "religious person" regarding "preparation for the change." Laura, who had never before met the young man, Harvey, engaged him in honest conversation about the state of his condition. "I see you are very low and weak, and I do not wish to worry you with talking, but you have but little hope of being restored to health I should judge from your appearance." Harvey agreed and she continued. "Then your mind has been turned toward the future, and may the enlightening influence of the Holy Spirit lead you to the Great Physician of souls, who knows every desire of the heart, and is able to save to the uttermost, even at the eleventh hour."[13]

Harvey became teary and while Laura held his feverish hand she asked if it would be alright for her to read a few words from the Bible. He was quite happy for her to do so and when she asked if she may pray for him, Harvey was equally pleased. "Placing my hand on his forehead, I implored divine aid in leading this precious soul to the cleansing fountain, and that his faith might increase, and in its exercise be enabled to secure the pearl of great price." As she prepared to leave, Harvey reached for her hands and asked her to come back the following day. "He wept freely; and I left with the burden of that precious soul upon my heart."[14]

Shortly before his death Harvey accepted Christ and asked Laura to visit his cousin, George, and share the gospel with him as well. Laura agreed and several weeks later paid a visit to George, whom she found near death with cholera. George, like Harvey, was from a Christian home, but was reticent to allow anyone to talk to him about religion. However, he agreed to allow Laura to visit him and she told him how Harvey had found relief in Jesus.

George asked her to return the next day and when she did he had this to say, "I have tried to pray to God; then it seems as if Jesus Christ stands there, and if I pray to Jesus it don't feel quite clear, because I want to go to head-quarters, and I am confused, and don't know where to go or what to do, and so I've given it all up; for it's all dark before me, and I've concluded to die in the dark."[15]

Fortunately, Laura believed in the power of trialogues. "This sorrowful condition of unbelief brought secret prayer for divine guidance in words to place the divinity of the Lord Jesus as clearly as possible before him. I read a few passages where he manifested his power by miracles, 'that ye may know that the Son of man hath power on earth to forgive sins.' He heard me attentively, and suddenly exclaimed: 'Now I see it; now I see it; now I've got a foothold. Now I can pray. I want you to pray for me.'"[16]

Laura was refreshingly honest. Whether confronting men and women in favor of slavery or comforting the dying, she looked to God and His Word, where she continuously pointed others. She had a profound impact on the hearts and minds of both the wealthy and the lowly.

Betsie ten Boom: Living and Dying for Christ

The ten Boom name is most often associated with Corrie ten Boom, the Dutch watchmaker's daughter who found herself unwittingly leading a cell of the underground resistance that aided Jews in the escape from Nazis. However, there is another ten Boom, Betsie (1885-1944), who had a profound role in shaping her younger sister, Corrie. Within the first two pages of her book, *The Hiding Place*, Corrie mentions Betsie eight times.[17] Betsie, being seven years older than Corrie, often looked after Corrie, helping her with the basics such as making sure she was dressed properly and neatly. Throughout their lives Betsie was not only an earthly sister to Corrie, but also a spiritual sister, a spiritual friend who prodded, helped, guided, sustained, and chastised Corrie, much of the time by simply being a presence in her life and by modeling godliness.

Betsie grew up in a devoutly Christian home. She and her siblings saw the faith modeled by both their parents and by three of their aunts who lived with them at various times. Betsie, her two sisters and her brother all became believers and it is that faith that both propelled them into the nightmare of the holocaust and also saw them through it. Although Betsie died inside a Nazi prison camp, her legacy lived on through the work that Corrie was able to accomplish once she was released from prison.

Hospitality and Presence: Paving the Way for Spiritual Friendship

Betsie possessed a sense of hospitality that not only met the physical needs of those around her, but also the emotional ones. She astutely paid attention to the details of her surroundings including the people with whom she interacted and she seemed to instinctively know what would help the current situation and the people in it.

Betsie had been running the watch shop and Corrie had been running the household, but a cold that threatened to turn into pneumonia sent Betsie to bed, leaving Corrie to run the shop. They quickly learned that they had "divided the work backwards. It was astonishing, once we'd made the swap, how well everything went. The house had been clean under my care; under Betsie's it glowed. She saw beauty in wood, in pattern, in color, and helped us to see it too."[18] The change in duties benefited the community as well as their immediate family. "The soup kettle and the coffee pot on the back of the stove, which I never seemed to find time for, were simmering again the first week Betsie took over, and soon a stream of postmen and police, derelict old men and shivering young errand boys were pausing inside our alley door to stamp their feet and cup their hands around hot mugs, just as they'd done when Mama was in charge."[19]

Not surprisingly Corrie still leaned on Betsie when it came to nurturing relationships with the shop's customers. "One thing in the shop I never learned to do as well as Betsie, and that was to care about each person who stepped through the door. Often when a customer entered I would slip out the rear door and up to Betsie in the kitchen. 'Betsie! Who is the woman with the Alpina lapel-watch on a blue velvet band—stout, around fifty?'

"'That's Mrs. Van den Keukel. Her brother came back from Indonesia with malaria and she's been nursing him. Corrie,' as I sped back down the stairs, 'ask her how Mrs. Rinker's baby is!'"[20]

Even in the face of danger and uncertainty, Betsie was ready to meet the needs of others. The night that war shattered their world Corrie was jolted awake by the sound of bombs. She ran first to her father's room and then to Betsie's. Knowing that others would likely soon be up and in need of comfort "Betsie had long since moved… where she would be nearer the kitchen and the doorbell."[21]

Part of Betsie's welcoming charm was her ability to read people and help ease the tension they might be feeling. One evening two years after the invasion, a Jewish woman came to their home looking for help. Betsie told her they had "four empty beds upstairs" and that her "problem will be choosing which one to sleep in!" Then to Corrie's astonishment she added, "First though, give me a hand with the tea things." Corrie was amazed. "Betsie never let anyone help in her kitchen: 'I'm just a fussy old maid,' she'd say. But Mrs. Kleermaker had jumped to her feet with pathetic eagerness and was already stacking plates and cups…. "²² Betsie sat aside her own desires in order to offer their new friend some sense of normalcy. No doubt such a mundane task as clearing tea cups helped to quiet the poor woman's soul and keep her mind occupied with something other than her desperate situation.

Over time the ten Booms took on seven permanent residents, those, who for one reason or another, were such a grave risk to harbor that they could not find safe houses for them. Corrie referred to them as "the nucleus of our happy household. That it could have been happy, at such a time and in such circumstances, was largely a tribute to Betsie. Because our guests' physical lives were so very restricted, evenings under Betsie's direction became the door to the wide world. Sometimes we had concerts, with Leendert on the violin, and Thea, a truly accomplished musician, on the piano. Or Betsie would announce 'an evening of Vondel' (the Dutch Shakespeare), with each of us reading a part. One night a week she talked Eusie into giving Hebrew lessons, another night Meta taught Italian."²³

Even in prison Betsie managed to turn a cell into a "home." Corrie had the fortunate opportunity to walk past Betsie's cell when the door was open. "For unbelievably, against all logic, this cell was charming….The straw pallets were rolled instead of piled in a heap, standing like little pillars along the walls, each with a lady's hat atop it. A headscarf had somehow been hung along the wall. The contents of several food packages were arranged on a small shelf…. Even the coats hanging on their hooks were part of the welcome of that room, each sleeve draped over the shoulder of the coat next to it like a row of dancing children."²⁴

In addition to having a knack for turning any environment into a welcoming resting place, Betsie was a master in the fine art of practicing presence. Before the war one of her aunts was diagnosed with diabetes which was, at the time, "a death sentence as surely as tuberculosis had been."[25] Corrie was taught how to administer a test to monitor the aunt's blood sugar level. When the day came that the test results indicated imminent death Corrie ran downstairs to the shop. "'Betsie!' she cried. 'Oh Betsie, it's black! How are we going to tell her? What are we going to do?' Betsie came swiftly from behind the desk and put her arms around me."[26]

The night the war erupted in Holland Corrie experienced a terrible dream, more like a vision, of her loved ones being carried away by the Nazis. "'Betsie!' I cried, jumping up, pressing my hands to my eyes. 'Betsie, I've had such an awful dream!' I felt her arm around my shoulder. 'We'll go down to the kitchen where the light won't show, and we'll make a pot of coffee.'"[27] Repeatedly Corrie sought the comfort of her sister's presence. "One night I tossed for an hour while dogfights raged overhead, streaking my patch of sky with fire. At last I heard Betsie stirring in the kitchen and ran down to join her.… For an hour we sipped our tea and talked, until the sound of planes died away and the sky was silent."[28]

The practice of presence was truly a godsend as they faced new horrors. When they were finally caught by the Nazis their journey to prison began. Early in the process when their father was taken away from them Corrie said simply, "Betsie's hand slipped around mine."[29] The sisters were initially kept in separate cells, those four months being their first separation in fifty-three years. As they were being evacuated from Scheveningen, Corrie spotted Betsie and made her way to her sister. The scene brought to life the truth that shared sorrow is endurable sorrow. "At the very steps of the train I reached out and seized Betsie's hand. Together we climbed onto the train, together found seats in a crowded compartment, together wept tears of gratitude… it seemed to me that I could bear whatever happened with Betsie beside me."[30]

Trust and Hope: Seeing Life with Faith Eyes

Betsie repeatedly reminded Corrie what it meant to trust in their all-knowing, all-powerful God. She didn't do this by preaching or lecturing, but by living out her faith while she comforted her sister and sought to infuse her with hope and courage. When Corrie told Betsie about her disturbing dream on the night the Nazis first attacked Holland, she asked Betsie whether she was just imagining things because she was frightened. "Betsie's finger traced a pattern on the wooden sink worn smooth by generations of ten Booms. 'I don't know,' she said softly. 'But if God has shown us bad times ahead, it's enough for me that He knows about them. That's why He sometimes shows us things, you know—to tell us that this too is in His hands.'"[31]

One night some months later, they were awakened by bombing. Corrie joined Betsie downstairs until the fighting stopped. After they talked, Corrie went back to bed where she cut her hand on a ten-inch piece of metal that had landed in her bed. She ran back downstairs to Betsie, who bandaged her hand. "'Betsie, if I hadn't heard you in the kitchen—' But Betsie put a finger on my mouth. 'Don't say it, Corrie! There are no "if's" in God's world. And no places that are safer than other places. The center of His will is our only safety—O Corrie, let us pray that we may always know it!'"[32] Betsie graciously offered her sister comfort and gently wrapped it in guidance she could cling to in the future.

After being imprisoned for months with no end in sight Corrie felt as though she could not persevere. She lamented their condition and asked her sister how much longer they would have to endure. She was stunned at Betsie's response. "Perhaps a long, long time. Perhaps many years. But what better way could there be to spend our lives?" Corrie stared at her and asked what she was talking about. "Corrie, if people can be taught to hate, they can be taught to love! We must find the way, you and I, no matter how long it takes...."[33]

Corrie continued the narrative. "She went on, almost forgetting in her excitement to keep her voice to a whisper, while I slowly took in the fact that she was talking about our guards. I glanced at the matron seated at the desk ahead of us. I saw a gray uniform and a visored hat; Betsie saw a wounded human being." She was amazed and "wondered, not for the first time, what sort of a person she was, this sister of mine...what kind of road she followed while I trudged beside her on the all-too-solid earth."[34]

At one point during their ordeal they moved to more permanent quarters, but they were horribly crowded in their new barracks. "Here there was not even a common language and among exhausted, ill-fed people quarrels erupted constantly."[35] This was particularly true at night when spaces that were designed for four people now held nine. "In the dark I felt Betsie's hands clasp mine. 'Lord Jesus,' she said aloud, 'send Your peace into this room. There has been too little praying here. The very walls know it. But where You come, Lord, the spirit of strife cannot exist...'" Just as Betsie expected, prayer made a difference. "The change was gradual, but distinct. One by one the angry sounds let up. ... I lay back on the sour straw and knew there was one more circumstance for which I could give thanks. Betsie had come to Barracks 28."[36]

Thanksgiving and Forgiveness: Imparting Hard Lessons

While in prison they discovered it was one of their own countrymen who had betrayed them. Corrie's rage welled within her, but not so with Betsie. "What puzzled me all this time was Betsie. She had suffered everything I had and yet she seemed to carry no burden of rage. 'Betsie!' I hissed one dark night when I knew that my restless tossing must be keeping her awake.... 'Betsie, don't you feel anything about Jan Vogel? Doesn't it bother you?'" Her response was not what Corrie expected. "Oh yes, Corrie! Terribly! I've felt for him ever since I knew—and pray for him whenever his name comes into my mind. How dreadfully he must be suffering!"[37]

Corrie lay silently for a long time "in the huge shadowy barracks restless with the sighs, snores, and stirrings of hundreds of women. Once again I had the feeling that this sister with whom I had spent all my life belonged somehow to another order of beings. Wasn't she telling me in her gentle way that I was as guilty as Jan Vogel? Didn't he and I stand together before an all-seeing God convicted of the same sin of murder? For I had murdered him with my heart and with my tongue."[38]

As the night wore on, Corrie prayed. "'Lord Jesus,' I whispered into the lumpy ticking of the bed, 'I forgive Jan Vogel as I pray that You will forgive me. I have done him great damage. Bless him now, and his family...' That night for the first time since our betrayer had a name I slept deep and dreamlessly until the whistle summoned us to roll call."[39]

Once again they were moved to new quarters. They learned quickly that the place was infested with fleas. Corrie bemoaned their situation and turned to Betsie wondering how they can "live in such a place!" Betsie's response of "Show us. Show us how," was so matter-of-fact that Corrie did not realize immediately that her sister is praying. "More and more the distinction between prayer and the rest of life seemed to be vanishing for Betsie." A moment later Betsie very excitedly exclaimed that God had already given them the answer in their Bible reading from the morning. She had Corrie reread the passage until she finally interrupted her.[40]

> "That's it, Corrie! That's His answer. 'Give thanks in all circumstances!' That's what we can do. We can start right now to thank God for every single thing about this new barracks!"
> I stared at her, then around me at the dark, foul-aired room.
> "Such as?" I said.
> "Such as being assigned here together."
> I bit my lip. "Oh yes, Lord Jesus!"
> "Such as what you're holding your hands." I looked down at the Bible. "Yes! Thank You, dear Lord, that there was no inspection when we entered here! Thank You for all the women, here in this room, who will meet You in these pages."
> "Yes," said Betsie, "Thank You for the very crowding here. Since we're packed so close, that many more will hear!" She looked at me expectantly. "Corrie!" she prodded.
> "Oh, all right. Thank You for the jammed, crammed, stuffed, packed, suffocating crowds."
> "Thank You," Betsie went on serenely, "for the fleas and for—"The fleas! This was too much. "Betsie,

there's no way even God can make me grateful for
a flea."
"Give thanks in *all* circumstances," she quoted. "It
doesn't say 'in pleasant circumstances.' Fleas are part
of this place where God has put us."
And so we stood between piers of bunks and gave
thanks for fleas. But this time I was sure Betsie
was wrong.[41]

For some reason unknown to the sisters, the prisoners had much
more freedom in these barracks than they'd had in other situations.
They eventually found out that the guards would not enter this area
because they didn't want to get fleas.[42]

In all things Betsie sought to keep her eyes focused on Jesus and
she did her best to impart this to her sister. Although Betsie became
ill and continued to grow weaker, she was still required to engage in
hard labor. One day a "young and well-fed" guard became angry with
Betsie because of the small amount of dirt she was able to shovel. The
guard grabbed the shovel from Betsie and proceeded to make fun
of her in front of the other guards and prisoners. Then "snatching
the leather crop from her belt she slashed Betsie across the chest and
neck." After the immediate shock of the incident Corrie looked at
Betsie. "Betsie saw where I was looking and laid a bird-thin hand
over the whip mark. 'Don't look at it, Corrie. Look at Jesus only.' She
drew away her hand: it was sticky with blood."[43]

Shortly after this incident Betsie died in the prison, but not
before passing on to her sister a vision of the healing and reconciling
work for which Corrie is so well known.

Listening to the Silenced Voices

When we listen to the silenced voices of women like Laura Haviland
and Betsie ten Boom we hear the message of unrelenting courage and
comfort in the face of grave danger. The message is distinct and it is
rooted in the unshakable faith that God and His Word are true and
faithful. They did not rely on their own power or strength, but on
God's. These two women spoke hard truth, but did so lovingly.

Laura went toe-to-toe with slave owners and their sympathizers. The hearts of some softened. The hearts of others remained hardened. Some wanted to see her dead, yet others came to respect her even while continuing to disagree with her.

Betsie, in her mild-mannered way, gently rebuked and instructed her sister, helping to shape her future as one who would decry the evils of the Nazi regime to the world. Betsie poured herself into Corrie's life, continuously pointing her back to Christ, back to God's Word, and back to truth and righteousness.

Learning Together from Our Great Cloud of Witnesses

1. Laura Haviland was quick to confront inconsistencies in people's words and actions. While she was firm and would not back down, she was gracious and respectful.
   a. How readily and willingly do you confront similar incongruencies?
   b. What is your usual style of confrontation? How effective has that been?

2. Laura was willing to engage strangers as well as friends in challenging truth-based, grace-filled conversations. As a result, she was sometimes able to turn adversaries into advocates.
   a. Are you more likely to confront friends or strangers on spiritual matters? Why do you suppose that is?
   b. How well would you rate yourself in being able to combine grace with truth in the midst of difficult or confrontational conversations?

3. The Lord called Laura to minister in some of life's hardest places, from the deathbed to the battlefield. In what difficult places or situations might the Lord be calling you?
   a. What situations would you least want to venture into? What about them repels you?
   b. What relationally challenging situations are most exciting to you? What about them motivates you?

4. Betsie ten Boom poured into her sister, Corrie, throughout Corrie's life.
   a. Who has poured into your life and what difference has that made?
   b. In whose life are you investing?

5. During some tremendously appalling times Betsie was able not only to keep her eyes focused on Jesus, but she was also consistently able to redirect Corrie to the Savior. When you are

in crushing circumstances, how do you typically respond? What can you learn from Betsie's unwavering focus?

6. Betsie left a legacy through Corrie that will be remembered for generations. What legacy will you leave? For what do you want to be remembered?

7. In what ways do Laura and Betsie inspire you?

Endnotes

Notes for Introduction

1. Ranft, *A Woman's Way*, 6.
2. Edwards, *Spiritual Friend*, 67.
3. MacHaffie, *Her Story*, xi.
4. Chesterton, *Orthodoxy*, 52-53.
5. Kellemen and Edwards, *Beyond the Suffering*.

Notes for Chapter 1

1. Ranft, *A Woman's Way*, 1.
2. Oden, *In Her Own Words*, 11.
3. Oden, *Whatever Happened to History?*, 7.
4. Oates, *Protestant Pastoral Counseling*, 11.
5. Clebsch, *Pastoral Care in Historical Perspective*, xii.
6. Miller-McLemore, "The Living Human Web," in Moessner, *Through the Eyes of Women*, 18-19.
7. Forbes, *Women of Devotion through the Centuries*, 41.
8. Cowman, *Streams in the Desert*, 13.
9. Clark, *Women in the Early Church*, 181.
10. Compare the model explained in Kellemen and Edwards, *Beyond the Suffering*.
11. Lane, *Christian Spirituality*, 1-2.
12. McNeil, *A History of the Cure of Souls*, 85.
13. Lake, *Clinical Theology*, 21.
14. Kellemen, *Soul Physicians*, 22.
15. Clebsch, 4.
16. Leech, *Soul Friend*, 98.
17. Oden, *Care of Souls in the Classic Tradition*, 10.
18. Kellemen, *Spiritual Friends*, 47.
19. Ray, "The Life of Susannah Spurgeon," in Spurgeon, *Free Grace and Dying Love*, 149.
20. Ibid.
21. Ibid., 150.
22. Ibid., 158, emphasis added.
23. Oden, *Phoebe Palmer*, 3, 10.
24. Palmer, *The Way of Holiness*, 100-101.
25. Wheatley, *The Life and Letters of Phoebe Palmer*, 30.
26. Ibid., 31.
27. Blauvelt, "Women and Revivalism," in Ruether, *The Colonial and Revolutionary Period*, 334.

28. Ibid., 335.
29. Wideman, *My Soul Has Grown Deep*, 369.
30. Ibid., 376
31. Ibid.
32. Ibid., 382.
33. Clarke, *Memoirs of the Wesley Family*, 398.

Notes for Chapter 2

1. Thiebauz, *The Writings of Medieval Women*, 8.
2. Ibid., 3.
3. "The Martyrdom of Perpetua," in Wilson-Kastner, *A Lost Tradition*, 19.
4. Ibid., 20.
5. Ibid.
6. Ibid., 22.
7. Ibid., emphasis added.
8. Ibid., 20.
9. Ibid., 23.
10. Ibid., 26-27, emphasis added.
11. Ibid., 27.
12. Ibid., 28.
13. Ibid., emphasis added.
14. Ranft, *A Woman's Way*, 26.
15. St. Basil, *St. Basil's Letters*, 2:76.
16. Gregory of Nyssa, *The Life of Saint Macrina*, paragraphs 962c-d.
17. Ibid., paragraph 964a.
18. Ibid., paragraph 972c.
19. Ibid., paragraph 972d.
20. Gregory of Nazianzus, "Funeral Oration on His Father," in Broderick, *The Catholic Encyclopedia*, oration 18, paragraph 8.
21. Ibid., paragraph 11, emphasis added.
22. Gregory of Nazianzus, "Funeral Oration on His Sister Gorgonia," in Broderick, oration 8, paragraph 11, emphasis added.
23. Ibid., oration 8, paragraph 5.
24. Gregory of Nazianzus, "Funeral Oration on His Father," oration 18, paragraph 11.
25. Ibid., paragraph 12.
26. Saint Chrysostom, "Treatise on the Priesthood," in Schaff, *Nicene and Post-Nicene Fathers*, vol. 9, book 1, paragraph 5.
27. Ibid.
28. Ibid., emphasis added.
29. Ranft, 44.
30. Clark, *Women in the Early Church*, 246.

31. Ibid., 247.
32. Ibid., 252.
33. Ibid., 253.
34. Ibid., 247.
35. Ibid., 254.
36. Ibid., 254-255.
37. Ibid., 257-258.

Notes for Chapter 3

1. MacHaffie, *Her Story*, xi.
2. Gregory of Nazianzus, "Funeral Oration on His Sister Gorgonia," in Schaff, *Nicene and Post-Nicene Fathers*, 7:240.
3. Sawyer, *Women and Religion in the First Christian Centuries*, 17.
4. Ibid., 30.
5. Gregory of Nazianzus, 7:238.
6. Ibid, 7:239.
7. Ibid., 7:239-240.
8. Ibid., 7:241.
9. Ibid.
10. Ibid., 7:242.
11. Ibid., 7:243.
12. Ibid., 7:244.
13. Ibid.
14. Gregory of Nyssa, *The Life of Saint Macrina*, paragraph 966b.
15. Ibid., paragraph 966c.
16. Ibid.
17. Ibid., paragraph 970b.
18. Ibid., paragraph 974c.
19. Oden, *In Her Own Words*, 48.
20. Gregory of Nyssa, paragraphs 978a-c.
21. Ibid., paragraphs 982a-c
22. Ibid., paragraphs 984c-986b.
23. "The Life of Olympias," in Clark, *Jerome, Chrysostom, and Friends*, 127-128.
24. Ibid., 128-129.
25. Swan, *The Forgotten Desert Mothers*, 107.
26. "The Life of Olympias," 132-133.
27. Ibid., 137.
28. Ibid., 133.
29. Ibid., 139.
30. Ibid.
31. Ibid., 134.
32. Saint Chrysostom, "Letters," in Schaff, *Nicene and Post-Nicene Fathers*, 9:297.

33. Ibid., 9:298.
34. "The Life of Olympias," 134-135.
35. Saint Chrysostom, 9:289.
36. Ibid.
37. Ibid.
38. Ibid., 9:293.
39. Ibid., 9:297.

Notes for Chapter 4

1. Swan, *The Forgotten Desert Mothers*, 35.
2. Ibid., 39.
3. Ibid., 15.
4. Kraemer, *Maenads, Martyrs, Matrons, Monastics*, 121.
5. Swan, 6-9.
6. Ibid., 9.
7. Ibid., 8-9.
8. Ward, *The Desert Fathers*, ix-xi.
9. Ibid., viii.
10. Swan, 11.
11. Ibid.
12. Wright, *Desert Listening*, 12.
13. Swan, 12
14. Ibid.
15. Ibid., 13.
16. Kraemer, 124.
17. Ibid., 123.
18. Ibid.
19. Swan, 42.
20. Ibid., 20.
21. Ward, 65, emphasis added.
22. Ibid., 105.
23. Ruether, *Women and Redemption*, 63.
24. Jerome, "Letters and Select Works," in Schaff, *Nicene and Post-Nicene Fathers*,
    vol. 6, letter 127, paragraph 4.
25. Ibid., paragraph 5.
26. Ibid., paragraph 6, emphasis added.
27. Ibid., paragraph 7, emphasis added.
28. Ibid.
29. Ibid., paragraph 8, emphasis added.
30. Ibid., emphasis added.
31. Ibid., emphasis added.
32. Ibid., paragraph 10, emphasis added.

33. Ibid.
34. Ibid., paragraph 13.
35. Ibid., paragraph 14.
36. Ibid., letter 108, paragraph 1.
37. Ibid., paragraph 5.
38. Ibid.
39. Ibid., paragraph 20.
40. Ibid.
41. Ibid.
42. Ibid.
43. Ibid.
44. Ibid., paragraph 15.
45. Ibid., paragraph 18.
46. Ibid.
47. Ibid.
48. Ibid.
49. Ibid., emphasis added.

Notes for Chapter 5

1. Radegund of Poitiers, "The Fall of Thuringia," in Thiebauz, *The Writings of Medieval Women*, 96.
2. Ibid.
3. Palladius, *The Lausiac History*, translated by Clarke, preface, paragraph 1.
4. Ibid, paragraphs 2-4.
5. Palladius, *The Lausiac History*, translated by Meyer, 21.
6. Ibid., 22.
7. Ibid., 23, 24.
8. Palladius, in Clarke, chapter XLVI, paragraph 1.
9. Ibid., paragraph 3-4.
10. Ibid., paragraph 6.
11. Ibid., chapter LIV, paragraphs 1-2.
12. Ibid., paragraph 3.
13. Ibid., paragraph 4.
14. Ibid., paragraphs 4-5.
15. Ibid., chapter LV, paragraphs 1-2.
16. Clark, *Women in the Early Church*, 217.
17. Palladius, in Clarke, chapter LV, paragraph 3.
18. Ibid., chapter LVI, paragraph 1.
19. Rudolph, "The Life of Saint Leoba," in Talbot, *The Anglo-Saxon Missionaries in Germany*, 204-205.
20. Ibid., 206-207.
21. Ibid., 207.

22. Ibid., 208.
23. Ibid.
24. Ibid.
25. Ibid., 208-209.
26. Ibid., 210-211.
27. Ibid., 211.
28. Ibid.
29. Ibid., 214, emphasis added.
30. Ibid.
31. Ibid., 214-215.
32. Ibid., 222-223.
33. Ibid., 223.
34. Ibid., 223-224.
35. Dhuoda, "Dhuoda's Manual," in Wilson, *Medieval Women Writers*, 13.
36. Ibid.
37. Ibid., 12.
38. Ibid.
39. Ibid., 13.
40. Ibid., 16, emphasis added.
41. Ibid., 15.
42. Ibid., emphasis added.
43. Ibid., 16.
44. Ibid., 18.
45. Ibid.
46. Ibid., 19.
47. Ibid., 20.
48. Ibid., 21.
49. Ibid.
50. Ibid., 22.
51. Ibid.

Notes for Chapter 6

1. Harris, *Birgitta of Sweden*, 19.
2. Ibid., 168-169.
3. Powers, *Medieval Women*, 1.
4. Wilson, *Medieval Women Writers*, vii.
5. Lamprecht von Regensburg, quoted in Brunn, *Women Mystics in Medieval Europe*, xiii-xiv.
6. Ibid., xiv.
7. Brunn, xiv.
8. Ibid., xv, xxviii.
9. Grant, *Sacred Legacy*, 51.
10. Hildegard, *Scivias*, 479.

11. Dronke, *Women Writers of the Middle Ages*, 186.
12. Ranft, *A Woman's Way*, 74.
13. Hildegard, *Letters of Hildegard of Bingen*, letter 35, 1:102.
14. Thiebauz, *The Writings of Medieval Women*, 349.
15. Ibid., 356.
16. Dronke, 149.
17. Turpin, *Women in Church History*, 92-93.
18. Wilson, 101.
19. Ibid., emphasis added.
20. Ibid., emphasis added.
21. Abelard and Heloise, *The Letters of Abelard and Heloise*, 119.
22. Hart, "Introduction," in Hadewijch, *Hadewijch*, 3.
23. Hadewijch, 107.
24. Ibid., 114.
25. Ibid.
26. Grant, 64-69.
27. Mechthild, *The Flowing Light of the Godhead*, 77.
28. Ibid., 223.
29. Armstrong, "Foreword," in Francis and Clare, *Francis and Clare*, xv.
30. Francis and Clare, 190-194.
31. Ibid., 193.
32. Ibid., 197.
33. Ibid., 200.
34. Oden, *In Her Words*, 148.
35. Ranft, 82.
36. Angela of Foligno, *Angela of Foligno*, 264.
37. Ibid., 266.
38. Ibid.
39. Ibid.
40. Ibid., 252.
41. Francis and Clare, 222.
42. Ibid.
43. Ibid., 221.
44. Ibid.
45. Mechthild, 192, emphasis added.
46. Ibid., 127.
47. Ibid., 210.
48. Marnau, "Introduction," in Gertrude of Helfta, *Gertrude of Helfta*, 5-7.
49. Gertrude of Helfta, 63.
50. Ibid.
51. Ibid., 64.
52. Ibid.
53. Schmidt, "Preface," in Mechthild, xxv.
54. Ibid., xxvi.

55. Armstrong, "Introduction," in Francis and Clare, 171.
56. Ibid., 184.
57. Francis and Clare, 190.
58. Ibid., 191.
59. Oden, 119.
60. Ibid.
61. Hadewijch, 62.

Notes for Chapter 7

1. Julian of Norwich, *Revelations of Divine Love*, 11.
2. Kempe, *The Book of Margery Kempe*, 78-79.
3. Leclercq, "Preface" in, Julian of Norwich, *Showings*, 2-3.
4. Spearing, "Introduction, in Julian of Norwich, *Revelations*, xiii.
5. Ibid., xiv.
6. Ruether, *Women and Redemption*, 104.
7. Spearing, in *Revelations*, viii-xii.
8. Ibid., xvii.
9. Kellemen, *Soul Physicians*, 384-386.
10. Spearing, in *Revelations*, xix.
11. Julian of Norwich, *Revelations*, 7.
12. Ibid., 9-10.
13. Ibid, 11.
14. Ibid., 15.
15. Ibid.
16. Ibid., 17.
17. Ibid., 37.
18. Ibid.
19. Ibid.
20. Ibid., 22.
21. Ibid., 19.
22. Ibid., 21-22.
23. Ibid., 80.
24. Ibid., 85.
25. Ibid., 22.
26. Ibid.
27. Ibid., 97.
28. Ibid.
29. Ibid.
30. Noffke, "Introduction," in Catherine of Siena, *The Dialogue*, 3.
31. Ibid., 3 7
32. Oden, *Classical Pastoral Care*, vol. 3, 14, from *Catherine of Siena: A Treatise of Discretion*, 69.

33. Ibid.
34. Oden, *Classical Pastoral Care*, vol. 1, 55, from *Catherine of Siena: A Treatise of Prayer*, 254.
35. Catherine of Siena, *The Letters of St. Catherine of Siena*, vol. 1, 54.
36. Ibid., 27.
37. Ibid., 86
38. Ibid., 86-87.
39. Ibid., 87, 88.
40. Ibid., 88.
41. Catherine of Siena, *The Dialogue*, 100.
42. Ibid., 277.
43. Catherine of Siena, *The Letters of St. Catherine of Siena*, vol. 1, 66.
44. Ibid.
45. Ibid., 109-110.
46. Ibid.
47. Graef, *The Light and the Rainbow*, 250.
48. Ibid., 250-251.
49. Ibid., 251.
50. Catherine of Siena, *Saint Catherine of Siena As Seen in Her Letters*, 278.
51. Ibid., 132.
52. Catherine of Siena, *The Letters of St. Catherine of Siena*, vol. 1, 54.
53. Ibid, 40.
54. Ibid., 53.
55. Catherine of Siena, *The Dialogue*, 64.
56. Ibid., 65.
57. Ibid., 103.
58. Ibid., 278.
59. Ibid., 328.

Notes for Chapter 8

1. Bainton, *Women of the Reformation in Germany and Italy*, 9.
2. Dentiere, in Wilson, *Women Writers of the Renaissance and Reformation*, 278.
3. MacHaffie, *Her Story*, 99-100.
4. Ibid., 119.
5. Ibid, emphasis added.
6. Bainton, *Germany*,105-106, emphasis added.
7. Ibid., 97-98.
8. Ibid., 97.
9. MacHaffie, 120.
10. Bainton, *Germany*, 106.
11. Ibid.
12. MacHaffie, 120.

13. Bainton, *Germany*, 55.
14. Tucker, *Daughters of the Church*, 182.
15. Schaff, *The History of the Reformation*, 633.
16. MacHaffie, 92, emphasis added.
17. Bainton, *Germany*, 55.
18. Ibid.
19. Tucker, *Private Lives of Pastors' Wives*, 33
20. Ibid., emphasis added.
21. Ibid., 34.
22. Ibid.
23. Bainton, *Germany*, 61.
24. Ibid.
25. Ibid., 61, 63.
26. Ibid., 69.
27. Ibid.
28. Ibid., 72.
29. Ibid.
30. Ibid.
31. Bainton, *Women of the Reformation in France and England*, 7.
32. Tucker, *Private*, 40.
33. Peterson, *25 Surprising Marriages*, 488.
34. Van Halsema, *This Was John Calvin*, 113.
35. Peterson, "John Calvin's Search for the Right Wife," 13.
36. Peterson, *25 Surprising Marriages*, 494.
37. Ibid., 496.
38. Tucker, *Private*, 41-42.
39. Hyma, *Life of John Calvin*, 85.
40. Van Halsema, 147
41. Ibid., 148.
42. Peterson, "John Calvin's Search," 15.
43. Walker, *John Calvin*, 236.
44. Bainton, *Germany*, 23.
45. Ibid.
46. Ibid., 24.
47. Ibid., 26.
48. Ibid., 27.
49. Ibid., 26.
50. Ibid.
51. Ibid., 29.
52. Ibid., 30.
53. Kellemen, *Spiritual Care in Historical Perspective*, 70-74.
54. Bainton, *Germany*, 42, emphasis added.
55. Ibid., 37.

56. Ibid., 38.
57. Schwiebert, *Luther and His Times*, 584.
58. Bainton, *Germany*, 30.
59. Ibid., 39.
60. Tucker, *Private*, 27.
61. Bainton, *Germany*, 37.
62. Ibid., 42.
63. Wilson, 260.
64. Ibid., 276.
65. Ibid., 277.
66. Ibid.
67. Ibid., 278.

Notes for Chapter 9

1. Dubay, *Fire Within*, 302.
2. de Sales and de Chantal, *Frances de Sales,* 204-205.
3. Teresa of Avila, *The Collected Works of St. Teresa of Avila*, vol. 2, "The Way of Perfection," 51.
4. Ibid.
5. Kavanaugh, "Introduction," in Teresa of Avila, *The Collected Works of St. Teresa of Avila*, vol. 1, 15-16.
6. Ibid., 17-18.
7. Ibid., 33-35.
8. Teresa of Avila, *The Collected Works*, vol. 1, "The Book of Her Life," 67.
9. Dubay, 277.
10. Kavanaugh, in Teresa of Avila, *The Collected Works*, vol. 1, 32, words of her biographer.
11. Teresa of Avila, *The Collected Works*, vol. 1, "The Book of Her Life," 71.
12. Ibid., 61.
13. Ibid.
14. Ibid., 201.
15. Ibid.
16. Ibid., 201-202, emphasis added.
17. Ibid., 130.
18. Teresa of Avila, *The Collected Works*, vol. 2, "The Way of Perfection," 62.
19. Ibid., 66.
20. Ibid., 67.
21. Ibid.
22. Dubay, 284.
23. Teresa of Avila, *The Collected Works*, vol. 1, "The Book of Her Life," 206.
24. Teresa of Avila, *The Collected Works*, vol. 2, "The Way of Perfection," 67.
25. Teresa of Avila, *The Collected Works*, vol. 1, "The Book of Her Life," 92-93.

26. Dubay, 273-274.
27. Teresa of Avila, *The Collected Works*, vol. 1, "The Book of Her Life," 293.
28. Ibid., 294.
29. Ibid.
30. Ibid., 300.
31. Teresa of Avila, *The Collected Works*, vol. 2, "The Interior Castle," 309.
32. Ibid., 292.
33. Teresa of Avila, *The Collected Works*, vol. 1, "The Book of Her Life," 208-209.
34. Ibid., 208.
35. Ibid., 211.
36. Ibid., 254.
37. Ibid., 314.
38. Teresa of Avila, *The Collected Works*, vol. 2, "The Interior Castle," 343.
39. Teresa of Avila, *The Collected Works*, vol. 1, "The Book of Her Life," 82.
40. Teresa of Avila, *The Collected Works*, vol. 2, "The Interior Castle," 450.
41. Wright, "Introduction," in de Sales and de Chantal, 19, 25-26.
42. Ibid., 26-27.
43. Ibid., 29-30.
44. de Sales and de Chantal, 76.
45. Ibid.
46. Ibid.
47. Ibid., 206.
48. Ibid., emphasis added.
49. Ibid., 207.
50. Ibid., 216.
51. Ibid.
52. Ibid., 185.
53. Ibid., 186.
54. Ibid., 189.
55. Ibid., 188.
56. Ibid., 189.
57. Ibid.
58. Ibid., 190.
59. Ibid. 189.
60. Ibid., 190.
61. Ibid., 191.
62. Ibid., 194.
63. Ibid., 203.
64. Ibid., 201.
65. Ibid., 265.

Notes for Chapter 10

1. Packer, *A Grief Sanctified*, 149.
2. Packer, 76.
3. Packer, p. 21.
4. Ibid., 22.
5. Ibid., 47.
6. Ibid.
7. Ibid., 101.
8. Ibid., 67.
9. Ibid.
10. Ibid., 70.
11. Ibid., 76.
12. Ibid., 69.
13. Ibid., 70.
14. Ibid.
15. Ibid., 71-72.
16. Ibid., 118-119.
17. Ibid., p. 56.
18. Ibid.
19. Ibid., 13
20. Ibid., p. 197.
21. Ibid., p. 57.
22. Ibid., p. 149.
23. Wallace, "Susanna Wesley's Spirituality," 163.
24. Tucker, *Private Lives of Pastors' Wives*, 53.
25. Peterson, *25 Surprising Marriages*, 253.
26. Clarke, *Memoirs of the Wesley Family*, 327.
27. Ibid., 326.
28. Ibid., 329.
29. Ibid., 347.
30. Ibid., 347-376
31. Ibid., 347.
32. Ibid., 337.
33. Ibid., 347.
34. Ibid., 342-343.
35. Ibid., 385.
36. Ibid., 386.
37. Ibid., 387.
38. Ibid.
39. Ibid.
40. Ibid.
41. Ibid.

42. Ibid., 388.
43. Ibid.
44. Ibid., 389.
45. Ibid.
46. Ibid.
47. Ibid., 390.
48. Ibid., 391.
49. Ibid., 392.
50. Ibid., 393.
51. Ibid.
52. Ibid., 394.
53. Ibid., 337.
54. Ibid., 397.
55. Ibid., 397-398.
56. Ibid., 398.
57. Ibid., 399.
58. Ibid., 406.
59. Ibid., 409.
60. Ibid., 408.
61. Ibid., 409.
62. Ibid., 413.
63. Ibid., 414.
64. Ibid., 341-342.

Notes for Chapter 11

1. Gerstner, *Jonathan and Sarah*, vii.
2. Ray, "The Life of Susannah Spurgeon," in Spurgeon, *Free Grace and Dying Love*, 123.
3. Dodds, *Marriage to a Difficult Man*, 15.
4. Marsden, *Jonathan Edwards*, 93-94.
5. Dodds, 11-12.
6. Petersen, *25 Surprising Marriages*, 428.
7. Parks, *Memoir of the Life and Character of Samuel Hopkins*, 254.
8. Marsden, 111.
9. Dodds, 87.
10. Ibid., 160.
11. Ibid., 16, 99.
12. Oberg, *Benjamin Franklin, Jonathan Edwards, and the Representation of American Culture*, 119.
13. Parks, 255.
14. Ibid.
15. Peterson, 434.

16. Ibid.
17. Parks, 255.
18. Ibid., 22-23.
19. Ibid., 19.
20. Ibid.
21. Marsden, 242.
22. Ibid., 243.
23. Ibid., 243.
24. Petersen, 436.
25. Ibid., 436.
26. Marsden, 244
27. Ibid., 244-245.
28. Ibid., 248.
29. Petersen, 440.
30. Marsden, 362.
31. Dodds, 203.
32. Ibid., 58.
33. Petersen, 443.
34. Ibid., 444-445.
35. Burr, *The Journal of Esther Edwards Burr*, 289.
36. Ray, 128.
37. Ibid.
38. Ibid., 132-133.
39. Ibid., 133.
40. Ibid., 134.
41. Ibid.
42. Ibid., 134-135.
43. Ibid., 143.
44. Ibid.
45. Ibid., 144.
46. Ibid., 123.
47. Ibid., 165.
48. Ibid., 165-166.
49. Ibid., 166.
50. Ibid., 166-167.
51. Ibid., 168.
52. Ibid., 168-169.
53. Petersen, 67.
54. Ibid.
55. Spurgeon, *Free Grace and Dying Love*, 28.
56. Ibid.
57. Ibid., 29-30.
58. Ibid., 18.

59. Ray, 242-243
60. Ibid., 242.
61. Ibid., 246.
62. Ibid., 247.
63. Ibid.

Notes for Chapter 12

1. Collier-Thomas, *Daughters of Thunder*, 119.
2. Ibid., 120.
3. Readers can enjoy the empowering narratives of more than two-dozen African American women (and scores of African American men) narrated in Kellemen and Edwards, *Beyond the Suffering*.
4. Keckley, *Behind the Scenes*, xiv, xv.
5. Ibid., 17.
6. Ibid., xii.
7. Ibid., 23.
8. Ibid., 24.
9. Ibid.
10. Ibid., 25.
11. Ibid., 31.
12. Ibid., 35.
13. Ibid., 37.
14. Ibid., 98.
15. Ibid., 102, 103.
16. Ibid., 103-104.
17. Ibid., 104.
18. Ibid., 105.
19. Ibid., 109-110, emphasis added.
20. Ibid., 116.
21. Ibid., 119.
22. Ibid., 120.
23. Ibid., 187.
24. Ibid., 189.
25. Ibid.
26. Ibid., 191.
27. Ibid., 191-192.
28. Ibid., 192-193.
29. Ibid., 210.
30. Ibid., 24.
31. Ibid., 311.
32. Ibid., 332, 333.
33. Ibid., 338, 339.
34. Ibid., 347.
35. Ibid., 348-349.

36. Ibid., 362.
37. Albert, *The House of Bondage*, 1-2.
38. Ibid., 130.
39. Ibid., xxvii.
40. Foster, "Introduction," in Albert, xxviii.
41. Blassingame, *Slave Testimony*, lxi.
42. Foster, "Introduction," in Albert, xxxi.
43. Albert., 27.
44. Ibid., 2.
45. Ibid., 15.
46. Ibid., 70.
47. Ibid., 28-29.
48. Ibid., 29.
49. Foster, "Introduction," in Albert, xxxvii.
50. A. E. P. Albert and Laura Albert, "Preface," in Albert, vi.
51. Albert, 16.
52. Ibid., 18.
53. Ibid., 45, emphasis added.
54. Ibid., 31, 32.
55. Ibid., 36.
56. Ibid., 47-48.
57. Ibid., 68.
58. Foster, "Introduction," in Albert, xxx.
59. Albert, 58.
60. Ibid., 1-2.
61. Ibid., 2.
62. Ibid., 22.
63. Ibid., 39.
64. Ibid., 40.
65. Ibid., 49.
66. Ibid., 58-59.
67. Ibid., 129.
68. Ibid., 143.
69. Ibid., 144-145.
70. Ibid., 146-147.
71. Ibid., 161.
72. Ibid., 161.
73. Collier-Thomas, 119.
74. Ibid.

Notes for Chapter 13

1. Stowe, *Life of Harriet Beecher Stowe*, 181.
2. Knowles, *Memoir of Mrs. Ann H. Judson,* 320.
3. Knowles, 13.

4. Ibid., 16.
5. Ibid., 28.
6. Ibid., 43-44.
7. Ibid., 37.
8. Ibid., 50-52.
9. Ibid., 82.
10. Ibid., 42.
11. Ibid., 43.
12. Ibid., 49.
13. Ibid., 320-321.
14. Ibid., 321.
15. Ibid., 320.
16. Ibid., 81.
17. Ibid.
18. Ibid.
19. Ibid., 81-82.
20. Ibid., 251.
21. Poel, *Life of Amelia Wilhelmina Sieveking*, 6.
22. Ibid., 6, 12, 16-17.
23. Ibid., 23.
24. Ibid., 31.
25. Ibid., 253.
26. Sieveking, *The Principles of Charitable Work*, viii.
27. Ibid., 243.
28. Ibid., 256.
29. Sieveking, 6.
30. Ibid., 5.
31. Ibid.
32. Poel., 110.
33. Ibid., 74-75.
34. Ibid., 215-216.
35. Sieveking, 26.
36. Ibid., 93.
37. Ibid., 104.
38. Ibid., 104.
39. Ibid., 104-105.
40. Ibid., 45-46.
41. Ibid., 100.
42. Ibid., 100-101.
43. Ibid., 101.
44. Ibid., 455.

Notes for Chapter 14

1. Ruffing, *Elisabeth Leseur*, 169-170.

2. Jackson, *Letters to a Young Christian*, 50.
3. Ibid., 2, 10.
4. Ibid., 10-11.
5. Ibid., 17-18.
6. Ibid., 25.
7. Ibid., 25-26.
8. Ibid., 26.
9. Ibid., 57.
10. Ibid., 84.
11. Ibid., 159-160.
12. Ibid., 101, 103-104.
13. Anderson, *Memoir of Catharine Brown*, 71-72.
14. Ibid., 72-73.
15. Ibid., 73.
16. Ibid.
17. Ibid., 74.
18. Ibid., 138-139.
19. Ibid., 139.
20. Ibid., 144.
21. Ibid., 148.
22. Jackson, 2.
23. Jackson, 13.
24. Ibid., 25.
25. Ibid.
26. Ibid., 25-26.
27. Ibid., 26.
28. Ibid., 65.
29. Ibid.
30. Ibid., 60.
31. Leseur, *My Spirit Rejoices*, 7.
32. Ruffing, *1-2.*
33. Leseur. 4.
34. Ruffing, 68.
35. Leseur, 25.
36. Ruffing, 192.
37. Ibid., 195.
38. Ibid.
39. Ibid., 192.
40. Ibid., 206-207.
41. Ibid., 64.
42. Ibid., 44.
43. Ibid., 234.
44. Ibid., 245-246.
45. Leseur, 27.

Notes for Chapter 15

1. Dyer, *Pandita Ramabai*, 104.
2. Wurmbrand, Sabina, *The Pastor's Wife*, 34.
3. Haviland, *A Woman's Life Work*, 10, 13, 22, 25-27.
4. Ibid. 34, 35.
5. Ibid., 132, 133.
6. Ibid., 133.
7. Ibid., 135.
8. Ibid., 141, 142.
9. Ibid., 142, 143.
10. Ibid., 143
11. Ibid., 130.
12. Ibid., 143-145.
13. Ibid., 125.
14. Ibid.
15. Ibid., 128.
16. Ibid., 128.
17. ten Boom, *The Hiding Place*, 9-10.
18. Ibid., 53.
19. Ibid., 52-53.
20. Ibid., 55.
21. Ibid., 62.
22. Ibid., 77.
23. Ibid., 102-103.
24. Ibid., 150-151.
25. Ibid., 37.
26. Ibid., 41.
27. Ibid., 63.
28. Ibid., 66-67.
29. Ibid., 131.
30. Ibid., 157.
31. Ibid., 63.
32. Ibid., 67.
33. Ibid., 161
34. Ibid.
35. Ibid., 182.
36. Ibid.
37. Ibid., 165.
38. Ibid.
39. Ibid.
40. Ibid., 180.
41. Ibid., 180-181.
42. Ibid., 189-190.
43. Ibid., 186.

BIBLIOGRAPHY

Abelard and Heloise. *The Letters of Abelard and Heloise.* Translated by Betty Radice. New York: Penguin Books, 1986.

Albert, Octavia, ed. *The House of Bondage or Charlotte Brooks and Other Slaves.* Reprint edition. New York: Oxford University Press, 1988.

Amt, Emilie, ed. *Women's Lives in Medieval Europe: A Sourcebook.* New York: Routledge, 1993.

Anderson, Rufus. *Memoir of Catherine Brown: A Christian Indian of the Cherokee Nation 1825.* Boston: Samuel T. Armstrong, 1825.

Andrews, William, ed. *Sisters of the Spirit: Three Black Women's Autobiographies of the Nineteenth Century.* Bloomington: Indiana University Press, 1986.

Angela of Foligno. *Angela of Foligno: Complete Works.* Translated by Paul Lachance. New York: Paulist Press, 1993.

_____. *The Book of Divine Consolation of the Blessed Angela of Foligno.* Translated by Mary Steegman. New York: Cooper Square Publishers, 1966.

Bainton, Roland. *Women of the Reformation in France and England.* Minneapolis: Augsburg, 1973.

_____. *Women of the Reformation in Germany and Italy.* Minneapolis: Augsburg, 1971.

_____. *Women of the Reformation from Spain to Scandinavia.* Minneapolis: Augsburg, 1977.

Bettenson, Henry, ed. *The Early Christian Fathers: A Selection from the Writings of the Fathers from St. Clement of Rome to St. Athanasius.* Translated by Henry Bettenson. New York: Oxford University Press, 1959.

_____. ed. *The Latter Christian Fathers: A Selection from the Writings of the Fathers from St. Cyril of Jerusalem to St. Leo the Great.* London: Oxford University Press, 1970.

Blassingame, John, ed. *Slave Testimony: Two Centuries of Letters, Speeches, Interviews, and Autobiographies.* Baton Rouge: Louisiana State University Press, 1977.

Bongie, Elizabeth, ed. *The Life of Blessed Syncletica by Pseudo-Athanasius.* Translated by Elizabeth Bongie. Toronto: Peregrina Publishing, 1995.

Brock, Sebastian, and Susan Harvey, eds. *Holy Women of the Syrian Orient.* Translated by Sebastian Brock and Susan Ashbrook. Berkeley: University of California Press, 1987.

Broderick, Robert, ed. *The Catholic Encyclopedia.* Revised and updated edition. Nashville: Thomas Nelson, 1990.

Brunn, Emilie, and Georgette Epiney-Burgard. *Women Mystics in Medieval Europe.* Translated by Sheila Hughes. New York: Paragon House, 1989.

Burr, Esther Edwards. *The Journal of Esther Edwards Burr: 1954-1757.* New Haven: Yale University Press, 1984.

Byrne, Lavinia, ed. *The Hidden Tradition: Women's Spiritual Writings Rediscovered.* New York: Crossroad, 1991.

Callahan, Virginia. "The Life of Macrina." *Ascetical Works.* In *The Fathers of the Church, a New Translation.* Vol. 58. Washington, DC: Catholic University of America Press, 1947.

Cameron, Averil, and Amelie Kurt, eds. *Images of Women in Antiquity: Addresses, Essays, Lectures.* Detroit: Wayne State University Press, 1983.

Carretta, Vincent. *Unchained Voices: An Anthology of Black Authors in the English-Speaking World of the Eighteenth Century.* Lexington: University Press of Kentucky, 1996.

Catherine of Genoa. *Catherine of Genoa: Purgation and Purgatory. The Spiritual Dialogue.* Translated by Serge Hughes. New York: Paulist Press, 1979.

Catherine of Siena. *The Dialogue.* Translated by Suzanne Noffke. New York: Paulist Press, 1980.

_____. *The Dialogue of Catherine Siena.* Translated by A. Thorold. Rockford, IL: Tan Books & Publishing, Inc., 1907.

_____. *The Letters of Catherine of Siena.* Vol. 1. Translated by Suzanne Noffke. Tempe, AZ: Arizona Center for Medieval and Renaissance Studies, 2000.

_____. *St. Catherine of Siena as Seen in Her Letters.* Translated by V. Scudder. London: Dent, 1906.

Chantal, Jane. *Saint Jane Frances Fremyot de Chantal. Her Exhortations, Conferences and Instructions.* Translated from the Paris 1875 edition. Chicago: Loyola University Press, 1928.

Chesterton, G. K. *Orthodoxy.* Whitefish, MT: Kessinger, 2004.

Chittister, Joan. *The Friendship of Women: A Spiritual Tradition.* Franklin, WI: Sheed and Ward, 2000.

Clark, Elizabeth. *Ascetic Piety and Women's Faith: Essays on Late Ancient Christianity.* Vol. 20 of *Studies in Women and Religion.* Lewiston, NY: E. Mellen Press, 1986.

_____. *Jerome, Chrysostom and Friends: Essays and Translations.* Vol. 2 of Studies in Women and Religion. Lewiston, NY: E. Mellen Press, 1979.

_____. *The Life of Melania the Younger.* Vol. 14 of *Studies in Women and Religion.* Lewiston, NY: The Edwin Mellen Press, 1984.

_____. *Women in the Early Church.* Collegeville, MN: Liturgical Press, 1990.

Clark, Elizabeth, and Herbert Richardson, eds. *Women and Religion: The Original Sourcebook of Women in Christian Thought.* Revised and expanded edition. San Francisco: Harper, 1996.

Clarke, Adam. *Memoirs of the Wesley Family; Collected Principally from Original Documents.* New York: The Methodist Episcopal Church at the Conference Office, 1832.

Clebsch, William, and Charles Jaekle. *Pastoral Care in Historical Perspective.* New York: Harper and Row, 1964.

Collier-Thomas, Bettye. *Daughters of Thunder: Black Women Preachers and Their Sermons, 1850-1979.* San Francisco: Josey-Bass, 1998.

Connolly, R. H. *Didascalia Apostolorum: The Syriac Version Translated and Accompanied by the Verona Latin Fragments.* Oxford: Clarendon, 1929.

Corrigan, Kevin. "Saint Macrina: The Hidden Face Behind the Tradition," in *On Pilgrimage: The Best of Ten Years of Vox Benedictina.* Toronto: Peregrina Publishing, 1994.

Cowman, Lettie. *Streams in the Desert.* Revised edition. Grand Rapids: Zondervan, 1999.

de la Cruz, Sor Juana Ines. *A Sor Juana Anthology.* Translated by Alan Trueblood. Cambridge, MA: Harvard University Press, 1988.

de Sales, Francis and Jane de Chantal. *Francis de Sales, Jane de Chantal: Letters of Spiritual Direction.* Translated by Peronne Thibert. New York: Paulist Press, 1988.

Dodds, Elizabeth. *Marriage to a Difficult Man: The Uncommon Union of Jonathan and Sarah Edwards.* Philadelphia: Westminster Press, 1971.

Dronke, Peter. *Women Writers of the Middle Ages: A Critical Study of Texts from Perpetua to Marguerite Porete.* Cambridge, England: Cambridge University Press, 1984.

Dubay, Thomas. *Fire Within: St. Teresa of Avila, St. John of the Cross, and the Gospel—On Prayer.* San Francisco: Ignatius Press, 1989.

Dyer, Helen. *Pandita Ramabai: The Story of Her Life.* New York: Revell, 1900.

Edwards, Sarah, and Susannah Edwards. "Letter to Esther Edwards Burr." Original Manuscript in Franklin Trask Library, Andover Newton Theological School, Newton Centre, MA, nd.

Edwards, Tilden. *Spiritual Friend: Reclaiming the Gift of Spiritual Direction.* New York: Paulist Press, 1980.

Flinders, C. *Enduring Grace.* New York: Harper, 1993.

Foner, Philip, and Robert Branham, eds. *Lift Every Voice: African American Oratory, 1787-1900.* Tuscaloosa: University of Alabama Press, 1998.

Forbes, Cheryl. *Women of Devotion through the Centuries.* Grand Rapids: Baker Books, 2001.

Francis and Clare. *Francis and Clare: The Complete Works.* Translated by Regis Armstrong and Ignatius Brady. New York: Paulist Press, 1982.

Gaustad, Edwin, and Mark Noll, eds. *A Documentary History of Religion in America to 1877.* Third edition. Grand Rapids: Eerdmans, 2003.

Gerstner, Edna. *Jonathan and Sarah: An Uncommon Union.* Morgan, PA: Soli Deo Gloria Publications, 1996.

Gertrude of Helfta. *Gertrude of Helfta: The Herald of Divine Love.* Translated by Margaret Winkworth. New York: Paulist, 1993.

Graef, Hilda. *The Light and the Rainbow: A Study in Christian Spirituality from Its Roots in the Old Testament and Its Development through the New Testament and the Fathers to Recent Times.* Westminster, MD: The Newman Press, 1959.

Grant, Myrna. *Sacred Legacy: Ancient Writings from Nine Women of Strength and Honor.* Grand Rapids: Baker, 2003.

Gregory of Nyssa. *The Life of Saint Macrina.* Translated by W. K. Clarke. London: Society for Promotion of Christian Knowledge, 1916.

Gryson, Roger. *The Ministry of Women in the Early Church.* Collegeville, MN: Liturgical Press, 1976.

Hadewijch. Hadewijch: *The Complete Works.* Translation and introduction by Columba Hart. Preface by Paul Mommaers. New York: Paulist Press, 1980.

Haight, Anne, ed. *Hroswitha of Gandersheim: Her Life, Times, and Works, and a Comprehensive Bibliography.* New York: The Hroswitha Club, 1965.

Harris, Marguerite, ed. *Birgitta of Sweden: Life and Selected Revelations.* Translated by Albert Kezel. New York: Paulist Press, 1990.

Haviland, Laura. *A Woman's Life Work.* Fifth edition. Grand Rapids: S. B. Shaw, 1881.

Hildegard of Bingen. *Hildegard of Bingen's Book of Divine Works: With Letters and Songs.* Translated by M. Fox. Santa Fe, NM: Bear & Company, 1987.

_____. *Letters of Hildegard of Bingen.* Translated by Joseph Baird and Radd Ehrman. New York: Oxford University Press, 1994.

_____. *The Life and Visions of St. Hildegard.* Translated by Francisca Steele. London: Heath, Cranton, and Ousely, 1914.

_____. *Scivias.* Translated by Columba Hart and Jane Bishop. New York: Paulist Press, 1990.

Hiltner, Seward. *Preface to Pastoral Theology.* Nashville: Abingdon, 1958.

Holy Apostles Convent. *The Lives of the Spiritual Mothers.* Beuna Vista, CO: Holy Apostles Convent, 1991.

Hopkins, Samuel. *The Life and Character of Miss Susanna Anthony.* Worcester, MA: Leonard Worcester, 1796.

Hyma, Albert. *Life of John Calvin.* Grand Rapids: Eerdmans, 1943.

Jackson, Sarah. *Letters to a Young Christian.* Fourth edition. New York: American Female Guardian Society, 1852

Jacobs, Harriet. *Incidents in the Life of a Slave Girl.* New York: Dover, 2001.

Julian of Norwich. *Revelations of Divine Love.* Translated by Elizabeth Spearing. London: Penguin Books, 1998.

_____. *Showings.* Translated by Edmund Colledge and James Welsh. New York: Paulist Press, 1978.

Keckley, Elizabeth. *Behind the Scenes, or Thirty Years a Slave and Four Years in the White House.* Reprinted by the Schomburg Library of Nineteenth-Century Black Women Writers. Edited by Henry Gates, Jr., New York: Oxford University Press, 1988.

Kellemen, Robert. *Soul Physicians: A Theology of Soul Care and Spiritual Direction.* Revised edition. BMH Books: Winona Lake, IN, 2007.

_____. "Spiritual Care in Historical Perspective: Martin Luther as a Case Study in Christian Sustaining, Healing, Reconciling, and Guiding." Ph.D. Dissertation. Kent State University, 1997.

_____. *Spiritual Friends: A Methodology of Soul Care and Spiritual Direction.* Revised edition. BMH Books: Winona Lake, IN, 2007.

Kellemen, Robert, and Karole Edwards. *Beyond the Suffering: Embracing the Legacy of African American Soul Care and Spiritual Direction.* Grand Rapids: Baker, 2007.

Kemp-Welch, Alice. *Of Six Medieval Women with a Note on Medieval Gardens.* Williamstown, MA: Corner House Publishers, 1972.

Kempe, Margery. *The Book of Margery Kempe.* Revised edition. Translated by B. A. Windeatt. London: Penguin Books, 2004.

Knowles, James D. *Memoir of Mrs. Ann H. Judson, Late Missionary to Burmah.* Second edition. Boston: Lincoln & Edmands, 1829.

Kraemer, Ross, ed. *Maenads, Martyrs, Matrons, Monastics: A Sourcebook on Women's Religions in the Greco-Roman World.* Philadelphia: Fortress Press, 1988.

Lake, Frank. *Clinical Theology.* London: Darton, Longman, & Todd, 1966.

Lane, George. *Christian Spirituality: An Historical Sketch.* Chicago: Loyola University Press, 1984.

Laporte, Jean. *The Role of Women in Early Christianity.* (Studies in Women and Religion). Vol. 7. Lewiston, NY: E. Mellen, 1982.

Leech, Kenneth. *Soul Friend: The Practice of Christian Spirituality.* San Francisco: Harper and Row, 1977.

Lehmijoki-Gardner, Maiju, ed. *Dominican Penitent Women.* Translated by Maiju Lehmijoki-Gardner. New York: Paulist Press, 2005.

Leseur, Elisabeth. *My Spirit Rejoices: The Diary of a Christian Soul in an Age of Unbelief.* Manchester: Sophia Institute Press, 1996.

Lesko, Barbara, ed. *Women's Earliest Records: From Ancient Egypt and Western Asia.* Atlanta, GA: Scholars Press, 1989.

MacHaffie, Barbara. *Her Story: Women in Christian Tradition.* Second edition. Philadelphia: Fortress Press, 2006.

Mahoney, Irene, ed. *Marie of the Incarnation: Selected Writings.* New York: Paulist Press, 1989.

Maloney, George, ed. *Pilgrimage of the Heart: A Treasury of Eastern Christian Spirituality.* San Francisco: Harper and Row, 1983.

Marsden, George. *Jonathan Edwards: A Life.* New Haven: Yale University Press, 2003.

McNamara, JoAnn, and John Halborg, eds. *Sainted Women of the Dark Ages.* Durham, NC: Duke University Press, 1992.

McNeil, John. *A History of the Cure of Souls.* New York: Harper and Row, 1951.

Mechthild of Magdeburg. *The Flowing Light of the Godhead.* Translated by Frank Tobin. New York: Paulist Press, 1998.

_____. *The Revelations of Mechthild of Magdeburg, or the Flowing Light of the Godhead.* Translated by Lucy Menzies. London: Longman, Green, and Co., 1953.

Moessner, Jeanne, ed. *Through the Eyes of Women: Insights for Pastoral Care.* Minneapolis: Fortress Press, 1996.

Musurillo, Herbert. *The Acts of the Christian Martyrs.* Oxford: Clarendon Press, 1972.

Newman, B. *Sister of Wisdom: St. Hildegard's Theology of the Feminine.* Berkeley, University of California Press, 1987.

Oates, Wayne. *Protestant Pastoral Counseling.* Philadelphia: Westminster, 1962.

Oberg, Barbara, and Harry Stout, eds. *Benjamin Franklin, Jonathan Edwards, and the Representation of American Culture.* New York: Oxford University Press, 1993.

Oden, Amy, ed. *In Her Words: Women's Writings in the History of Christian Thought.* Nashville: Abingdon Press, 1994.

Oden, Thomas. *Care of Souls in the Classic Tradition.* Philadelphia: Fortress, 1983.

_____. *Pastoral Counsel.* Vol. 3 of Classical Pastoral Care. Grand Rapids: Baker, 1987.

_____. *Phoebe Palmer: Selected Writings.* New York: Paulist Press, 1988.

_____. "Whatever Happened to History?" *Good News,* January-February, 1993.

Packer, J. I. *A Grief Sanctified: Passing Through Grief to Peace and Joy.* Ann Arbor, MI: Vine Books, 1997.

Palladius. *The Lausiac History.* Translated by Robert Meyer. New York: Paulist Press, 1964.

_____. *The Lausiac History.* Translated by W. K. Clarke. London: Macmillan, 1918.

Palmer, Phoebe. *Tongues of Fire on Daughters of the Lord.* New York: Walter C. Palmer, Jr., 1869.

_____. *The Way of Holiness: With Notes by the Way.* New York: Lance and Tippett, 1845.

Park, Edwards. *Memoir of the Life and Character of Samuel Hopkins.* Second edition. Boston: Doctrinal Track and Book Society, 1854.

Peterson, William. "John Calvin's Search for the Right Wife." *Christian History and Biography* 5, no. 4 (1986): 12-15.

_____. *25 Surprising Marriages: Faith-Building Stories from the Lives of Famous Christians.* Grand Rapids: Baker, 1997.

Petrof, Elizabeth. *Medieval Women's Visionary Literature.* Oxford, England: Oxford University Press, 1986.

Poel, Emma. *Life of Amelia Wilhelmina Sieveking.* Edited by Catherine Winkworth. London: Longman, Roberts, and Green, 1863.

Porete, Marguerite. *Marguerite Porete: The Mirror of Simple Souls.* Translated by Ellen Babinski. New York: Paulist Press, 1992.

Powers, Eileen. *Medieval Women: Canto.* Cambridge, England: Cambridge University Press, 1997.

Ranft, Patricia. *A Woman's Way: The Forgotten History of Women Spiritual Directors.* New York: Palgrave, 2000.

Ruether, Rosemary. *Women and Redemption: A Theological History.* Minneapolis: Fortress Press, 1998

Ruether, Rosemary and Rosemary Keller, eds. *The Colonial and Revolutionary Period: A Documentary History.* Vol. 2 of *Women and Religion in America.* San Francisco: Harper and Row, 1983.

_____, eds. *The Nineteenth Century: A Documentary History.* Vol. 1 of *Women and Religion in America.* San Francisco: Harper and Row, 1981.

_____, eds. *1900-1968: A Documentary History.* Vol. 3 in *Women and Religion in America.* San Francisco: Harper and Row, 1990.

Ruffing, Janet, ed. *Elisabeth Leseur: Selected Writings.* New York: Paulist Press, 2005.

Sawyer, Deborah. *Women and Religion in the First Christian Centuries.* London: Routledge, 1996.

Schaff, Philip. *The History of the Reformation.* Vol. 7 of *The History of the Christian Church.* Reprint edition. Grand Rapids: Eerdmans, 1979.

Schaff, Philip, and Henry Wace, eds. *Gregory Nazianzus: Select Orations, Sermons, Letters; Dogmatic Treatises.* Series 2, Vol. VII of *Nicene and Post-Nicene Fathers.* Reprint edition.Grand Rapids: Eerdmans, 1955.

_____, eds. *Jerome: Letters and Select Works.* Series 2, Vol. VI of *Nicene and Post-Nicene Fathers.* Reprint edition. Grand Rapids: Eerdmans, 1972.

_____, eds. *St. Chrysostom: Treatise on the Priesthood, Ascetic Treatises, Select Homilies and Letters.* Series 1, Vol. IX of *Nicene and Post-Nicene Fathers.* Reprint edition. Grand Rapids: Eerdmans, 1954.

_____, eds. *The Soul and the Resurrection.* Series 2, Vol. V of *Nicene and Post-Nicene Fathers.* Reprint edition. Grand Rapids: Eerdmans, 1972.

Scholer, D. *Women in Early Christianity.* New York: Garland Publishing, 1993.

Schwiebert, E. G. *Luther and His Times.* St. Louis: Concordia, 1950.

Sieveking, Amelia Wilhelmina. *The Principles of Charitable Work—Love, Truth, and Order—As Set Forth in the Writings of Amelia Wilhelmina Sieveking.* Translated by Catherine Winkworth. London: Longman, Roberts, and Green, 1863.

Sijthoff, A. W. *Mediaeval Netherlands Religious Literature.* Translated and introduced by Eric Colledge. New York: London House and Maxwell, 1965.

Sisters of the Visitation. *The Spirit of Saint Jane Francis de Chantal as Shown in Her Letters.* Translated by the Sisters of Visitation. Harrow-on-the-Hill. New York: Longmans, Green and Co., 1922.

Spurgeon, Susannah. *Free Grace and Dying Love: Morning Devotions.* Including *The Life of Susannah Spurgeon* by Charles Ray. Edinburgh: The Banner of Truth Trust, 2006.

St. Basil. *St. Basil's Letters.* Translated by Agnes Way. Washington, DC: Catholic University of America Press, 1951.

St. Teresa. *The Collected Works of St. Teresa of Avila.* Vol. 1: "The Book of Her Life," "Spiritual Testimonies," and "Soliloquies." Translated by Kieran Kavanaugh and Otilio Rodriguez. Revised second edition. Washington, D. C.: Institute of Carmelite Studies Publications, 1987.

_____. *The Collected Works of St. Teresa of Avila.* Vol. II: "The Way of Perfection," "Meditations on the Song of Songs," and "The Interior Castle." Translated by Kieran Kavanaugh and Otilio Rodriguez. Washington, D. C., Institute of Carmelite Studies Publications, 1980.

_____. *Teresa of Avila: The Interior Castle.* New York: Paulist Press, 1979.

Stewart, Dorothy, ed. *Women of Prayer: An Anthology of Everyday Prayers from Women around the World.* Chicago: Loyola Press, 1999.

Stowe, Charles, ed. *The Life of Harriet Beecher Stowe.* London: Sampson Low, Marston, Searle, and Rivington, 1889.

Swan, Laura. *The Forgotten Desert Mothers: Sayings, Lives, and Stories of Early Christian Women.* New York: Paulist Press, 2001.

Talbot, Alice Mary, ed. *Holy Women of Byzantium: Ten Saints' Lives in English Translation.* Washington, D.C.: Dumbarton Oaks, 1996.

Talbot, C. H., ed. *The Anglo-Saxon Missionaries in Germany.* Translated by C. H. Talbot. New York: Sheed and Ward, 1954.

ten Boom, Corrie, John Sherrill, and Elizabeth Sherrill. *The Hiding Place.* Washington Depot, CN: Chosen Books, 1971.

Thiebauz, Marcelle. *The Writings of Medieval Women: An Anthology.* Second edition. New York: Garland Publishing, 1994.

Topping, Eva. *Saints and Sisterhood: The Lives of Forty-Eight Holy Women.* Minneapolis: Light and Life Publishing, 1990.

Truth, Sojourner. *Narrative of Sojourner Truth.* Battle Creek, MI: Published for the Author, 1878.

Tucker, Ruth. *Private Lives of Pastor's Wives.* Grand Rapids: Zondervan, 1988.

Tucker, Ruth, and Walter Liefeld. *Daughters of the Church: Women and Ministry from New Testament Times to the Present.* Grand Rapids: Zondervan, 1987.

Turpin, Joanne. *Women in Church History: 20 Stories for 20 Centuries.* Cincinnati: Saint Anthony Messenger, 1990.

Van Halsema, Thea. *This Was John Calvin.* Grand Rapids: Baker, 1981.

Voobus, Arthur. *The Didascalia Apostolorum in Syriac.* Louvain: Corpus Scriptorium Christianorum Orientaliusm, 1979.

Walker, Williston. *John Calvin: The Organizer of Reformed Protestantism, 1509-1564.* New York: Schocken, 1969.

Wallace, Charles, ed. *Susanna Wesley: The Complete Writings.* New York: Oxford University Press, 1997.

_____. "Susanna Wesley's Spirituality: The Freedom of a Christian Woman." *Methodist History* 22 (April 1984): 158-173.

Ward, Benedicta. *The Desert Christian: The Sayings of the Desert Fathers.* New York: Macmillan, 1975.

_____. *The Desert Fathers: Sayings of the Early Christian Monks.* Translated by Benedicta Ward. New York: Penguin, 2003.

_____. *Harlots of the Desert: A Study of Repentance in Early Monastic Sources.* Kalamazoo, MI: Cistercian Publications, 1987.

Warrack, G., ed. *Revelations of Divine Love.* London: Methuen & Company, 1901.

Wheatley, Richard. *The Life and Letters of Phoebe Palmer.* New York: Palmer and Hughes, 1884.

White, Caroline. *Christian Friendship in the Fourth Century.* Cambridge, England: Cambridge University Press, 1992.

Wideman, John. *My Soul Has Grown Deep: Classics of Early African-American Literature.* Philadelphia: Running Press, 2001.

Wilson, Katherine, ed. *Medieval Women Writers.* Athens, GA: University of Georgia Press, 1984.

_____, ed. *Women Writers of the Renaissance and Reformation.* Athens, GA: University of Georgia Press, 1987.

Wilson-Kastner, Patricia, Ronald Kastner, Ann Millin, Rosemary Rader, and Jeremiah Reedy, eds. *A Lost Tradition: Women Writers of the Early Church.* Washington, DC: University Press of America, 1981.

Wright, Wendy. "Desert Listening." *Weavings* 9:3 (May-June 1994): 8-12.

Wurmbrand, Sabina. *The Pastor's Wife.* Sixth edition. Bartlesville, OK: Living Sacrifice Books, 2003.

About Dr. Kellemen and RPM Ministries

Robert W. Kellemen, Ph.D., LCPC served for more than a decade as the founding Chairman of the Master of Arts in Christian Counseling and Discipleship Department at Capital Bible Seminary in Lanham, Maryland. He is now Professor-at-Large in that department.

Dr. Kellemen is the author of *Soul Physicians: A Theology of Soul Care and Spiritual Direction, Spiritual Friends: A Methodology of Soul Care and Spiritual Direction*, and *Beyond the Suffering: Embracing the Legacy of African American Soul Care and Spiritual Direction*. Bob has pastored three churches and serves as the Co-Director of the American Association of Christian Counselors' Biblical Counseling and Spiritual Formation Network (BCSFN). Bob and his wife, Shirley, live in Crown Point, Indiana. They have two adult children, Josh, who is married to Andi, and Marie, who is in college.

Bob is the founder and CEO of *RPM Ministries* (www.rpmministries.org). *RPM* is an acronym for *Resurrection Power Multipliers* which takes its name from the Apostle Paul's longing in Philippians 3:10 to know the power of Christ's resurrection.

RPM Ministries exists to empower Christians toward Christlikeness by relating God's truth to human relationships. It is Bob's passion through *RPM Ministries* to equip leaders to change lives with Christ's changeless truth through Christ-centered, comprehensive, compassionate, and culturally-informed ministry.

Through *RPM Ministries*, Bob offers conferences and seminars on Spiritual Friendship, Soul Care and Spiritual Direction, Biblical Counseling, African American Church History, Multi-cultural Ministry, Marriage, Parenting, Women's Soul Care, and Women's Church History.

Bob also provides consulting for churches and para-church ministries on equipping lay counselors and spiritual friends, vision catching and casting, change management, and conflict resolution.

To learn more about *RPM Ministries*, please visit: www.rpmministries.org. There you will find free resources, book reviews, blogs, quotes, articles, and much more.

To discuss scheduling a conference or consulting, please e-mail: rpm.ministries@gmail.com.